GERMAN LATE WAR ARMORED FIGHTING VEHICLES

GEORGE BRADFORD

STACKPOLE
BOOKS

Copyright © 2007 by George Bradford

Published by
STACKPOLE BOOKS
5067 Ritter Road
Mechanicsburg, PA 17055
www.stackpolebooks.com

All rights reserved, including the right to reproduce this book or portions thereof in any form or by any means, electronic or mechanical, including photocopying, recording, or by any information storage and retrieval system, without permission in writing from the publisher. All inquiries should be addressed to Stackpole Books, 5067 Ritter Road, Mechanicsburg, Pennsylvania 17055.

Cover design by Wendy A. Reynolds

Printed in the United States of America

10 9 8 7 6 5 4 3 2 1

FIRST EDITION

Library of Congress Cataloging-in-Publication Data

Bradford, George.
   German late war armored fighting vehicles / George Bradford. — 1st ed.
      p. cm. — (World War II AFV Plans)
   Includes bibliographical references.
   ISBN-13: 978-0-8117-3355-7
   ISBN-10: 0-8117-3355-6
   1. Armored vehicles, Military—Germany. 2. Tanks (Military science)—Germany. I. Title.

UG446.5.B6826 2007
623.7'475094309044—dc22
                              2007002681

Contents

StuG. 40, Ausf. G (Sd.Kfz. 142/1)	6
s.Pz.Sp.Wg. 2cm (Sd.Kfz. 234/1)	7
Pz.Kpfw. V, Panther Ausf. D (Sd.Kfz. 171)	8–9
Pz.Kpfw. VI P Tiger (P) (Sd.Kfz. 181)	10
Pz.Kpfw. Tiger I Ausf. E (Sd.Kfz. 181)	11–12
s.Pz.Sp.Wg. 7.5cm (Sd.Kfz. 234/3)	13–14
Berge-Ferdinand	15
Panzerjäger Ferdinand (Sd.Kfz. 184)	16–17
SturmPz. IV Brummbär (Sd.Kfz. 166)	18–19
Pz.Kpfw. IV Ausf. J (Sd.Kfz. 161/2)	20–21
Pz.Sp.Wg. II Ausf. L, Luchs (Sd.Kfz. 123)	22
Schwimmwagen K2s (Kfz. 1/20)	23
2cm FlaK38 auf Fahrgestell Zugkraftwagen 1t (Sd.Kfz. 10/4)	24
Jagdpanzer IV (Sd.Kfz. 162)	25
Sd.Kfz. 250/11 mit s.Panzerbüchse 41	26
s.Pz.Sp.Wg. 5cm Puma (Sd.Kfz. 234/2)	27
s.Ladungsträger BIV (Sd.Kfz. 301) Ausf. C	28
Sd.Kfz. 250/8 Neü Art mit 5cm PaK38	29
le.Gp.Kft.Wg. (Sd.Kfz. 250/9) Neü Art	30
Jagdpanzer 38(t) Hetzer	31
s.Pz.Sp.Wg. 7.5cm PaK40 (Sd.Kfz. 234/4)	32
Flammpanzer 38(t) Hetzer	33
Bergepanzer 38(t) Hetzer	34–35
Pz.Kpfw. Tiger I Ausf. E (Sd.Kfz. 181)	36
Opel Maultier Pz.Werfer 42 (Sd.Kfz. 4/1)	37
Panzer IV/70(A)	38–39
Sd.Kfz. 250/8 Neü mit 7.5cm KwK51	40
Panzer IV/70(V) (Sd.Kfz. 162/1)	41
StuG. 40, Ausf. G (Sd.Kfz. 142/1)	42
Pz.Kpfw. Panther Ausf. A (Sd.Kfz. 171)	43
Bergepanther (Sd.Kfz. 179)	44–45
Grille Ausf. M (Sd.Kfz. 138/1)	46
Sd.Kfz. 251/1 Ausf. D	47
Panzerjäger Elefant (Sd.Kfz. 184)	48–49
StuG. IV (Sd.Kfz. 167)	50–51
Pz.Beob.Wg. Panther	52
Jagdpanzer 38(t) Hetzer	53
Sd.Kfz. 251/21 Ausf. D	54
Sd.Kfz. 251/22 Ausf. D	55
Befehls-Panther Ausf. A (Sd.Kfz. 171)	56–57
Pz.Kpfw. V Panther Ausf. G	58–59
Pz.Kpfw. Tiger II (Porsche turret)	60–61
Pz.Kpfw. Tiger II (Henschel turret)	62
Jagdpanther (Sd.Kfz. 173)	63
Sturmmörser Tiger, 38cm RW61	64–66
Jagdtiger (Sd.Kfz. 186) (Henschel suspension)	68
Jagdtiger (Sd.Kfz. 186) (Porsche suspension)	69
Zug.Kf.Wg. 8t für V-2 Raketen	70
FlakPz. IV Ostwind I, 3.7cm FlaK	71
Panzerjäger Elefant (Sd.Kfz. 184)	72
Pz.Kpfw. Tiger I Ausf. E (Sd.Kfz. 181)	73
sIG 33/2 (Sf) auf Jagdpanzer 38(t)	74
FlakPz. IV Wirbelwind (Sd.Kfz. 161/4)	75
15cm Pz.Werfer 42 auf sWS	76
Jagdpanther (Sd.Kfz. 173)	77–78
NSU Springer (Sd.Kfz. 304)	79
sWS Armored Supply Vehicle	80
Ardelt 8.8cm PaK43/3 Waffenträger	81
Jagdpanzer 38(t) Starr	82
Panzerkampfwagen Maus	83–84
le.FlakPz. IV Kugelblitz	85
5.5cm FlakPz. Panther	86
Pz.Kpfw. V Panther Ausf F	87
Pz.Kpfw. E-100	88–89
BMM/CKD Kätzchen APC	90

Introduction

The fourth volume in this series of books on scale drawings of armored fighting vehicles of World War II is devoted to German military vehicles which appeared in the final years of the war. Many of these vehicles were quite unique, and are shown here roughly in chronological order of appearance on the scene. However, there was much overlap in vehicle production, and this makes it somewhat difficult to establish a sequence which is totally perfect.

Therefore, if you are looking for armored vehicles that came into German service after 1943, then you should be able to find them in this book. Vehicles encountered before early 1943 are covered in *German Early War Armored Fighting Vehicles*. Among the vehicles illustrated you will find some of the prototypes that never really saw action, plus some of the vehicles that were just too late to participate in the war. You will also find that we cover mainly armored fighting vehicles, but also with a few support vehicles that fought along side of them thrown in.

The ultimate purpose of this series of books is to try and present a sequence of World War II military vehicle plan view scale drawings all in one place. Most of these drawings display 4-view plans, but with some of the smaller vehicles we were able to show five or more views. However, no matter how well the plans are drawn it is always necessary to have sufficient photo reference books as well. There are a number of "walk around" and close up view series on the market to give the super detailers all the finer detail they could ask for.

Over the years, scale drawings of various armored vehicles have appeared in magazines and books, but never all in one place where they would be easy for the researcher or modeler to access them. Many different scales have fought for the limelight, but the more popular ones of late have boiled down to mainly 1:35, 1:48 and 1:72 in the armor modeling world. With this in mind we have tried to keep the drawings as large as possible with a preponderance of 1:35 scale drawings, supported by 1:48 scale where appropriate, and also for vehicles that are simply too big to fit on these pages comfortably as 1:35 scale drawings. The 1:72 scale plans are mainly used to fill out a page here and there, and give the modeler some choice.

You will also find a chart at the end of this book for reducing or enlarging any of these drawings to other popular scales. The quality and accuracy of modern photocopying should make it possible for you to achieve whatever final scale you require. However, in some cases where enlargement is required, you may only be able to squeeze one view onto letter size paper and may have to utilize 11" x 17" paper where available.

These drawings have been created using vector based drawing applications with line weights ranging from .25 point to 1 point, and thus should easily hold the finer detail when copying. The bulk of these drawings were done over a period of ten years and are currently among the most precise and accurate AFV drawings available. You will also notice a variance in the drawings as the art style changes slightly over the years, but eventually supports shading in the majority of the later works.

SCALE CONVERSIONS

REDUCING

1:35 to 1:48 Scale = 73%

1:35 to 1:76 Scale = 46%

1:35 to 1:72 Scale = 49%

1:35 to 1:87 Scale = 41%

1:48 to 1:76 Scale = 63%

1:48 to 1:72 Scale = 66%

1:48 to 1:87 Scale = 55%

1:72 to 1:76 Scale = 95%

ENLARGING

1:35 to 1:32 Scale = 109%

1:35 to 1:16 Scale = 218%

1:48 to 1:35 Scale = 138%

1:48 to 1:32 Scale = 150%

1:48 to 1:16 Scale = 300%

1:72 to 1:35 Scale = 207%

1:72 to 1:48 Scale = 150%

1:72 to 1:16 Scale = 450%

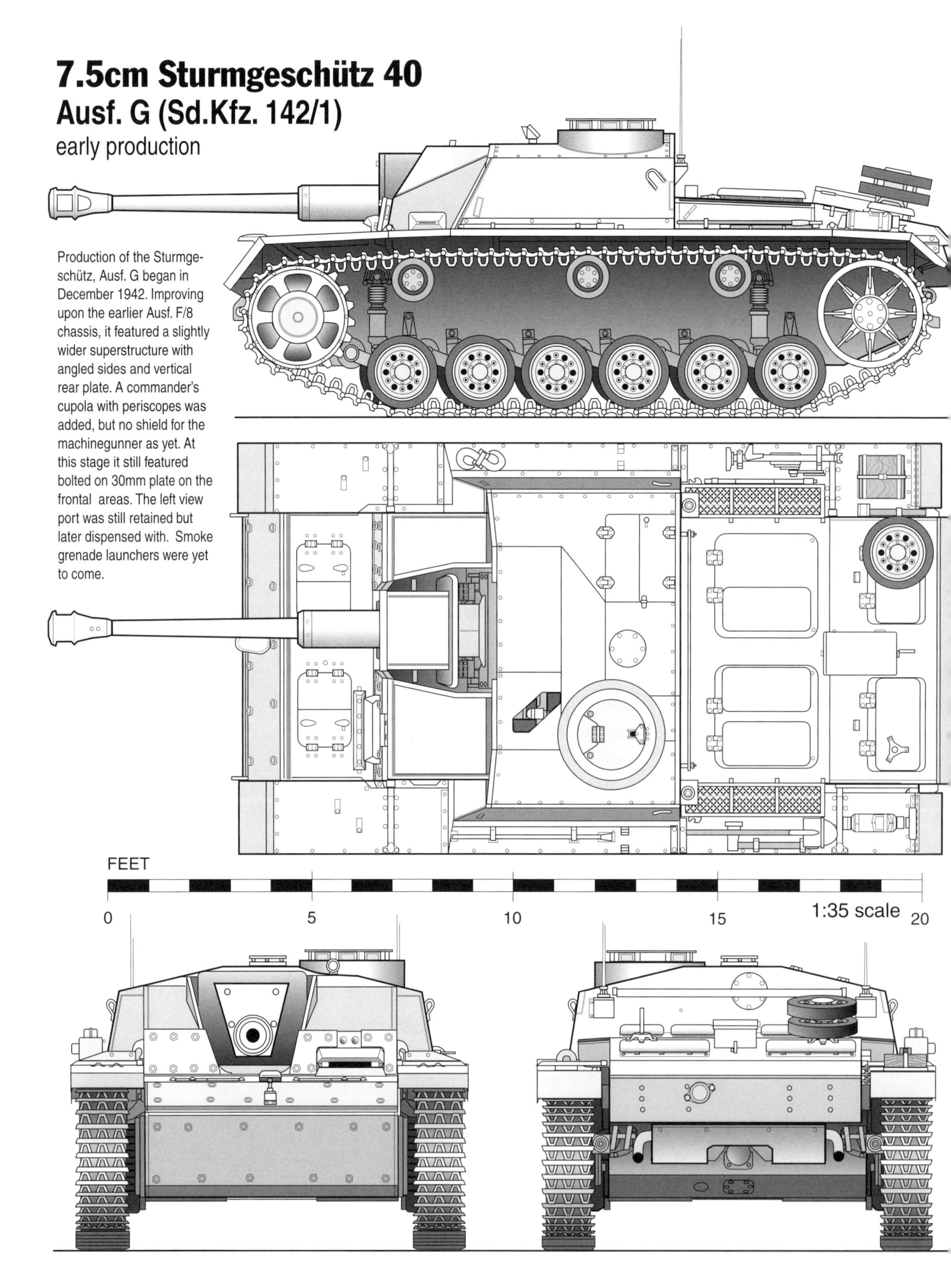

7.5cm Sturmgeschütz 40
Ausf. G (Sd.Kfz. 142/1)
early production

Production of the Sturmgeschütz, Ausf. G began in December 1942. Improving upon the earlier Ausf. F/8 chassis, it featured a slightly wider superstructure with angled sides and vertical rear plate. A commander's cupola with periscopes was added, but no shield for the machinegunner as yet. At this stage it still featured bolted on 30mm plate on the frontal areas. The left view port was still retained but later dispensed with. Smoke grenade launchers were yet to come.

FEET

0   5   10   15   20

1:35 scale

6   German Late War Armored Fighting Vehicles

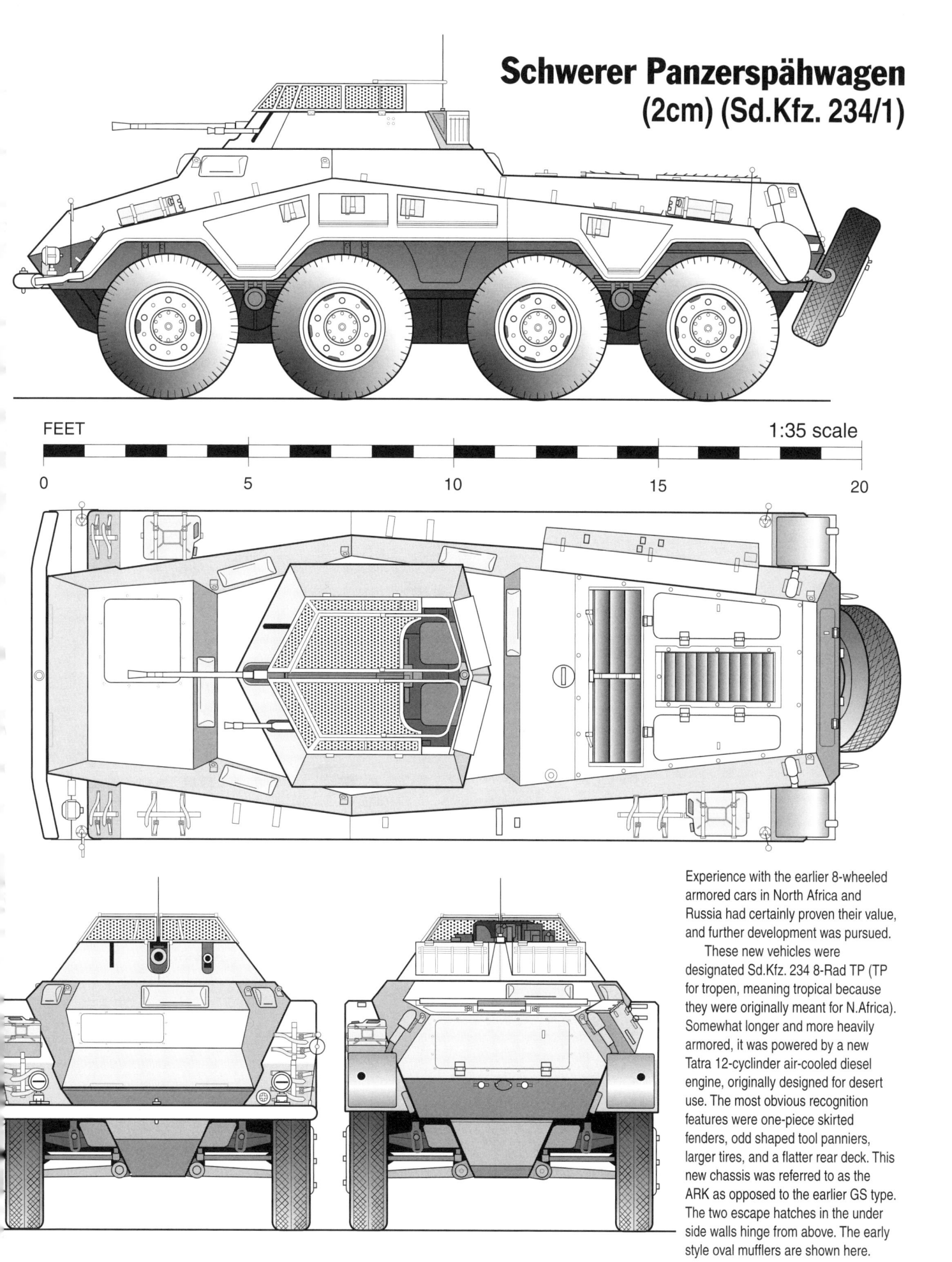

Schwerer Panzerspähwagen (2cm) (Sd.Kfz. 234/1)

FEET 1:35 scale

0   5   10   15   20

Experience with the earlier 8-wheeled armored cars in North Africa and Russia had certainly proven their value, and further development was pursued.

These new vehicles were designated Sd.Kfz. 234 8-Rad TP (TP for tropen, meaning tropical because they were originally meant for N.Africa). Somewhat longer and more heavily armored, it was powered by a new Tatra 12-cyclinder air-cooled diesel engine, originally designed for desert use. The most obvious recognition features were one-piece skirted fenders, odd shaped tool panniers, larger tires, and a flatter rear deck. This new chassis was referred to as the ARK as opposed to the earlier GS type. The two escape hatches in the under side walls hinge from above. The early style oval mufflers are shown here.

German Late War Armored Fighting Vehicles

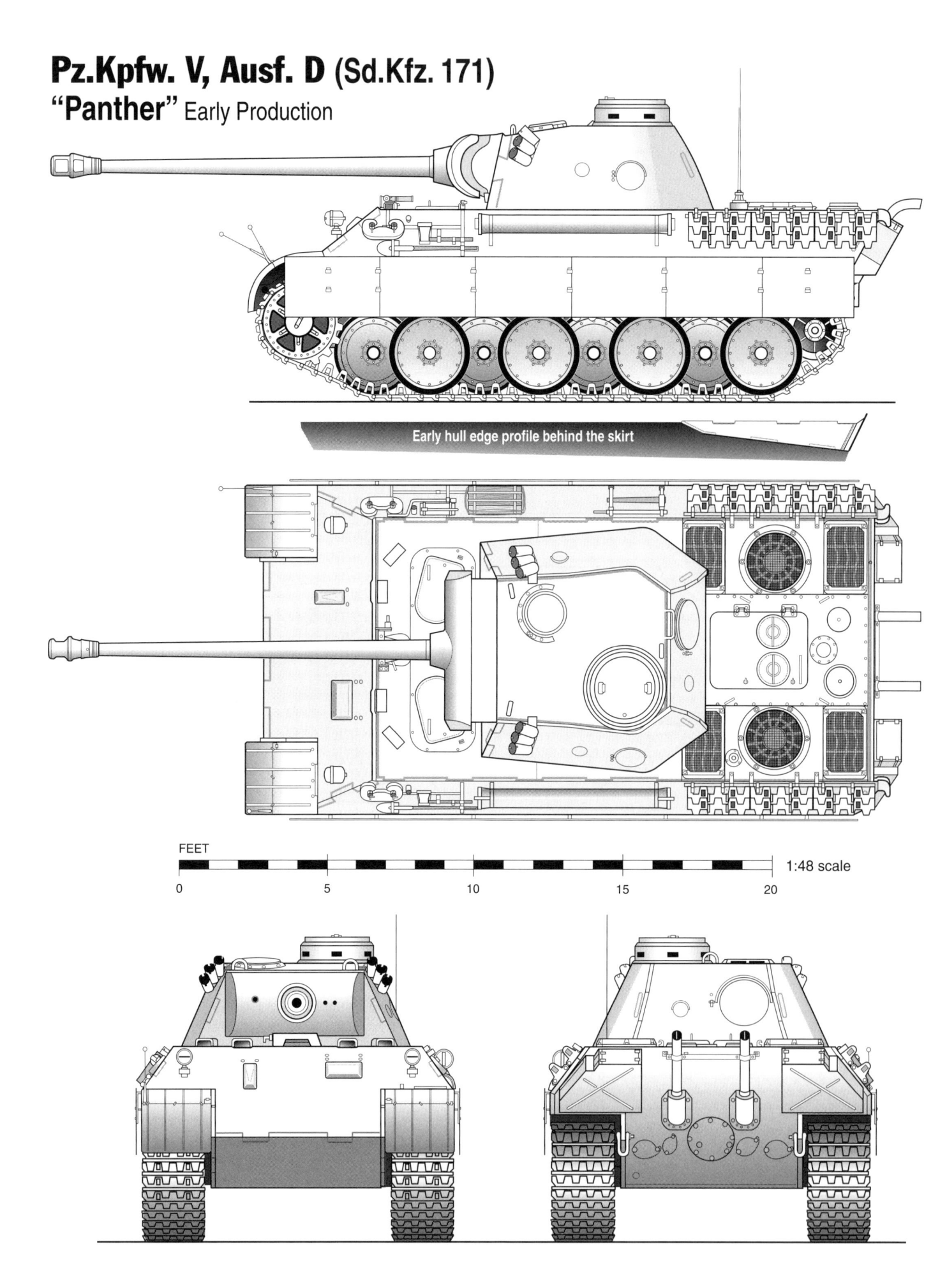

Pz.Kpfw. V, Ausf. D (Sd.Kfz. 171)
"Panther" Early Production

Early hull edge profile behind the skirt

FEET

1:48 scale

8 German Late War Armored Fighting Vehicles

An early Panther Ausf. D on display outside the factory in mid-1943.

A captured Panther Ausf. D on display in Moscow 1943, giving us a good look at the early cupola and position of smoke dischargers.

German Late War Armored Fighting Vehicles 9

Pz.Kpfw. VI P (Sd.Kfz.181), Typ 101, VK 4501(P), Tiger (P)

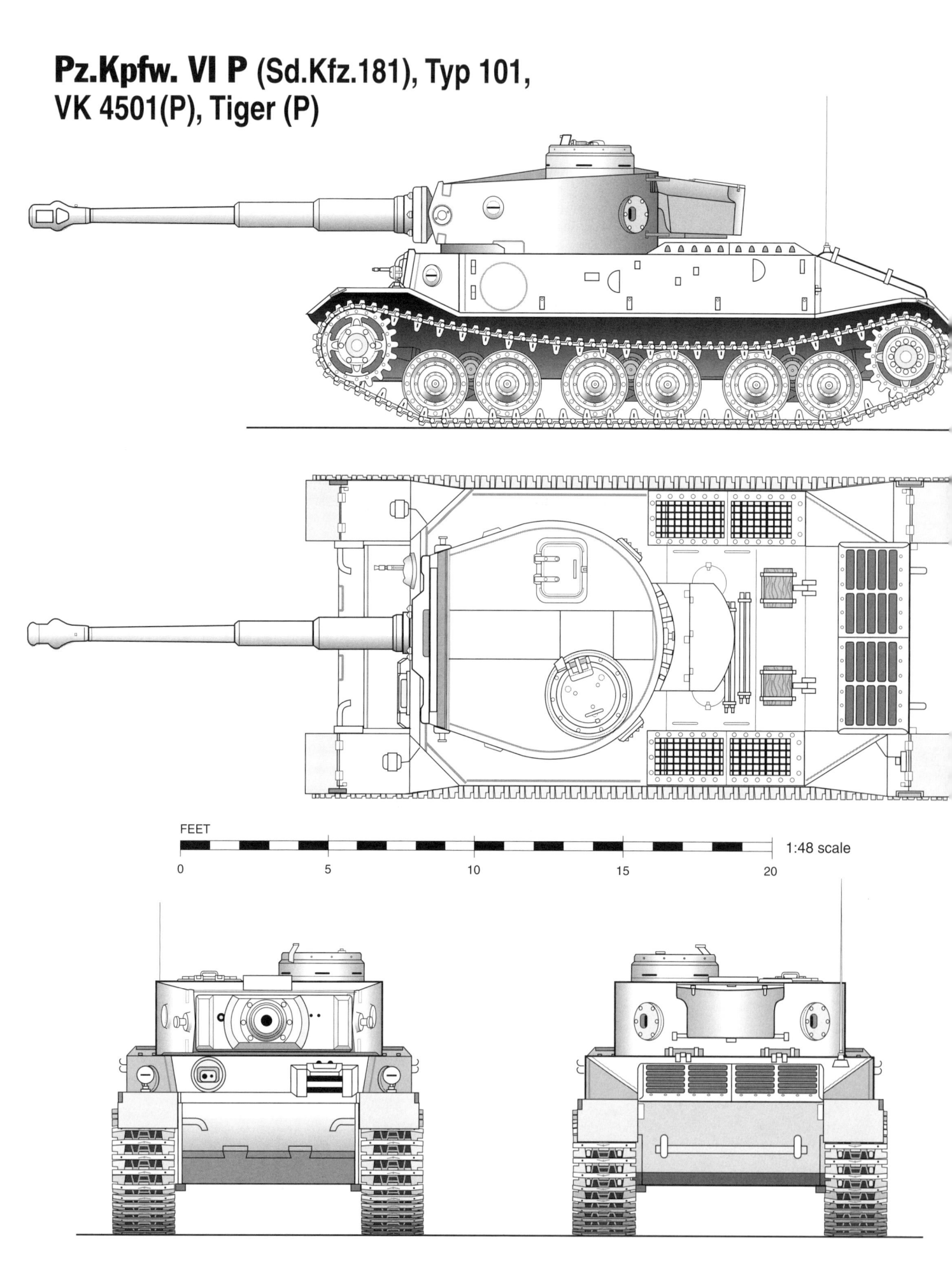

Pz.Kpfw. Tiger Ausf. E,
(Sd.Kfz. 181) early production

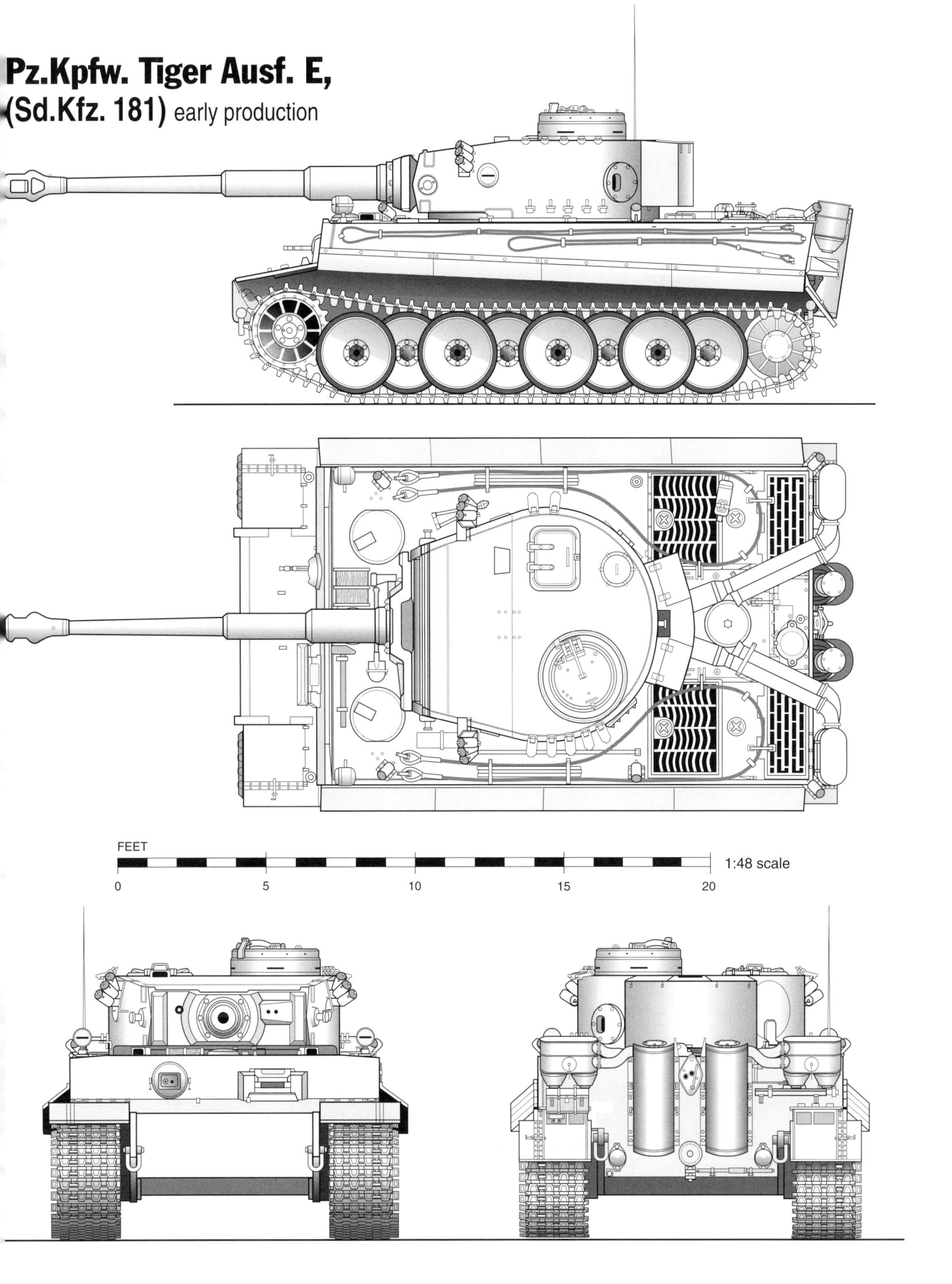

FEET
0   5   10   15   20
1:48 scale

German Late War Armored Fighting Vehicles   11

Pz.Kpfw. TIGER Ausf. E,
(Sd.Kfz. 181) early production

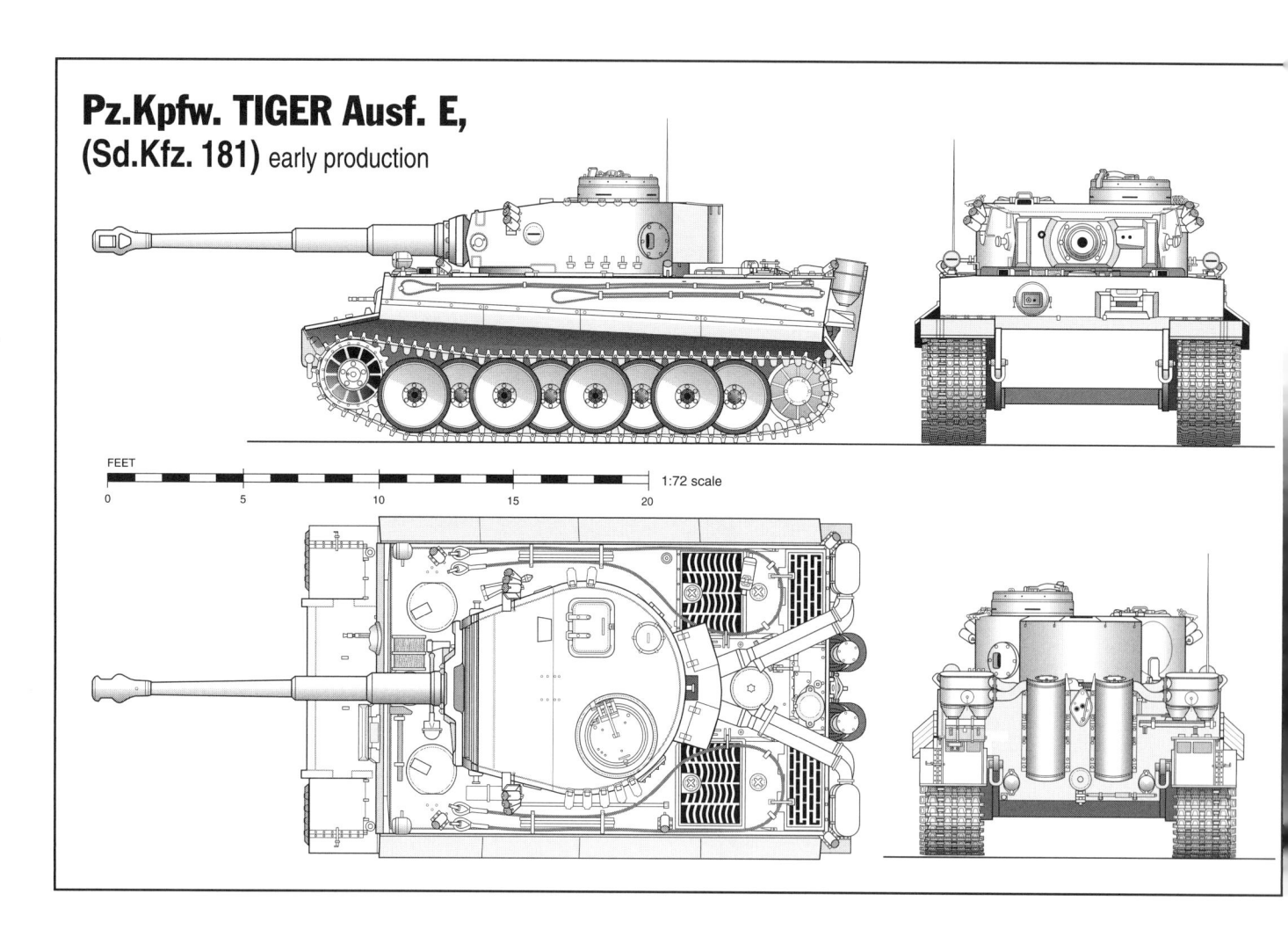

FEET
1:72 scale

A factory-fresh early Tiger Ausf. E leaving the building on transport tracks. You can see that the wider front fender flaps are in the raised position.

12 German Late War Armored Fighting Vehicles

Schwerer Panzerspähwagen (7.5cm) (Sd.Kfz. 234/3)

FEET

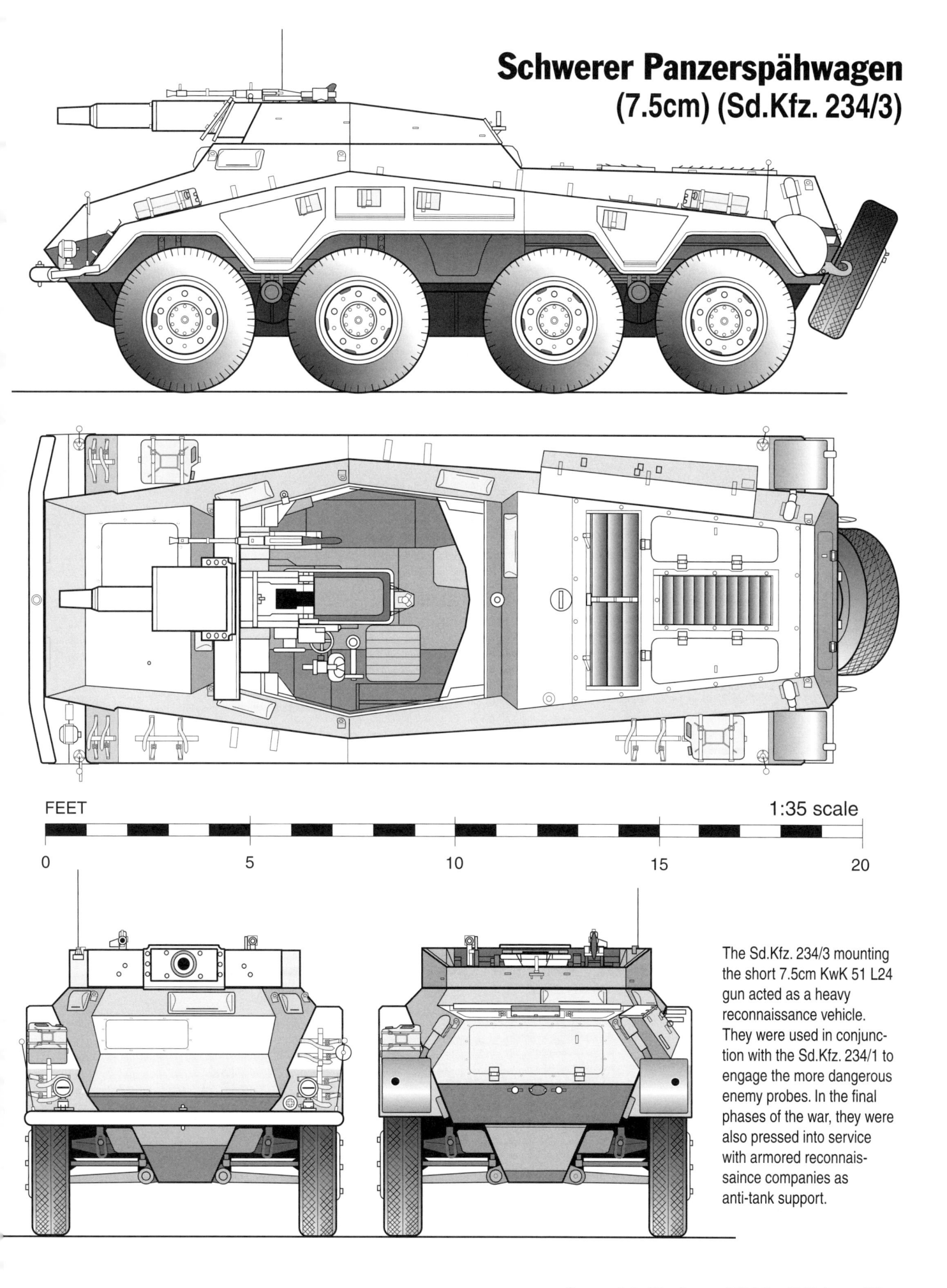

1:35 scale

0 5 10 15 20

The Sd.Kfz. 234/3 mounting the short 7.5cm KwK 51 L24 gun acted as a heavy reconnaissance vehicle. They were used in conjunction with the Sd.Kfz. 234/1 to engage the more dangerous enemy probes. In the final phases of the war, they were also pressed into service with armored reconnaissaince companies as anti-tank support.

German Late War Armored Fighting Vehicles 13

A rare shot of a German Sd.Kfz. 234/3 mounting the short 7.5 cm gun being inspected by Polish troops. Note that all four of the side panier stowage bin doors are hanging open.

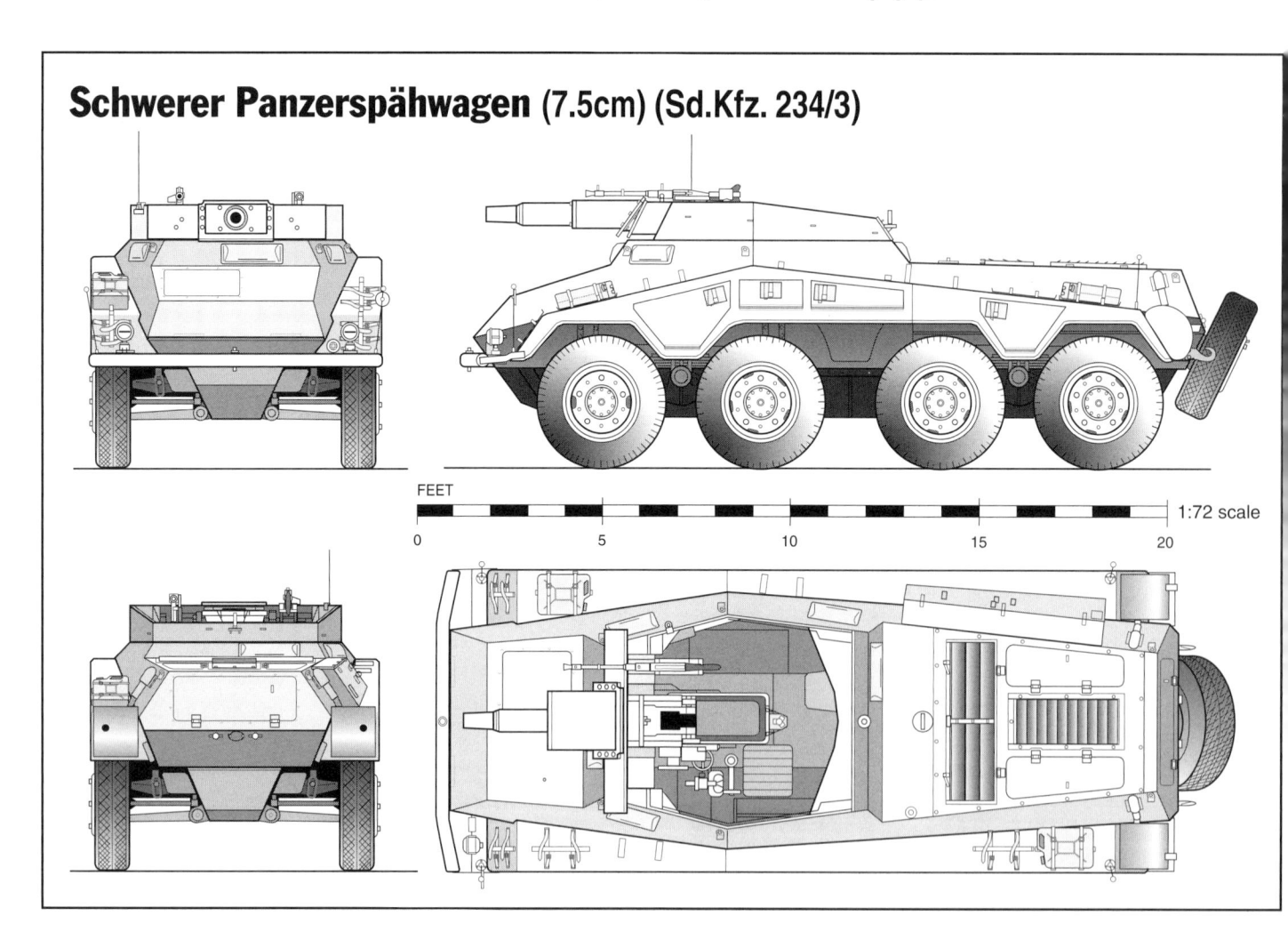

Schwerer Panzerspähwagen (7.5cm) (Sd.Kfz. 234/3)

Berge-Ferdinand
Bergepanzer Tiger (P), early

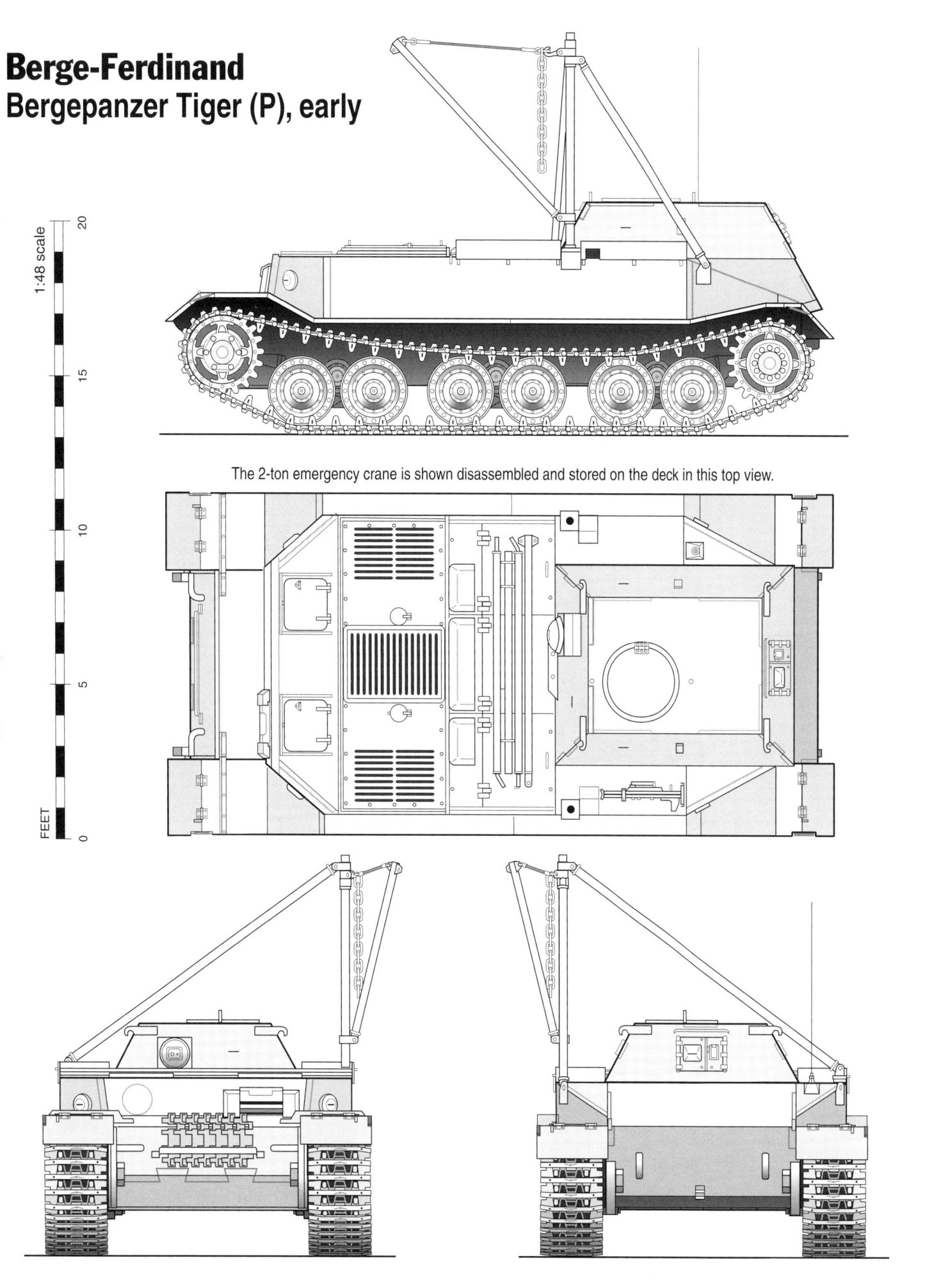

The 2-ton emergency crane is shown disassembled and stored on the deck in this top view.

German Late War Armored Fighting Vehicles 15

Panzerjäger Tiger (P) mit 8.8 Pak 43.2 (L/71)
(Sd.Kfz.184) "Ferdinand"

FEET   1:48 scale
0   5   10   15   20

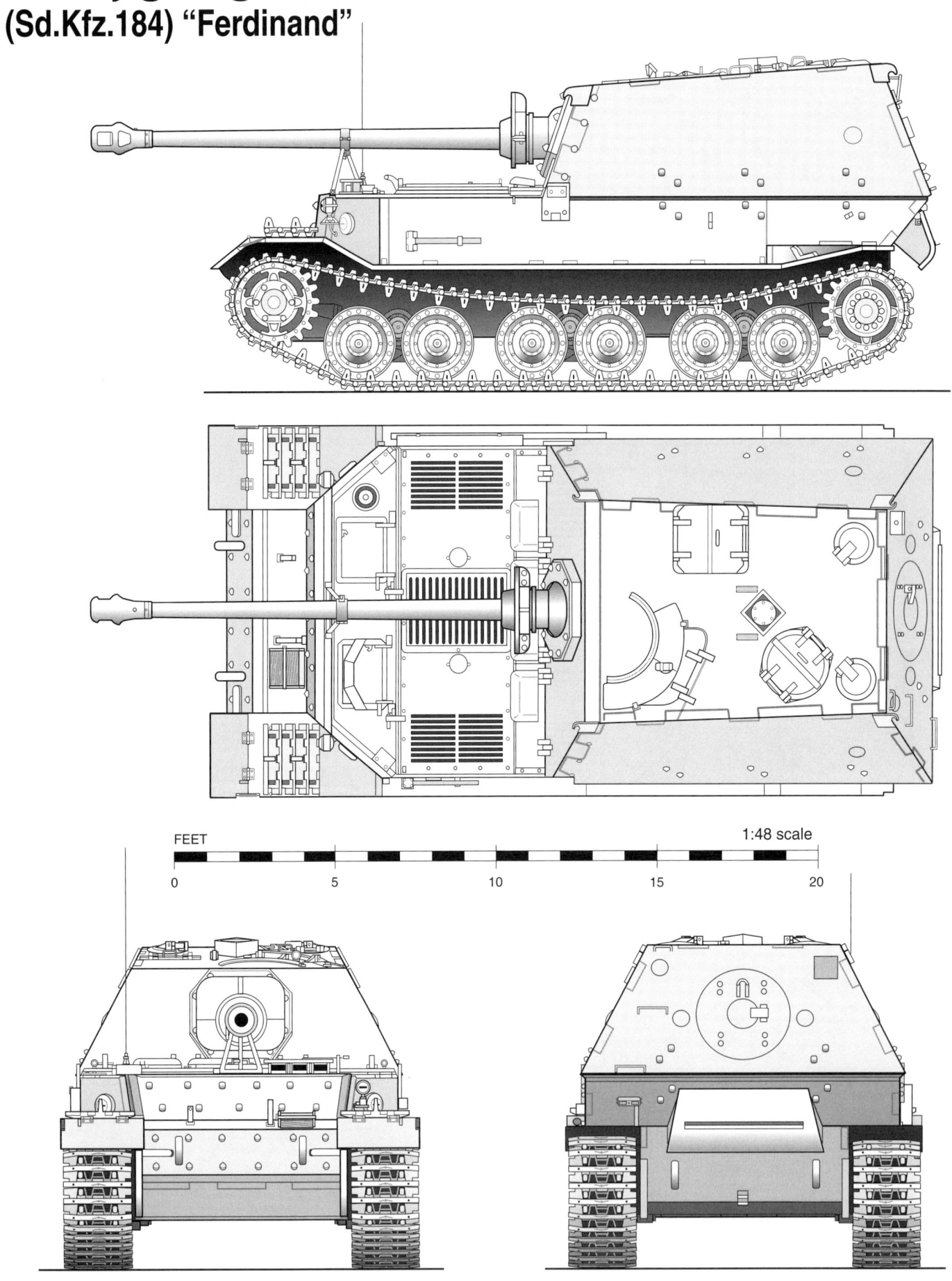

16   German Late War Armored Fighting Vehicles

Panzerjäger Tiger (P) mit 8.8 Pak 43.2 (L/71)
(Sd.Kfz.184) "Ferdinand"

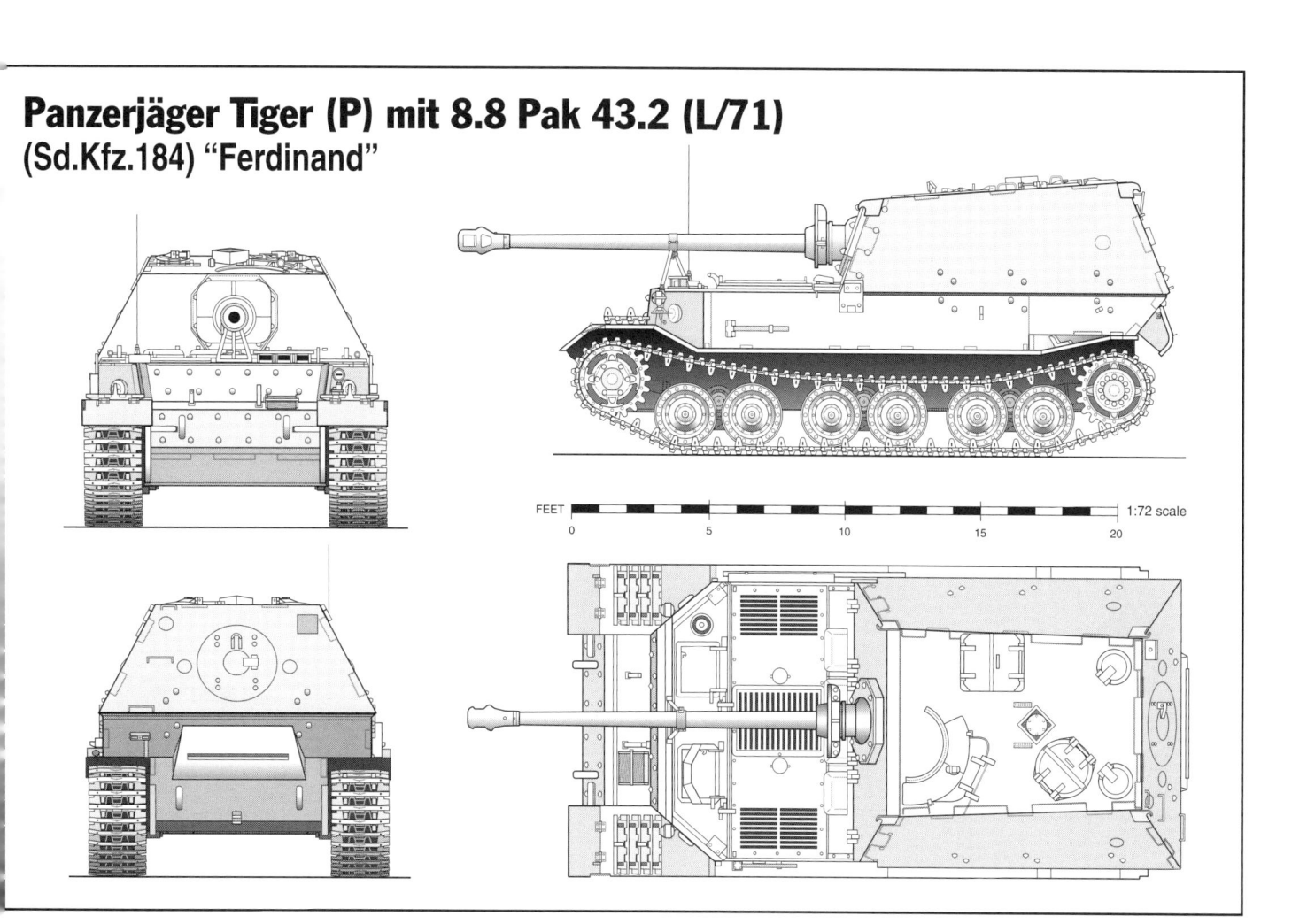

German Late War Armored Fighting Vehicles 17

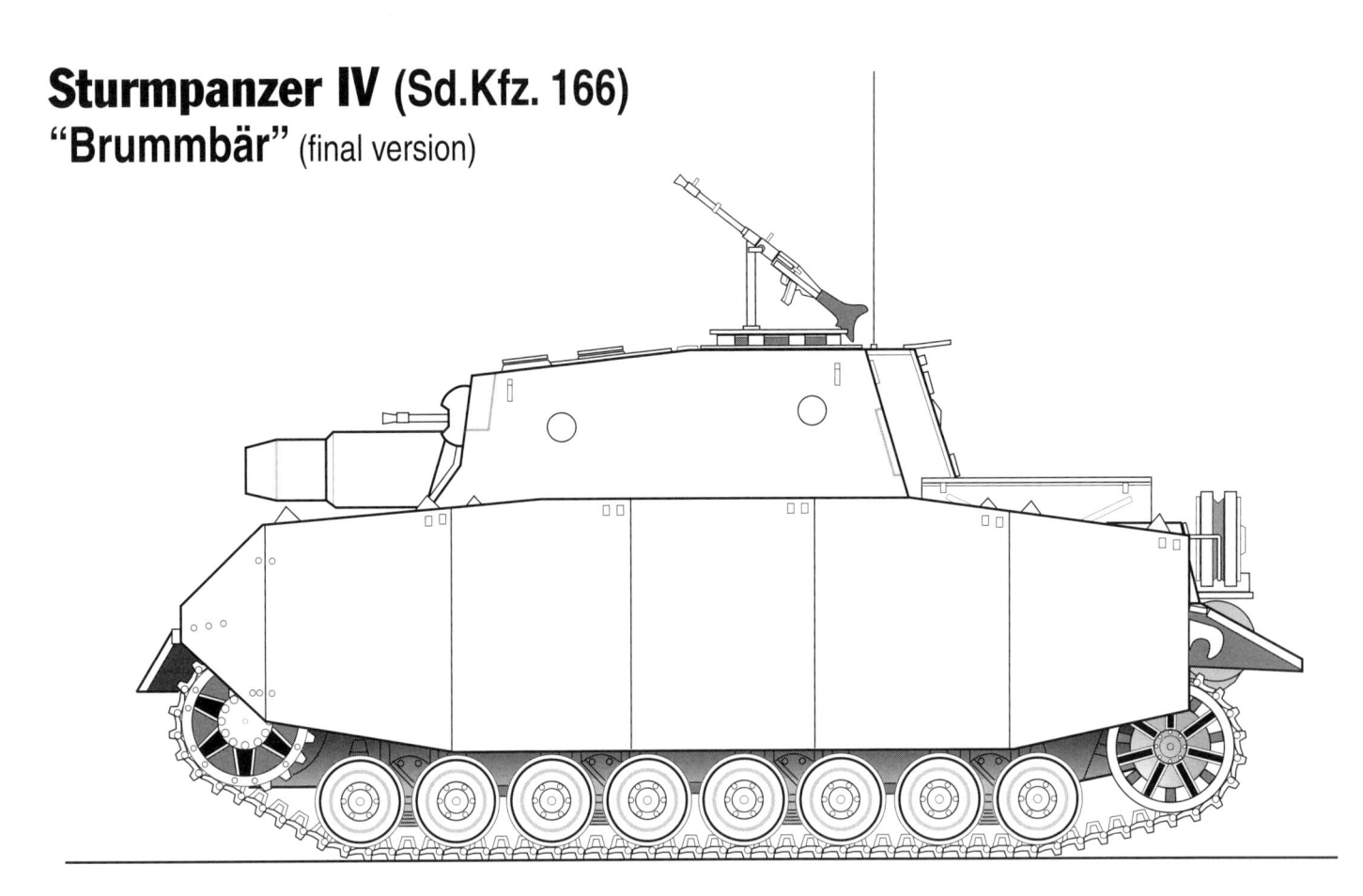

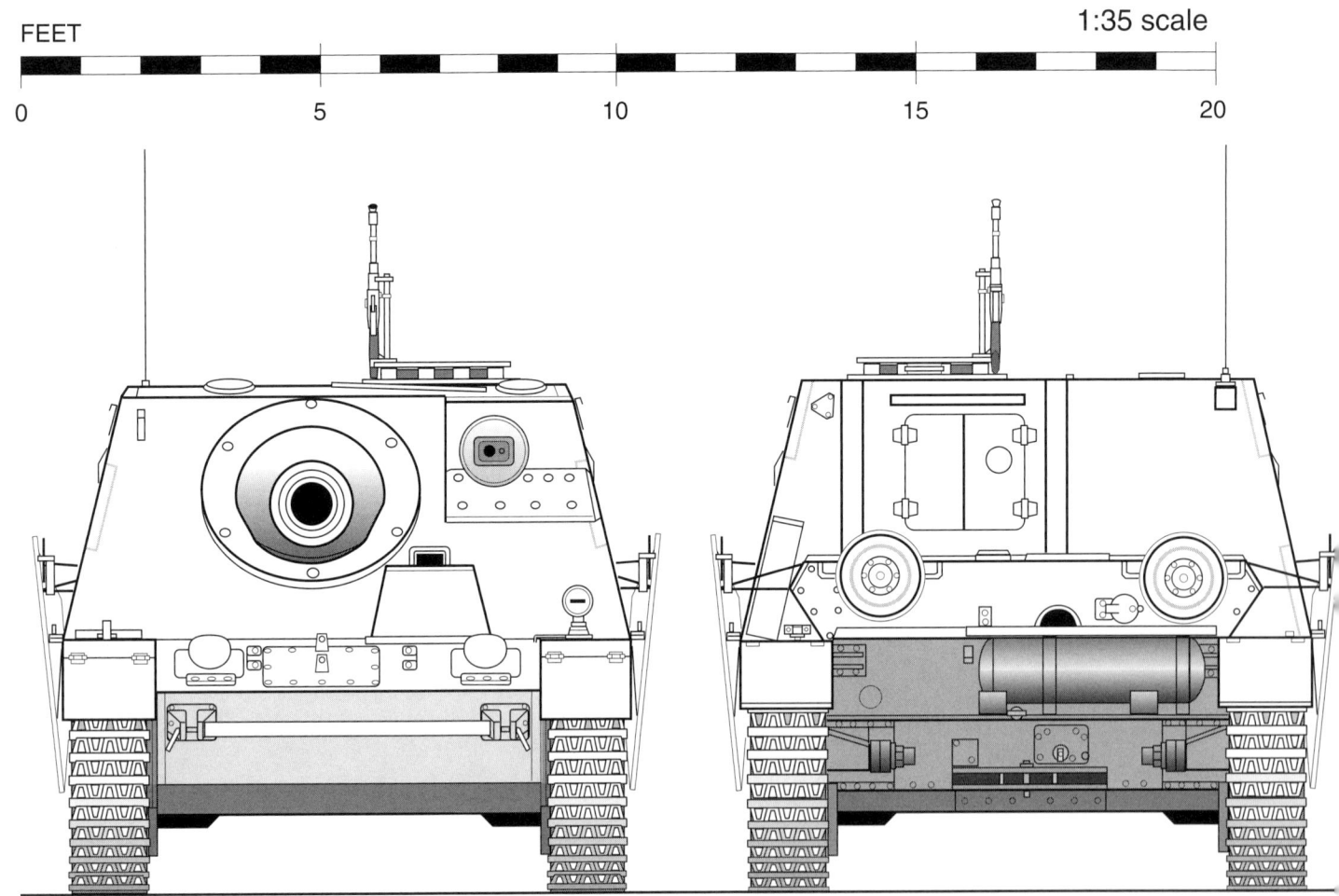

Sturmpanzer IV (Sd.Kfz. 166)
"Brummbär" (final version)

FEET 0 5 10 15 20   1:35 scale

18   German Late War Armored Fighting Vehicles

Sturmpanzer IV (Sd.Kfz. 166)
"Brummbär" (final version)

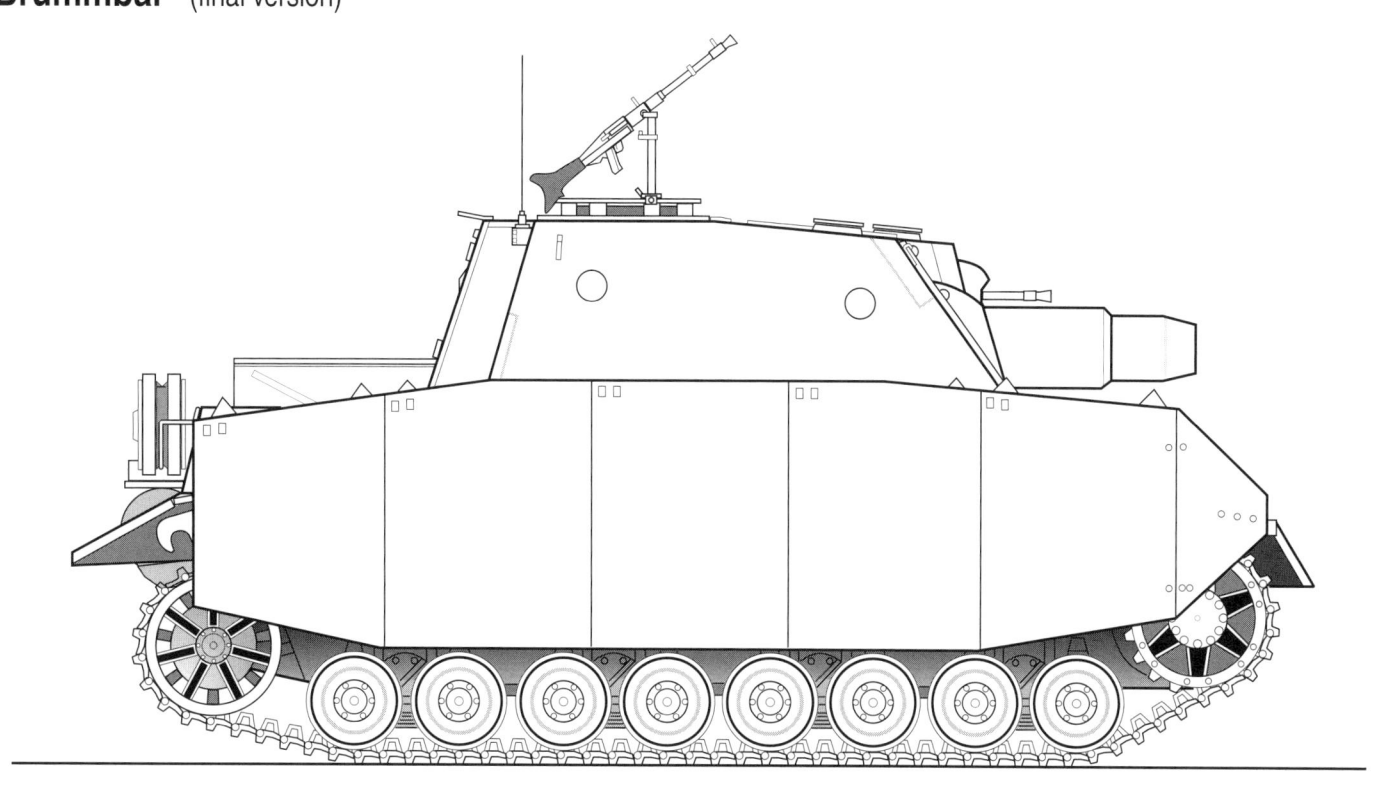

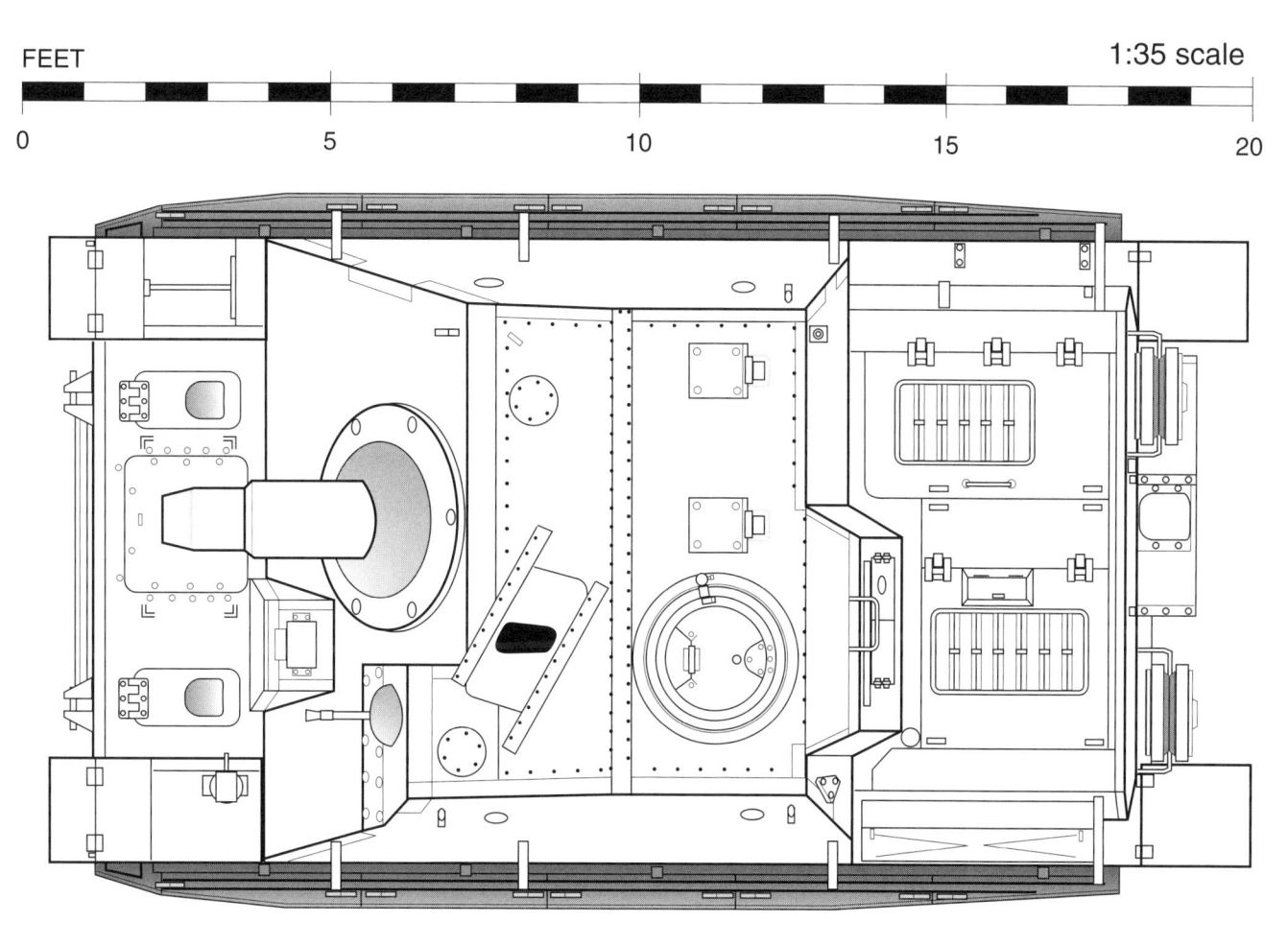

FEET

1:35 scale

0   5   10   15   20

German Late War Armored Fighting Vehicles   19

Pz.Kpfw. IV Ausf. J
(Sd.Kfz. 161/2) final production

The early Ausf. J carried the normal skirt plates, but the final models were fitted with wire mesh skirts. In order to show the return rollers and other detail, this drawing shows only the tubular metal supports on which the wire mesh skirts were mounted.

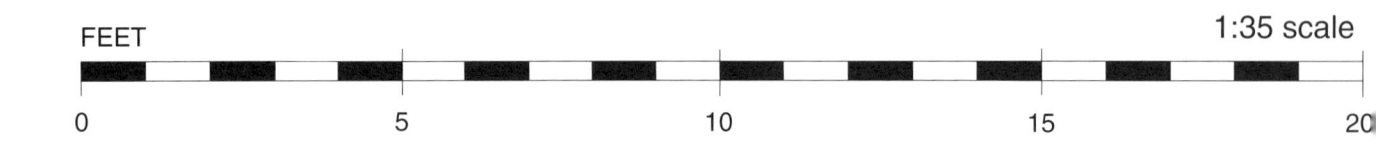

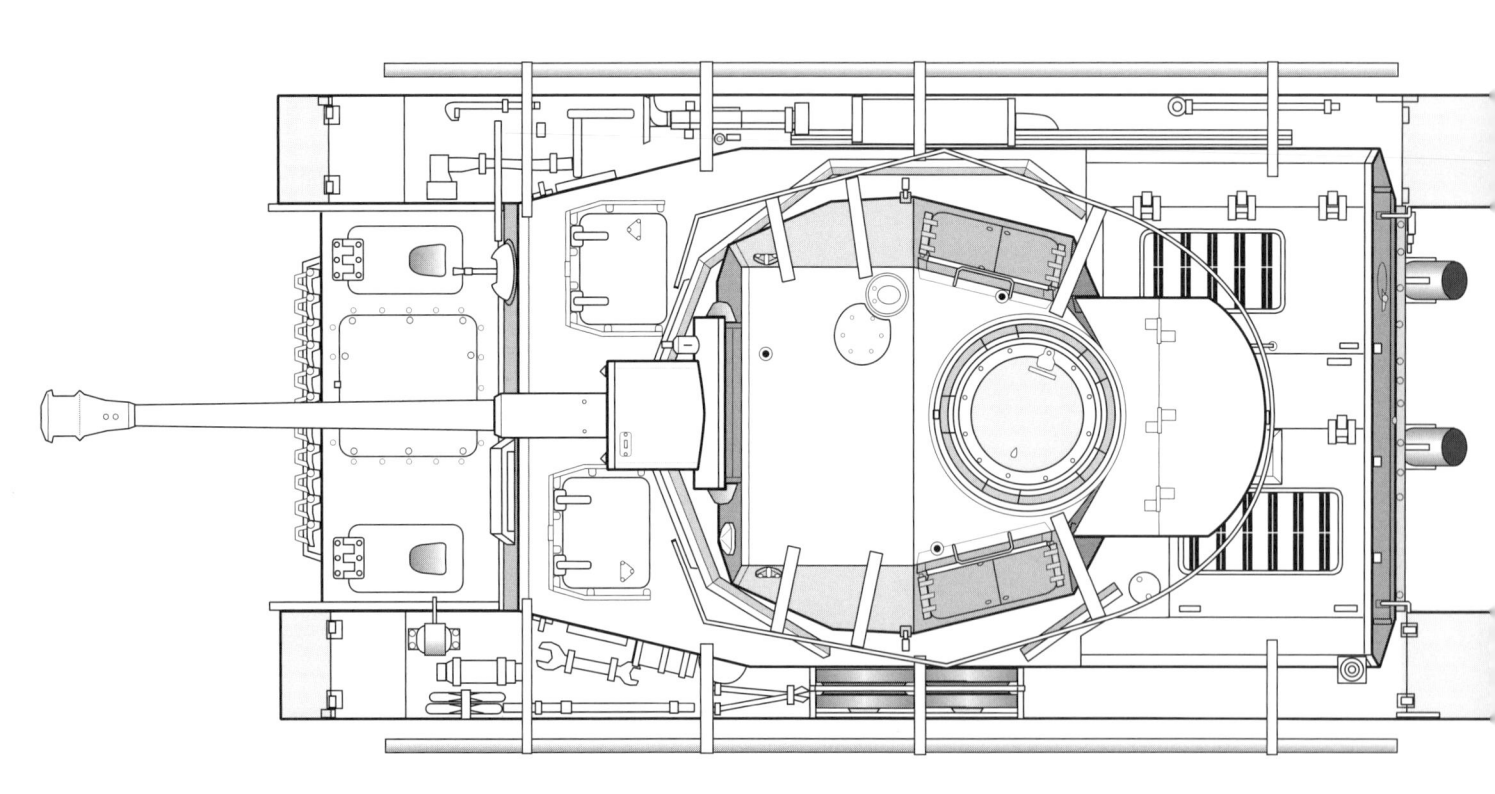

FEET 1:35 scale
0   5   10   15   20

20 German Late War Armored Fighting Vehicles

Pz.Kpfw. IV Ausf. J
(Sd.Kfz. 161/2) final production

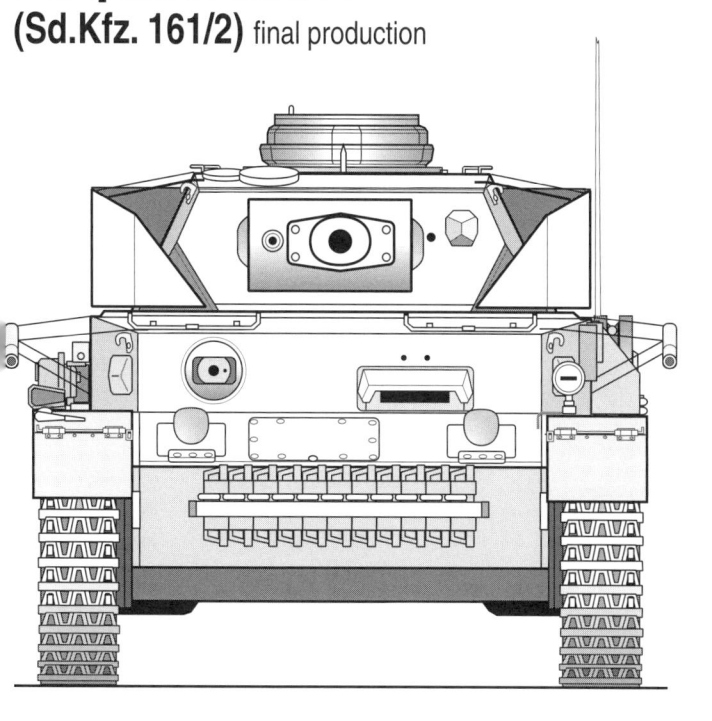

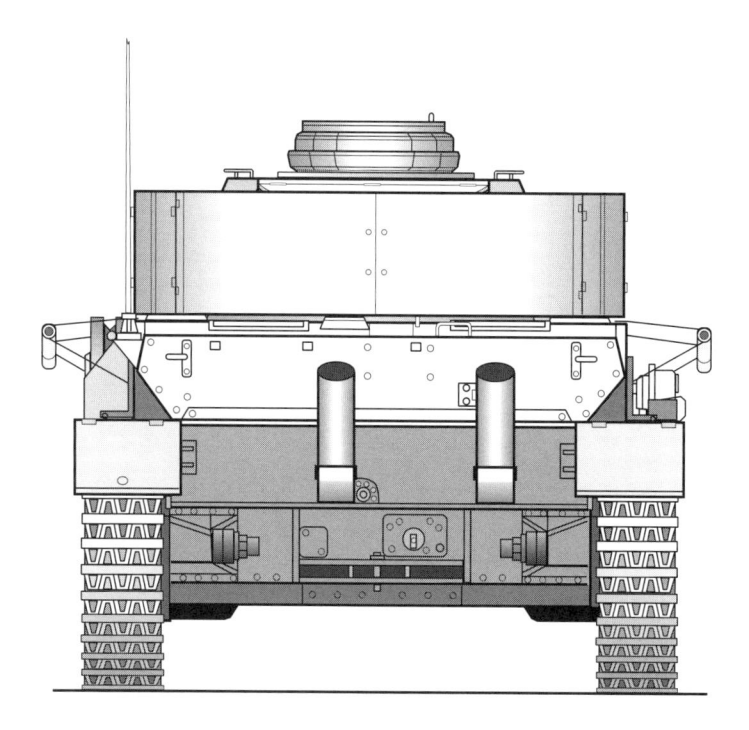

What appears to be a Pz.Kpfw. IV Ausf. H that was knocked out west of Salerno, Italy, in the vicinity of Cava on September 23, 1943.

German Late War Armored Fighting Vehicles

Panzerspähwagen II (2cm) "Luchs" (Sd.Kfz.123)

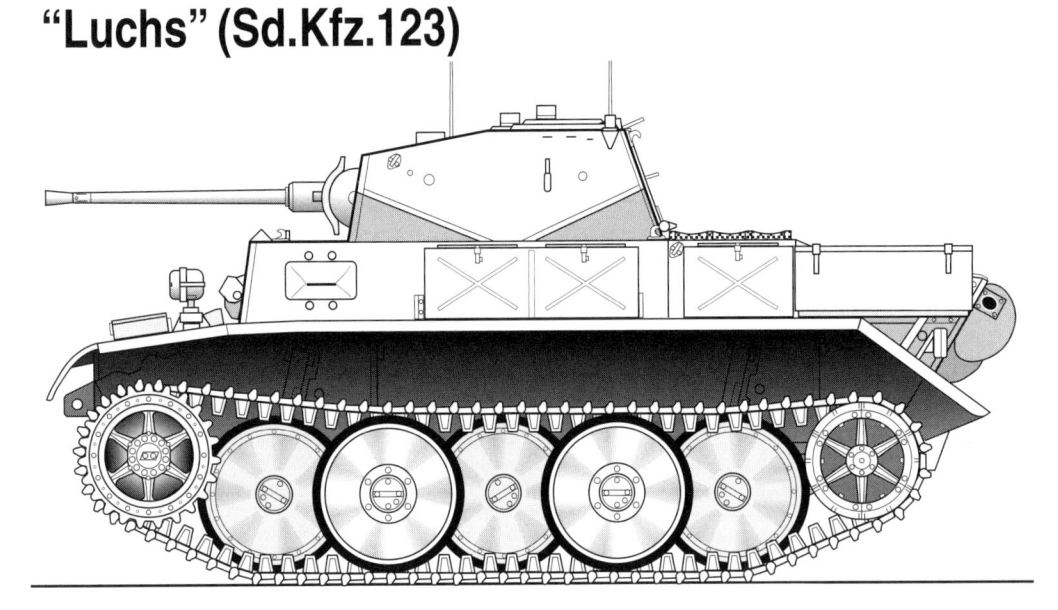

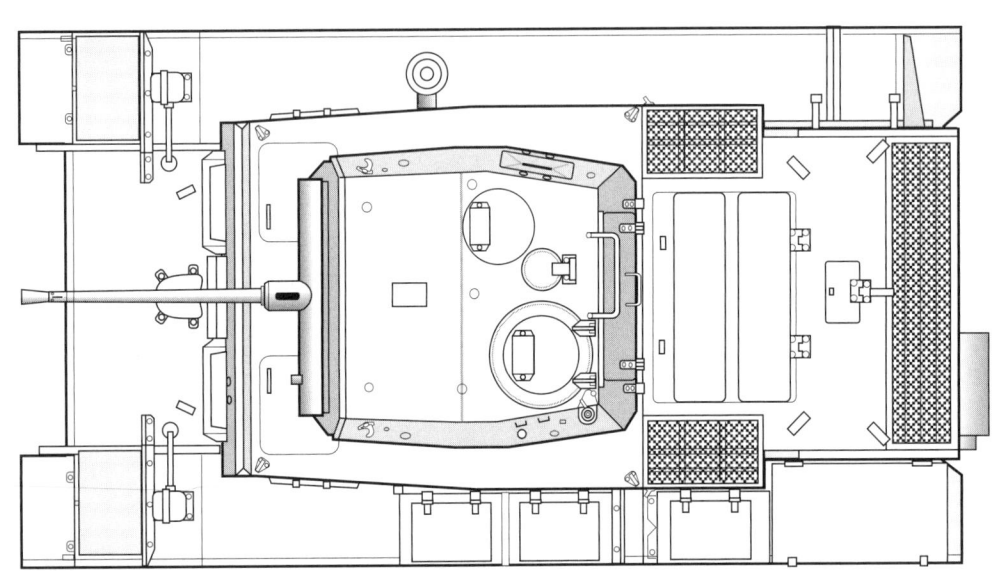

The "Luchs" was developed as a fully-tracked reconnaissance vehicle that could operate both on the road and off. The need for such a vehicle had been obvious ever since the Polish campaign of 1939, where recon vehicles had been restricted to roads mainly because of their poor cross-country performance.

The original contract order with M.A.N. was for 800 vehicles, with the first 100 fitted with the 2cm gun and then with the 5cm gun starting with the 101st vehicle. However, the "Luchs" did not prove as reliable as had been hoped and the production run ended at 100 vehicles, plus a few upgraded prototypes.

The first "Luchs" Kompanie was the 2.Panzer-Späh-Kompanie/ Panzer-Aufklärungs-Abteilung 9. This unit served in the 9.Panzerdivision on the Eastern Front as of June, 1943. At that time it was made up of 29 "Luchs" and 4 Sd.Kfz.250/1, but by August 17th it reported only 5 "Luchs" operational, and eventually was disbanded in late September, 1943.

The only other unit to use the "Luchs" at full company strength was the 2. Kompanie/ Panzer-Aufklärungs-Abteilung 4. This unit served with the 4.Panzerdivision on the Eastern Front from September, 1943.

A Luchs-Kompanie was later reestablished for the 9.Panzerdivision again, and renamed 1.Kompanie/Panzer-Aufklärungs-Abteilung 9. This unit saw action in Normandy trying to stem the Allied advances, but again 9.Panzerdivision had lost all its Luchs by late August, 1944. There were also a few more Luchs scattered around, but only in ones and twos.

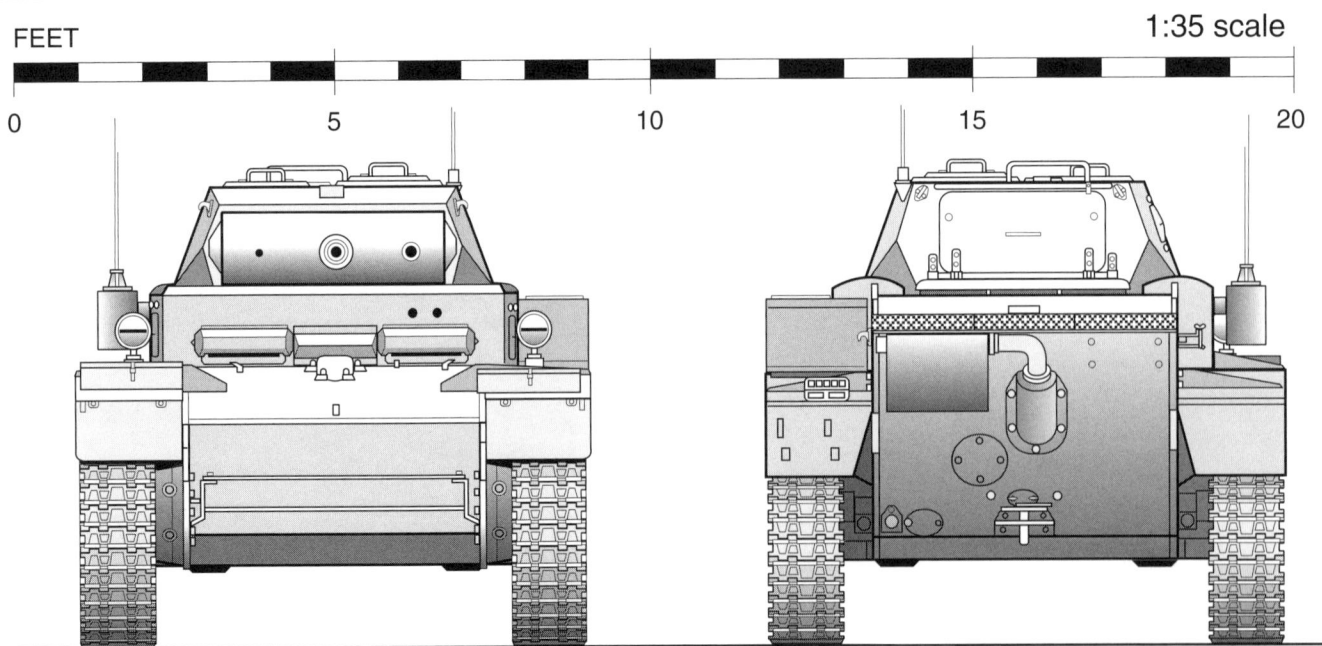

1:35 scale

22 German Late War Armored Fighting Vehicles

Schwimmwagen K2s Kfz. 1/20
(Volkswagen KdF. 166)

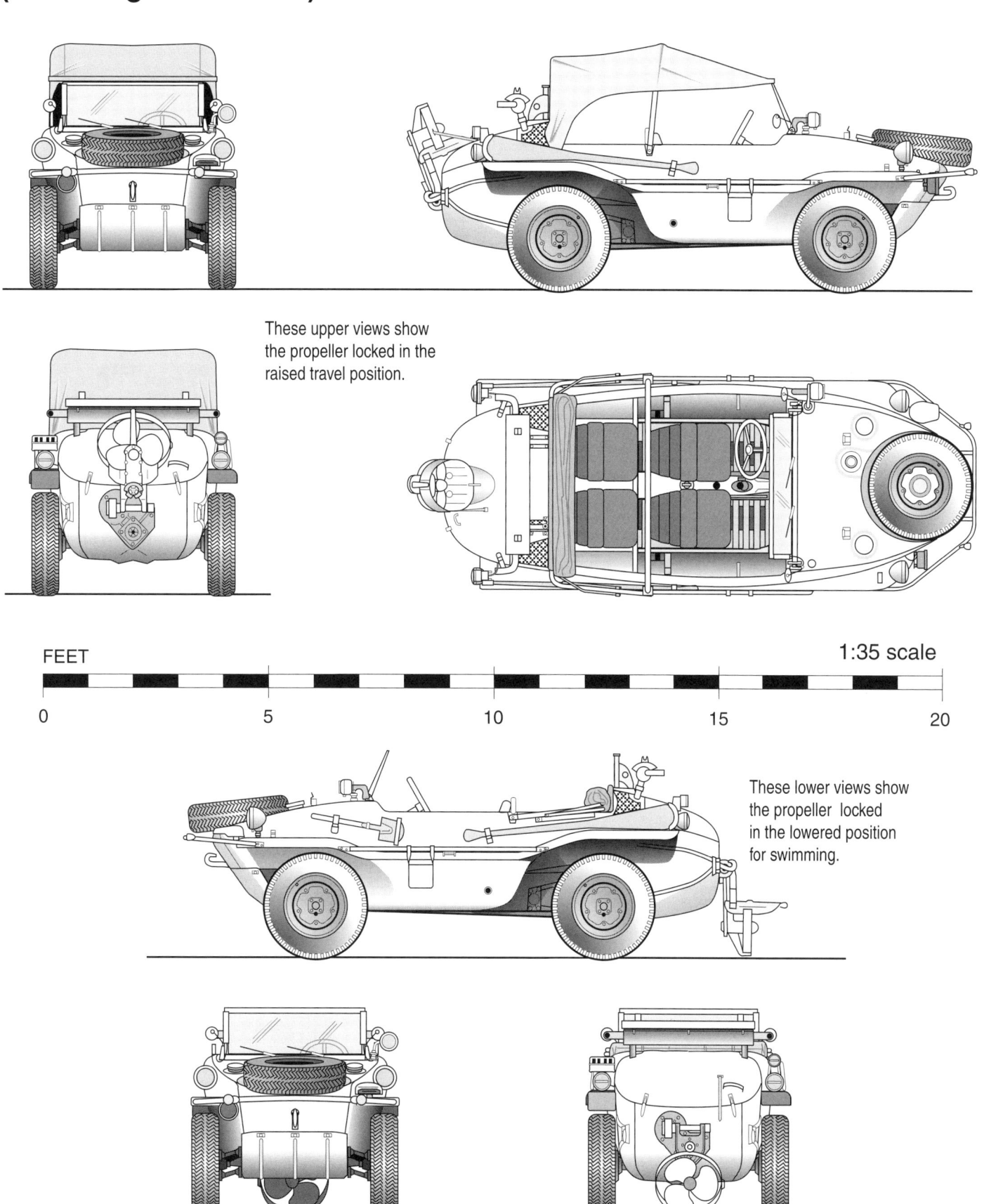

These upper views show the propeller locked in the raised travel position.

FEET 0 5 10 15 20   1:35 scale

These lower views show the propeller locked in the lowered position for swimming.

German Late War Armored Fighting Vehicles   23

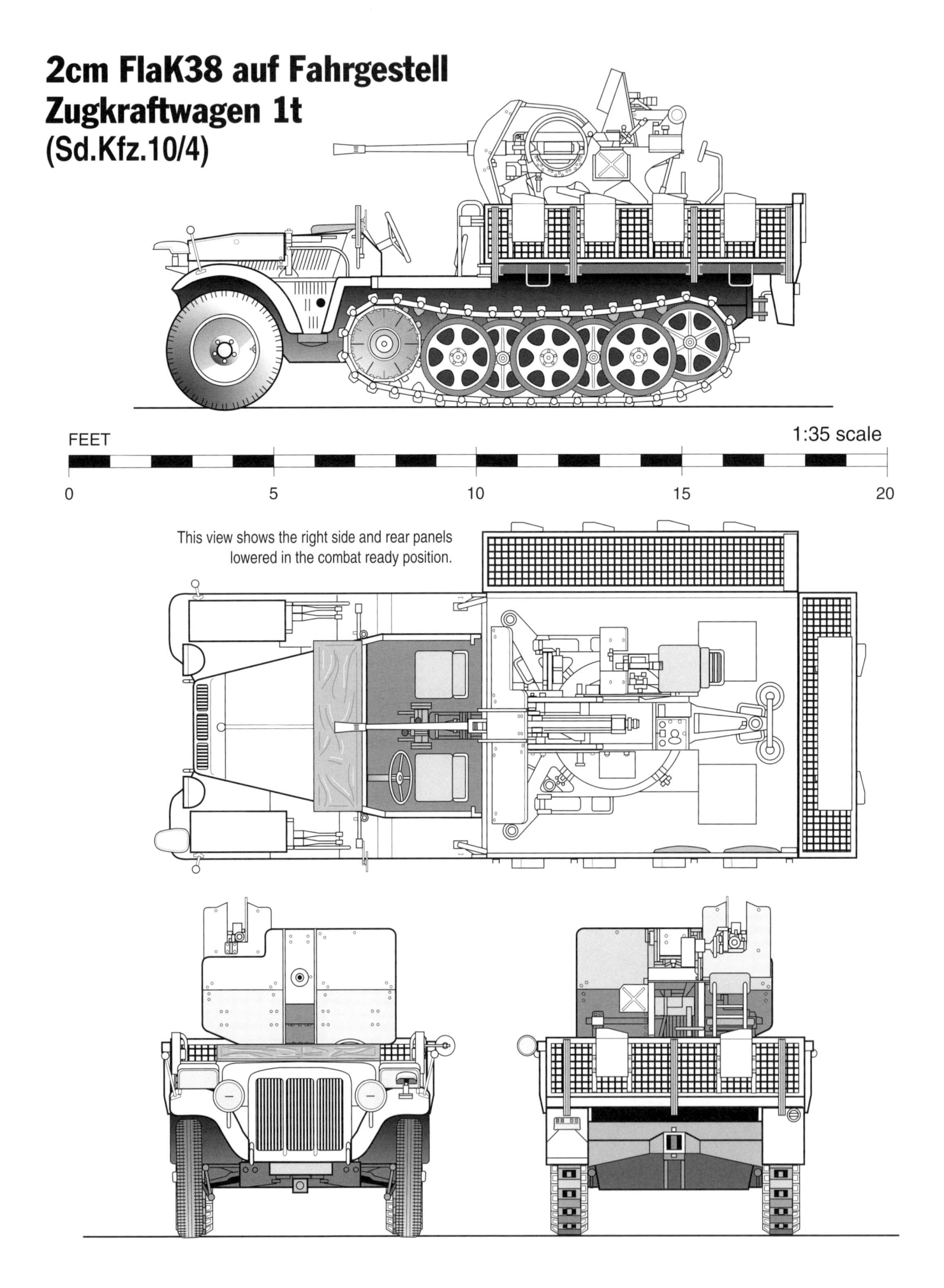

2cm FlaK38 auf Fahrgestell Zugkraftwagen 1t
(Sd.Kfz.10/4)

FEET

1:35 scale

0　　　　5　　　　10　　　　15　　　　20

This view shows the right side and rear panels lowered in the combat ready position.

24　German Late War Armored Fighting Vehicles

Jagdpanzer IV (Sd.Kfz. 162)

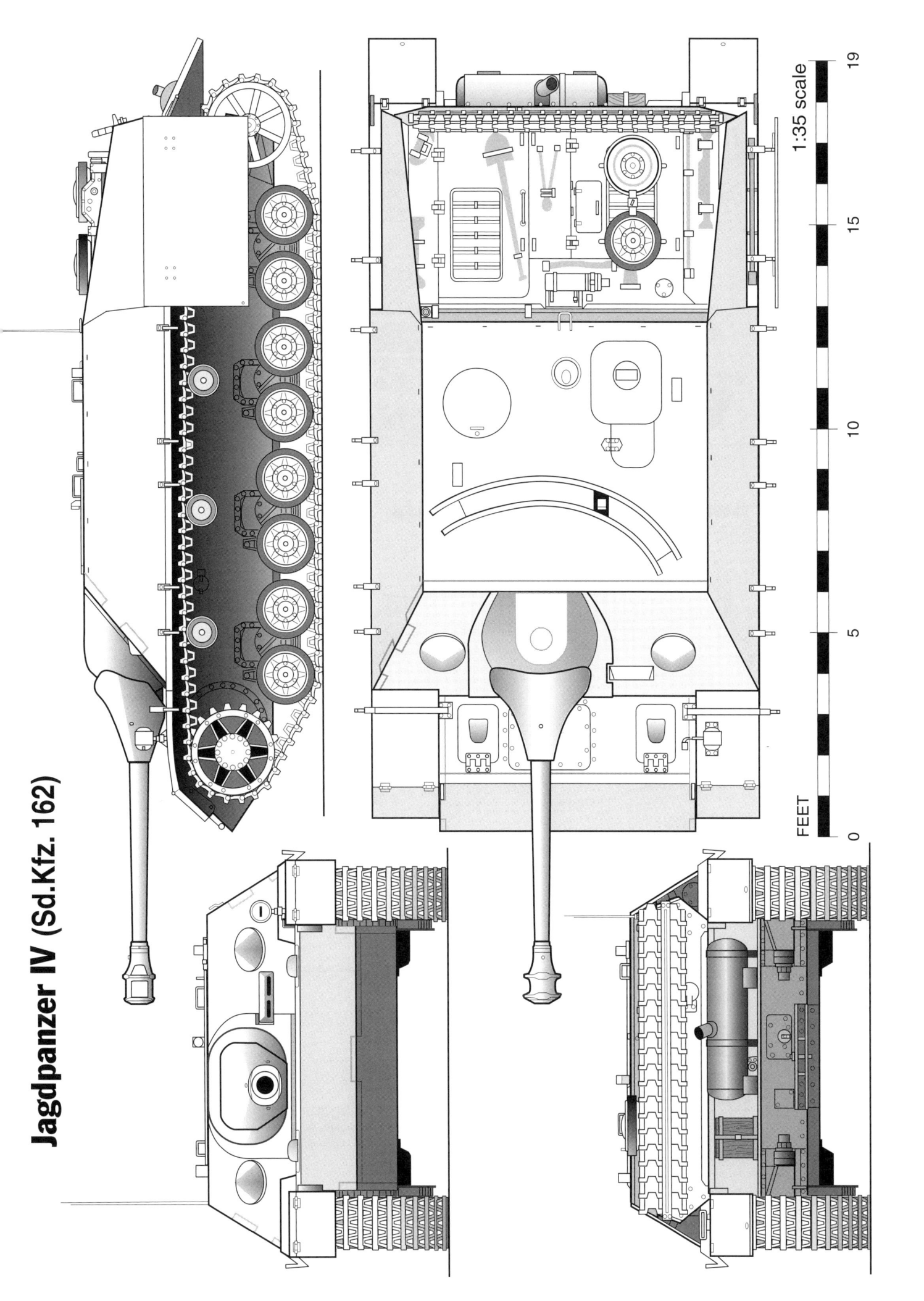

1:35 scale

FEET 0 5 10 15 19

Leichter Schützenpanzerwagen
(Sd.Kfz. 250/11)
with schwerer Panzerbüchse 41

FEET 1:35 scale
0   5   10   15   20

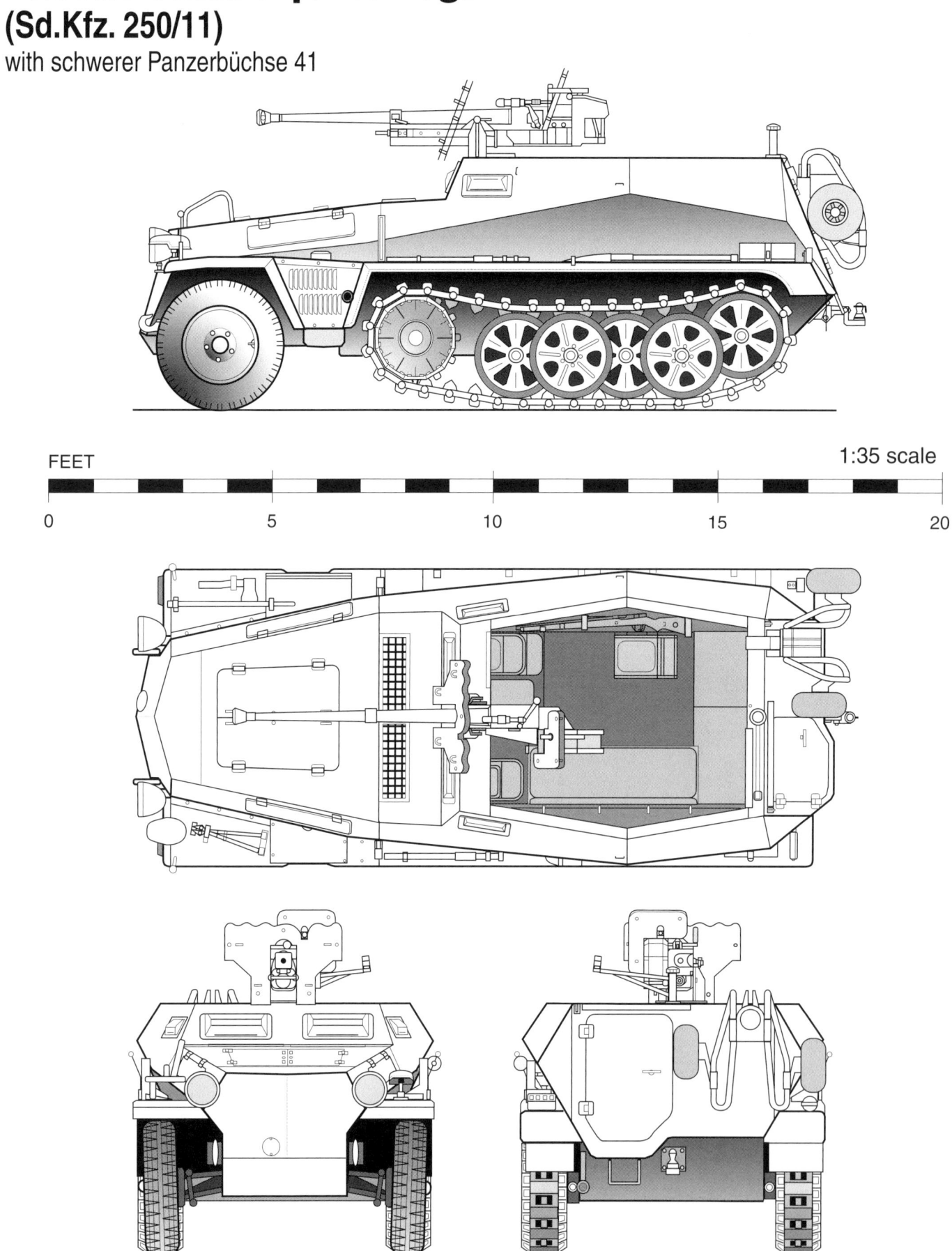

26   German Late War Armored Fighting Vehicles

Schwerer Panzerspähwagen (5cm)
(Sd.Kfz. 234/2) "Puma"

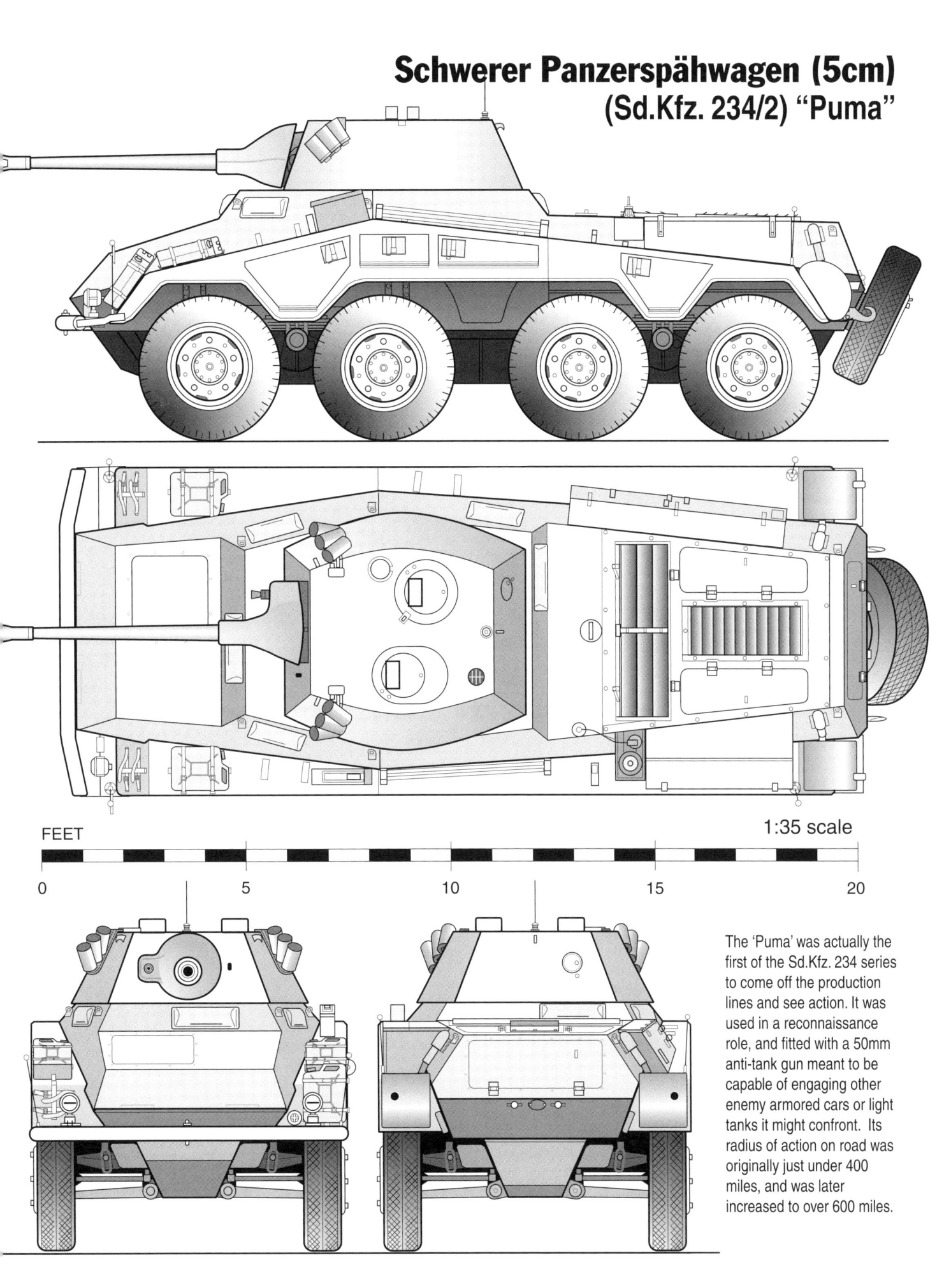

FEET

1:35 scale

The 'Puma' was actually the first of the Sd.Kfz. 234 series to come off the production lines and see action. It was used in a reconnaissance role, and fitted with a 50mm anti-tank gun meant to be capable of engaging other enemy armored cars or light tanks it might confront. Its radius of action on road was originally just under 400 miles, and was later increased to over 600 miles.

German Late War Armored Fighting Vehicles

Schwerer Ladungsträger (Sd.Kfz. 301) Ausf. C,
Sonderschlepper B IV

The B IV was a one-man vehicle provided with a radio-controlled guidance system. The driver would take it to a forward area, and then it would be guided to its target by an accompanying Tiger tank. It would then release its 500kg demolition charge, and be guided back to safety. The control Tigers Is carried an extra radio antenna on the right side of their turret.

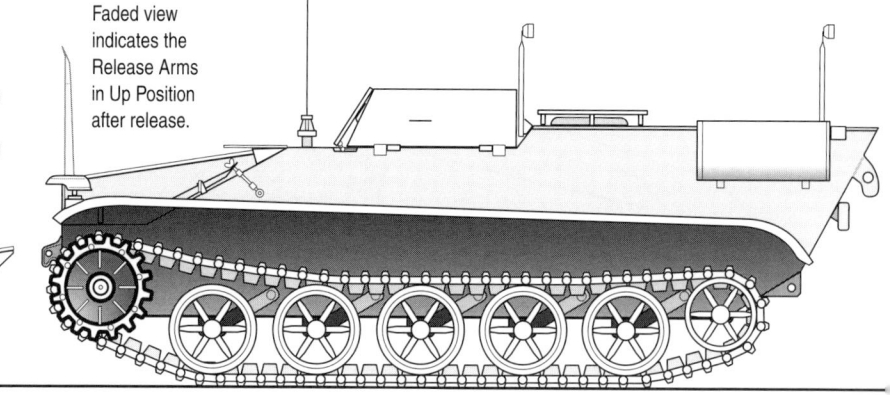

Faded view indicates the Release Arms in Up Position after release.

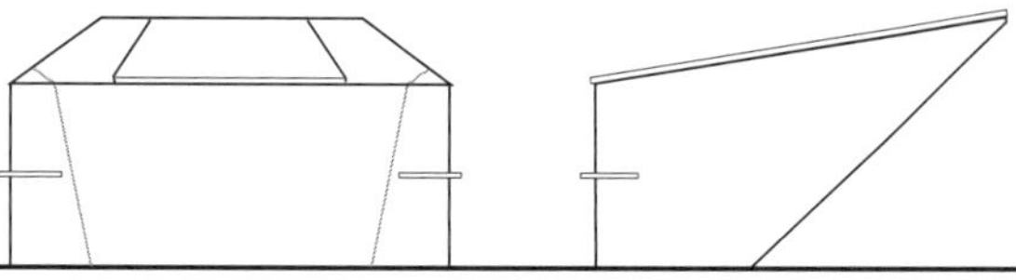

Front and side view of unloaded charge.

The idea of a remote-controlled vehicle to place charges and clear minefields was conceived early in the war, and Borgward began development of a B 1, tracked radio-controlled vehicle in 1940. This was followed by the B2, a slightly larger vehicle weighing 2.3 tons. By 1941 they had trialed the B IV and production of the 3.6 ton BIV Ausf. B began in May 1942. The B IV Ausf. C was a total redesign; longer, with increased wheel spacing, a larger engine, the driver's position moved to the left side, heavier armor, and a final weight of 4.85 tons. Production reached 616 of Ausf. A, 260 Ausf. B, and 305 of Ausf. C. The new dry pin steel track was introduced midway through the Ausf. B production run.

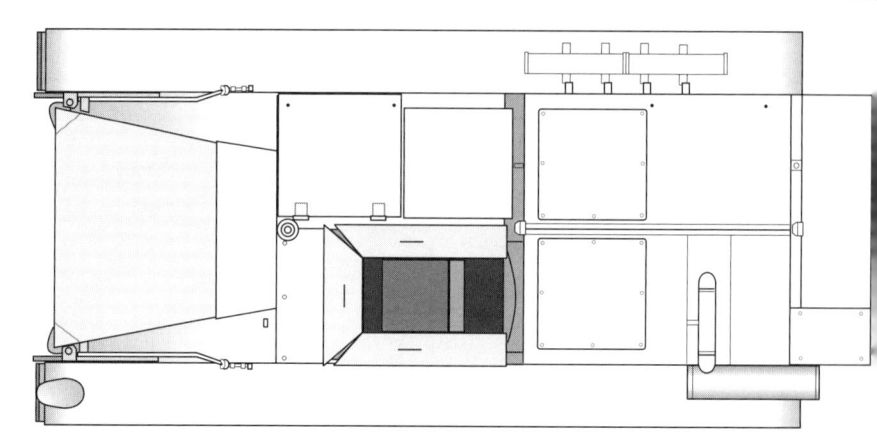

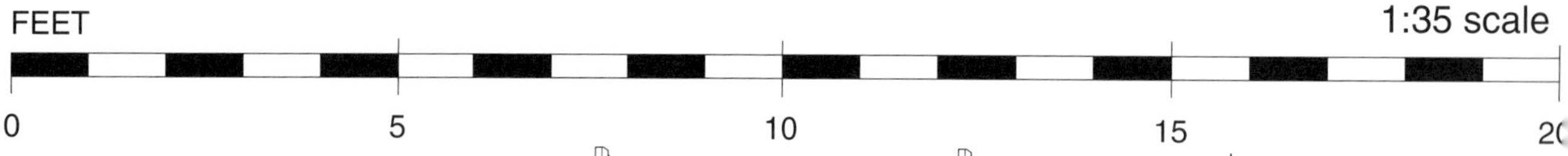

FEET   1:35 scale
0   5   10   15   20

These vehicles were first controlled by Pz.III tanks, then StuG.IIIs and finally by Tiger tanks. The first serious use of B IVs was with Panzer Abteilung (Funklenk) 300, using Pz.IIIs as control tanks. It was assigned to Heeres Gruppe Sud in mid-1942, but ended up with Heeres Gruppe Nord by Sept./42 and renumbered 301.

The next major Funklenk deployment was at Kursk, where the HQ of Pz.Abt.(FKL) 301 was assigned to Heeres Gruppe Mitte with three new companies: 312, 313 & 314. These independent companies were formed in Jan/43, and were all controlled from StuG.IIIs.

Eventually a 315, 316 Kp. were formed in Aug./43. By the time of the Anzio landings Pz.Abt.(FKL) 301 was using Tiger I 's as control tanks. Each Tiger controlled three B IVs. In Dec./43 Pz.Kp.313 was assigned to s.PzAbt.508 as its 3. Kompanie, and in Jan./44 the 314 was assigned to s.Pz.Abt.504 as its 3. Kompanie, and 316 was assigned to Panzer Lehr. In time several of these units were devastated, and eventually a Pz.Abt.(FKL) 302 was formed from their remnants. Late in the war a Pz.Abt.(FKL) 303 was organized by pulling together Pz.Kp.(FKL) 319, the 4, Kp./Pz.Abt.(FKL) 301, and 4.Kp./Pz.Abt.(FKL) 302.

The last unit to be formed from other remnants was Panzer Zug (FKL) 303 in Feb./45.

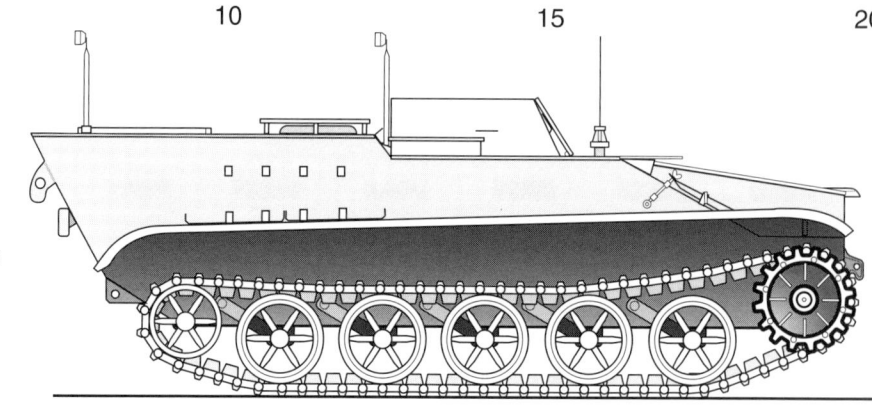

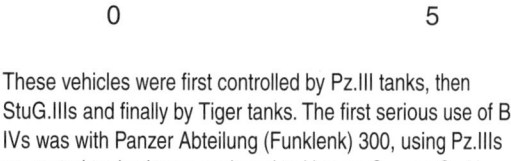

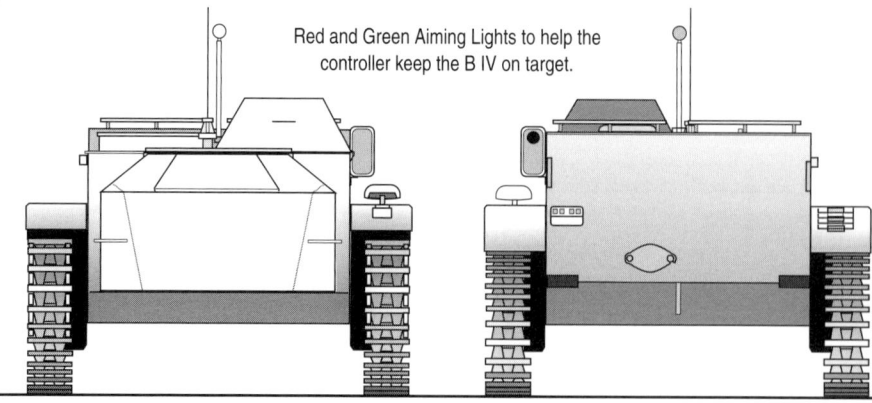

Red and Green Aiming Lights to help the controller keep the B IV on target.

28   German Late War Armored Fighting Vehicles

Leichter Schützenpanzerwagen
(Sd.Kfz. 250/8) Neü Art
(with 5cm PaK 38 Neü Ausf.)

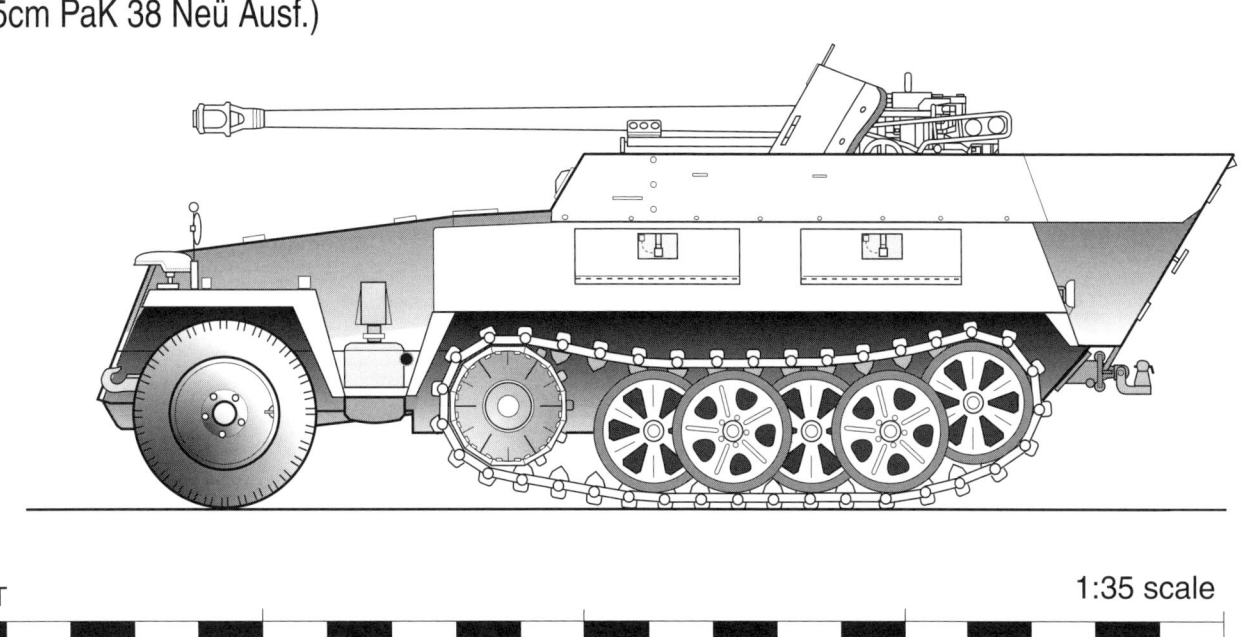

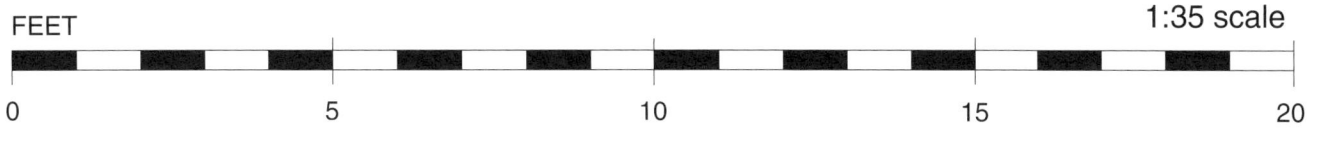

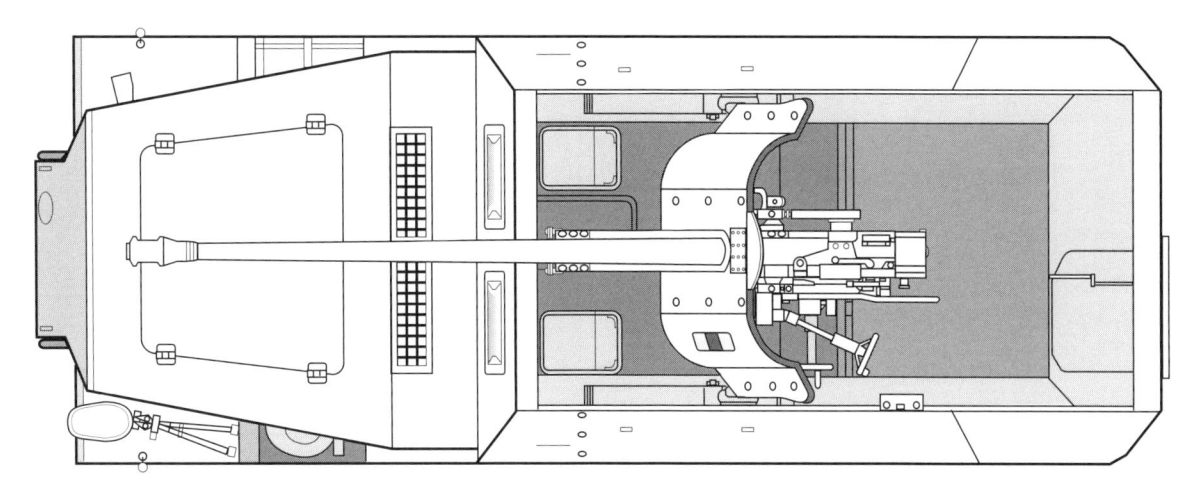

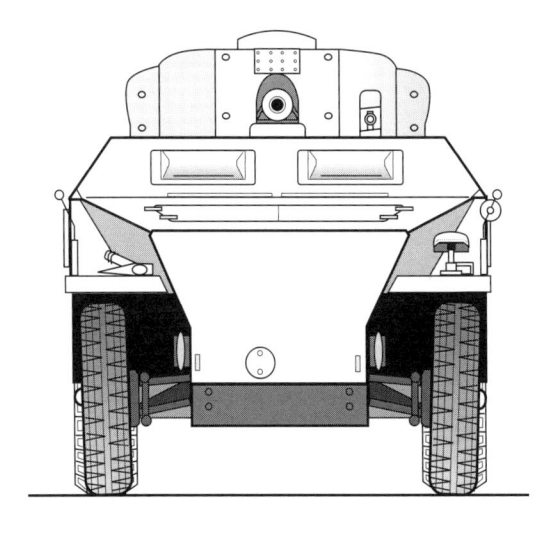

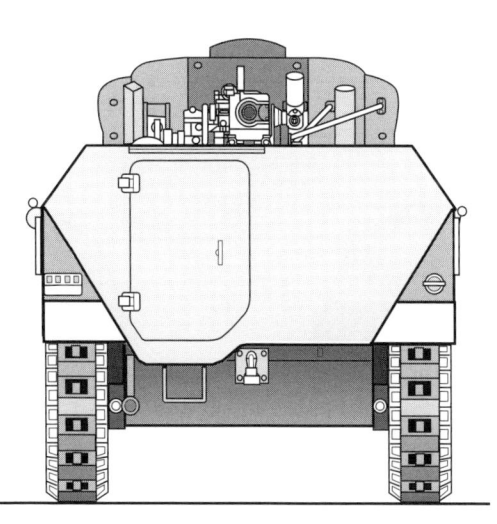

FEET

1:35 scale

0　　　　　5　　　　　　　　10　　　　　　　　15　　　　　　20

German Late War Armored Fighting Vehicles　29

Leichter Gepanzerter Kraftwagen
(Sd.Kfz. 250/9) Neü Art
(Semi-Tracked Armored Car)

FEET　　1:35 scale

0　　5　　10　　15　　20

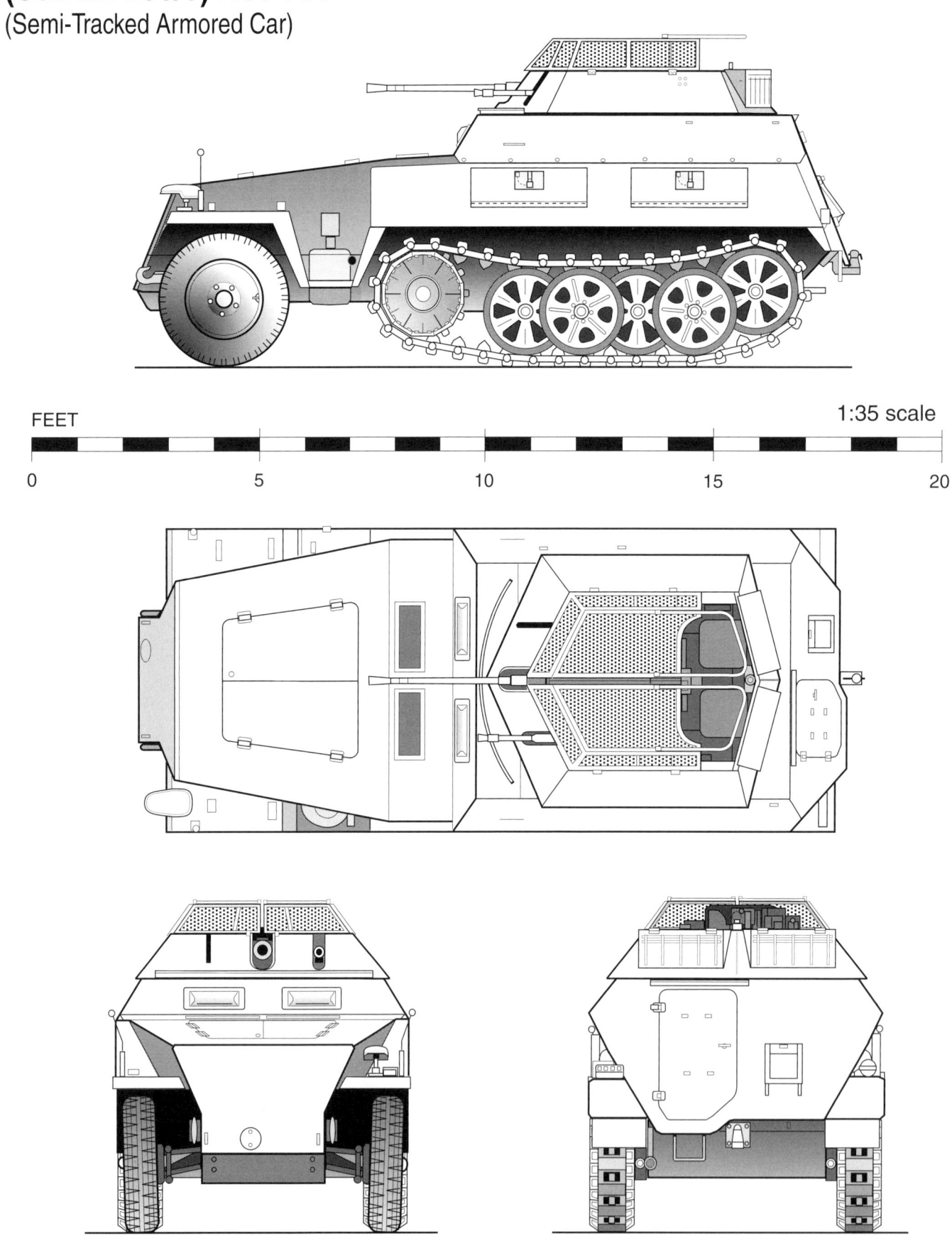

30　German Late War Armored Fighting Vehicles

Jagdpanzer 38(t) "Hetzer"
(Early production)

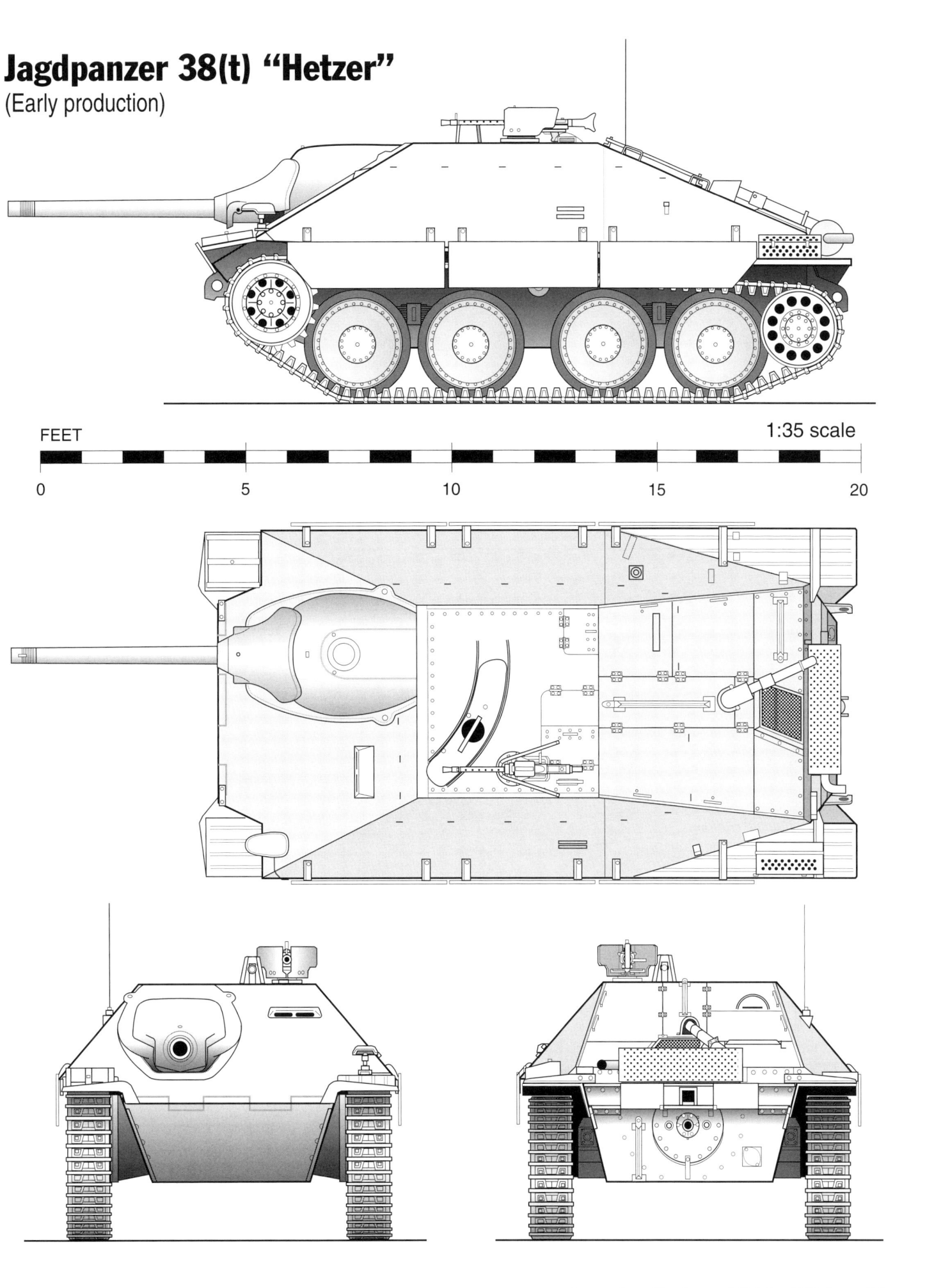

FEET 1:35 scale

German Late War Armored Fighting Vehicles 31

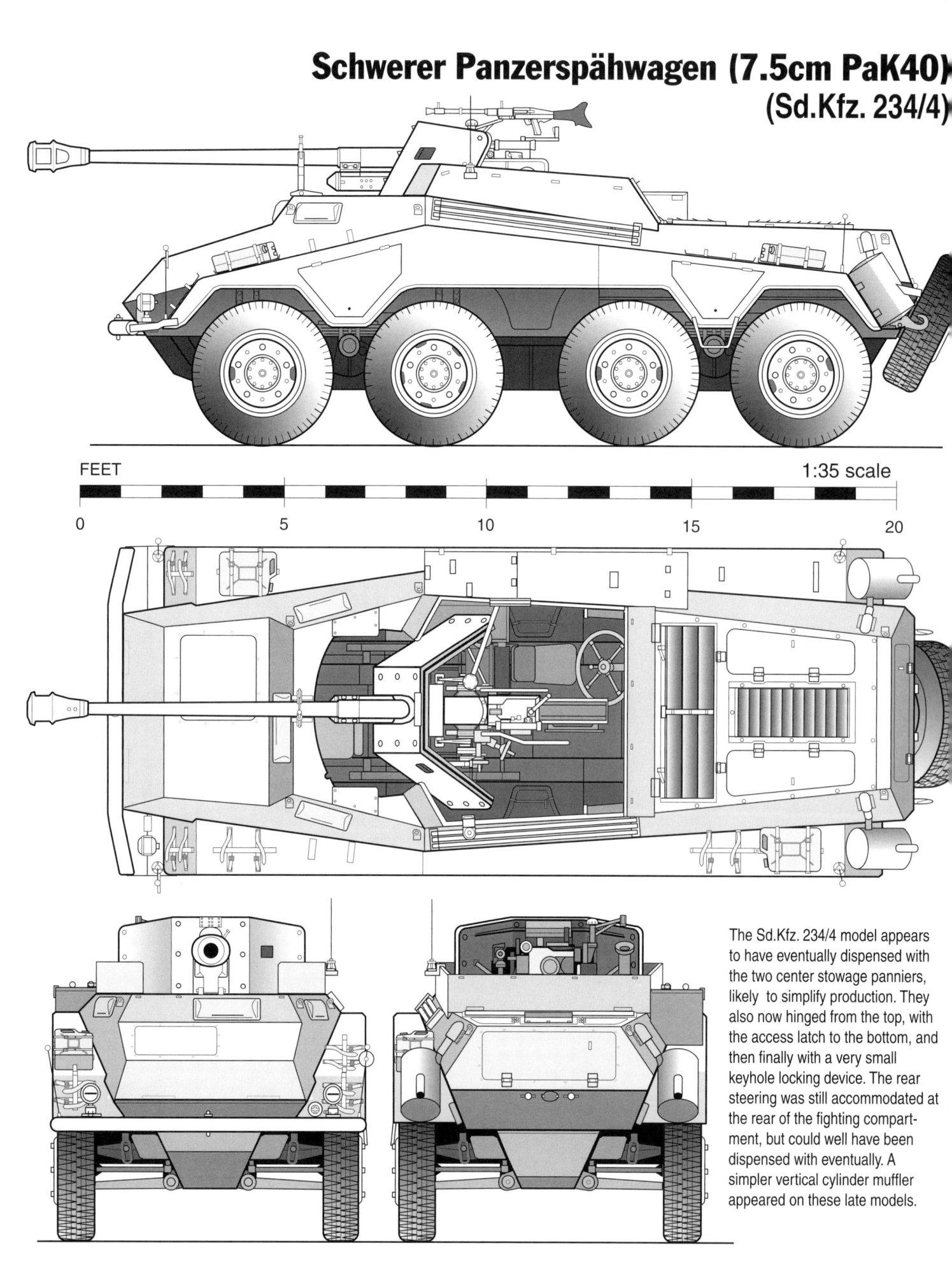

Schwerer Panzerspähwagen (7.5cm PaK40)
(Sd.Kfz. 234/4)

FEET 1:35 scale
0   5   10   15   20

The Sd.Kfz. 234/4 model appears to have eventually dispensed with the two center stowage panniers, likely to simplify production. They also now hinged from the top, with the access latch to the bottom, and then finally with a very small keyhole locking device. The rear steering was still accommodated at the rear of the fighting compartment, but could well have been dispensed with eventually. A simpler vertical cylinder muffler appeared on these late models.

32 German Late War Armored Fighting Vehicles

Flammpanzer 38(t) "Hetzer"

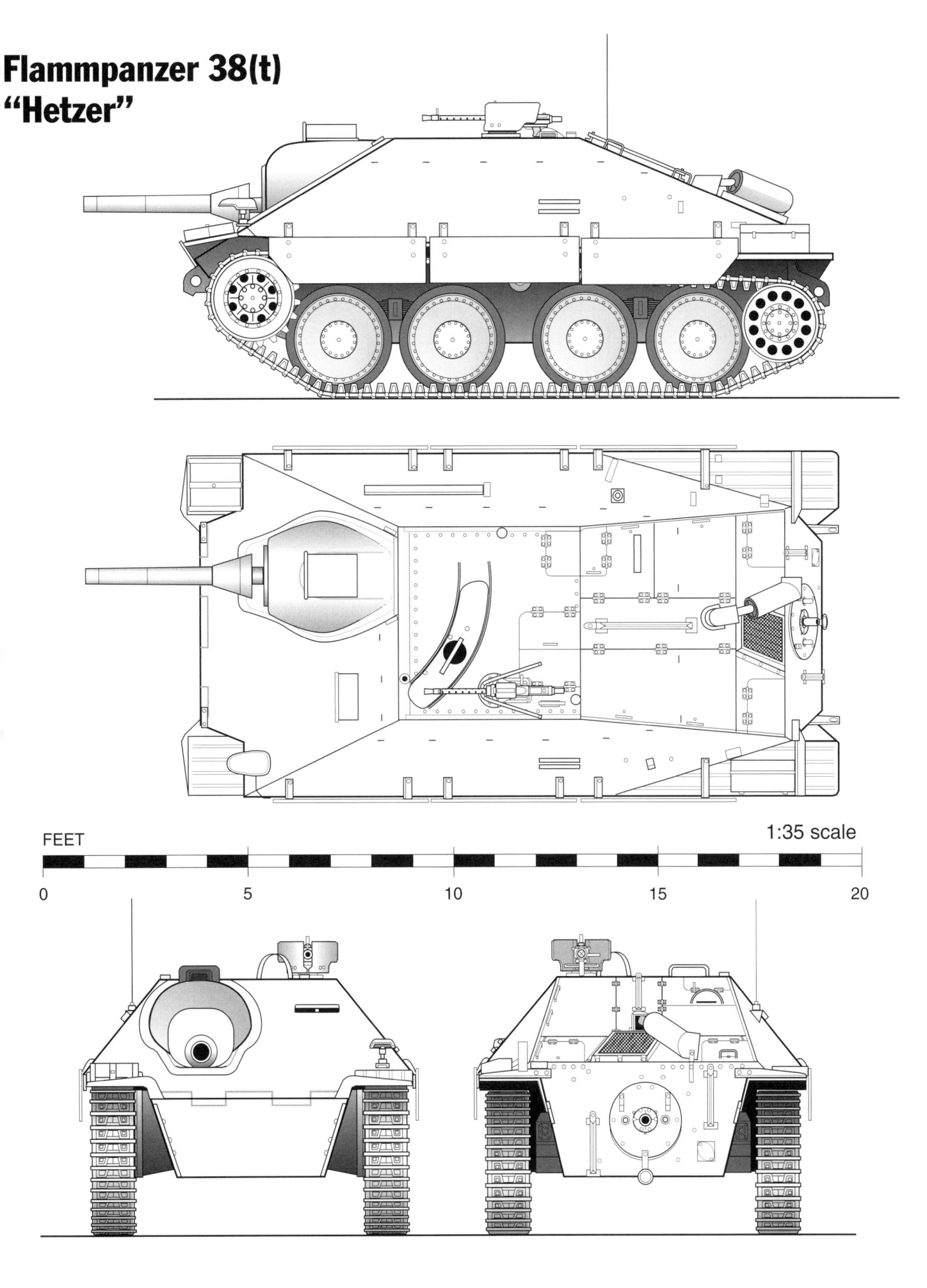

FEET

1:35 scale

German Late War Armored Fighting Vehicles 33

Bergepanzer 38(t) Hetzer

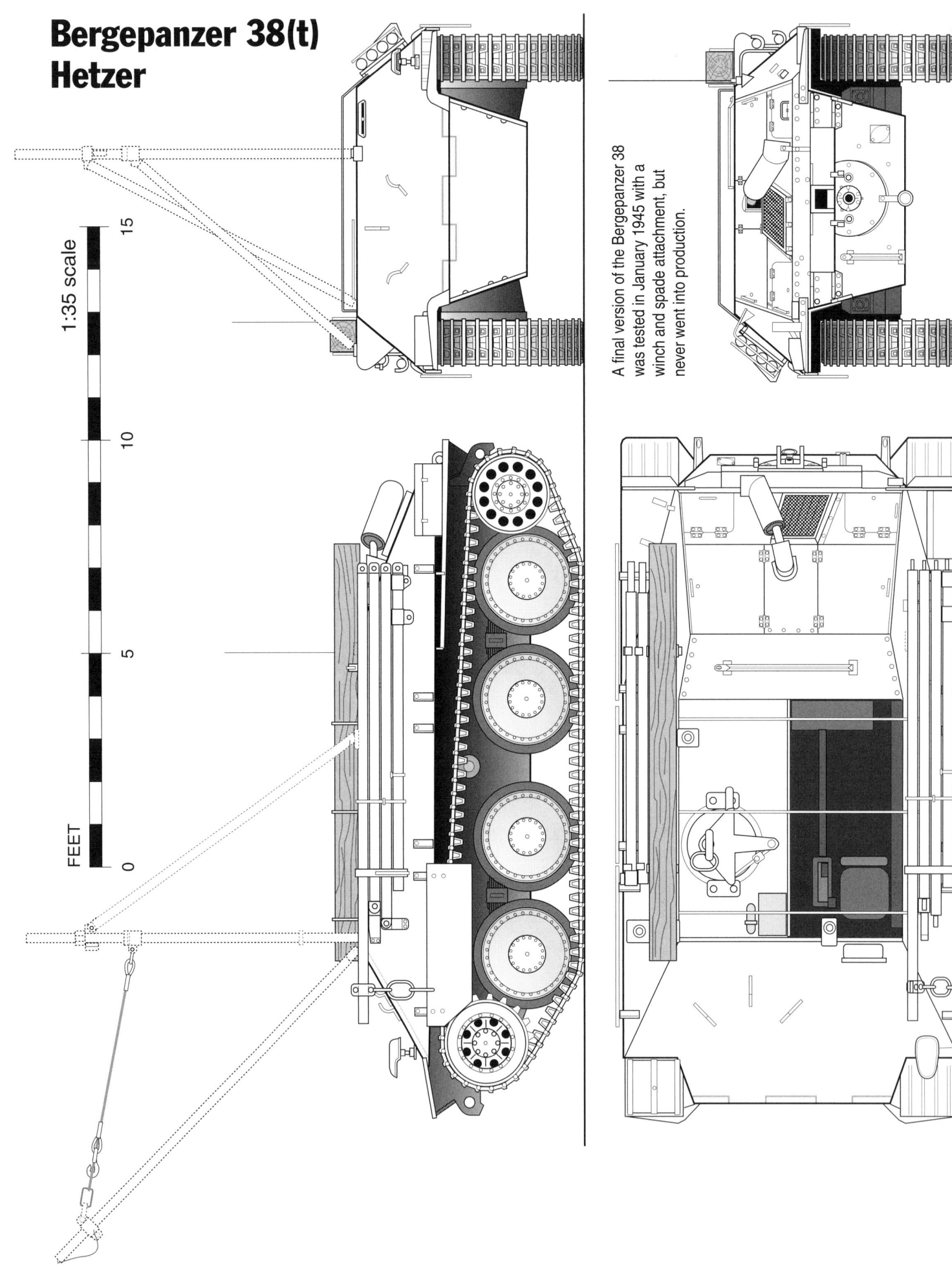

1:35 scale

FEET

A final version of the Bergepanzer 38 was tested in January 1945 with a winch and spade attachment, but never went into production.

34 German Late War Armored Fighting Vehicles

A pair of comparison shots showing the different muffler arrangements, early version above and later version below.

German Late War Armored Fighting Vehicles 35

Pz.Kpfw. Tiger Ausf. E,
(Sd.Kfz. 181) mid production

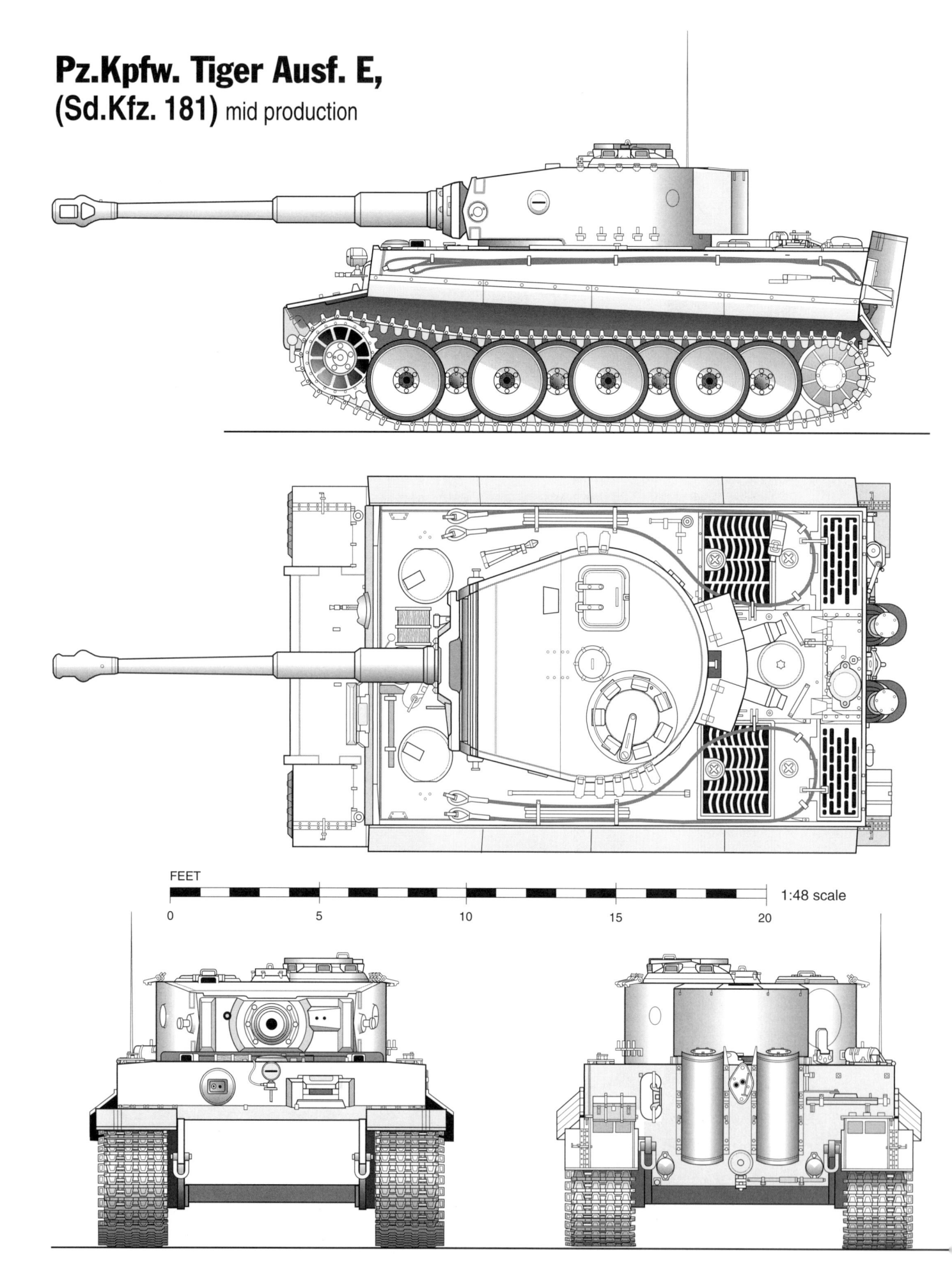

FEET
0   5   10   15   20
1:48 scale

36   German Late War Armored Fighting Vehicles

Opel "Maultier"
15cm Panzerwerfer 42 auf Sf
(Sd.Kfz. 4/1)

FEET

0   5   10   15   20

1:35 scale

Armored rad plates in the closed position.

German Late War Armored Fighting Vehicles 37

Panzer IV/70(A) Alkett interim production design

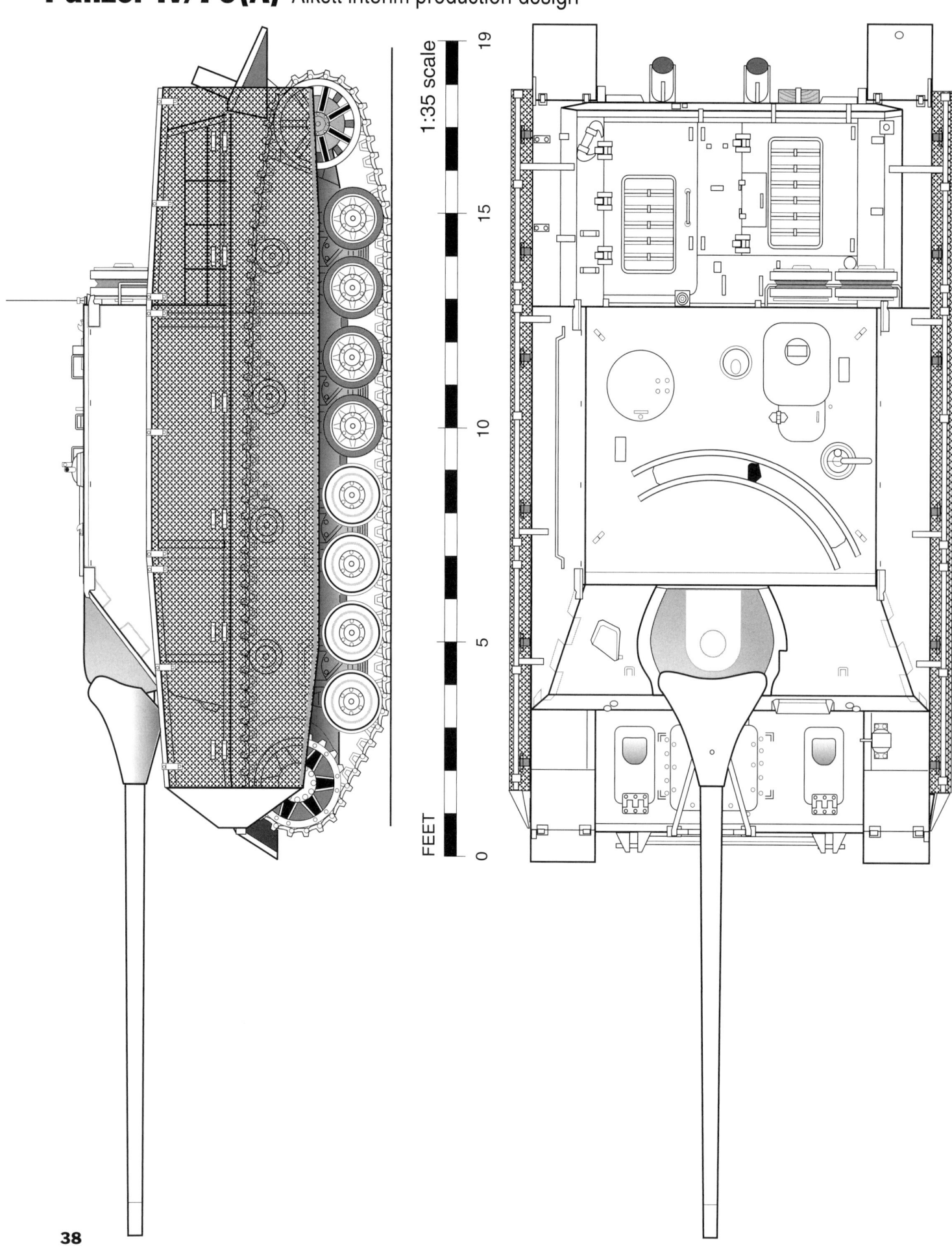

Panzer IV/70(A) Alkett interim production design

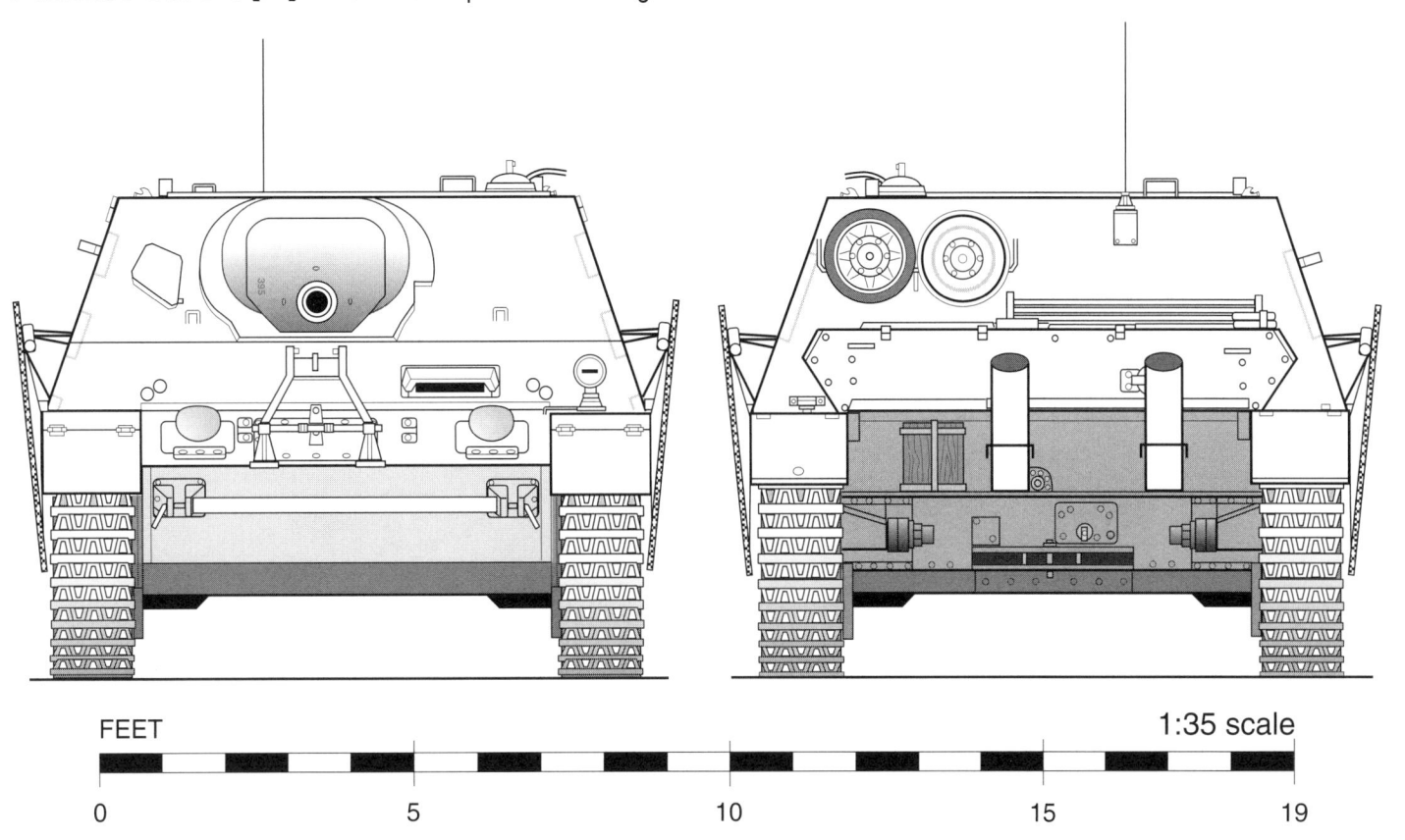

FEET 1:35 scale

This gaudily painted Pz.IV/70(A) is on display at the Saumur Armor Museum in France. The damage to the superstructure front existed at the time of its capture by French troops.

German Late War Armored Fighting Vehicles

Leichter Schützenpanzerwagen
(Sd.Kfz. 250/8) Neü
with 7.5 cm KwK51

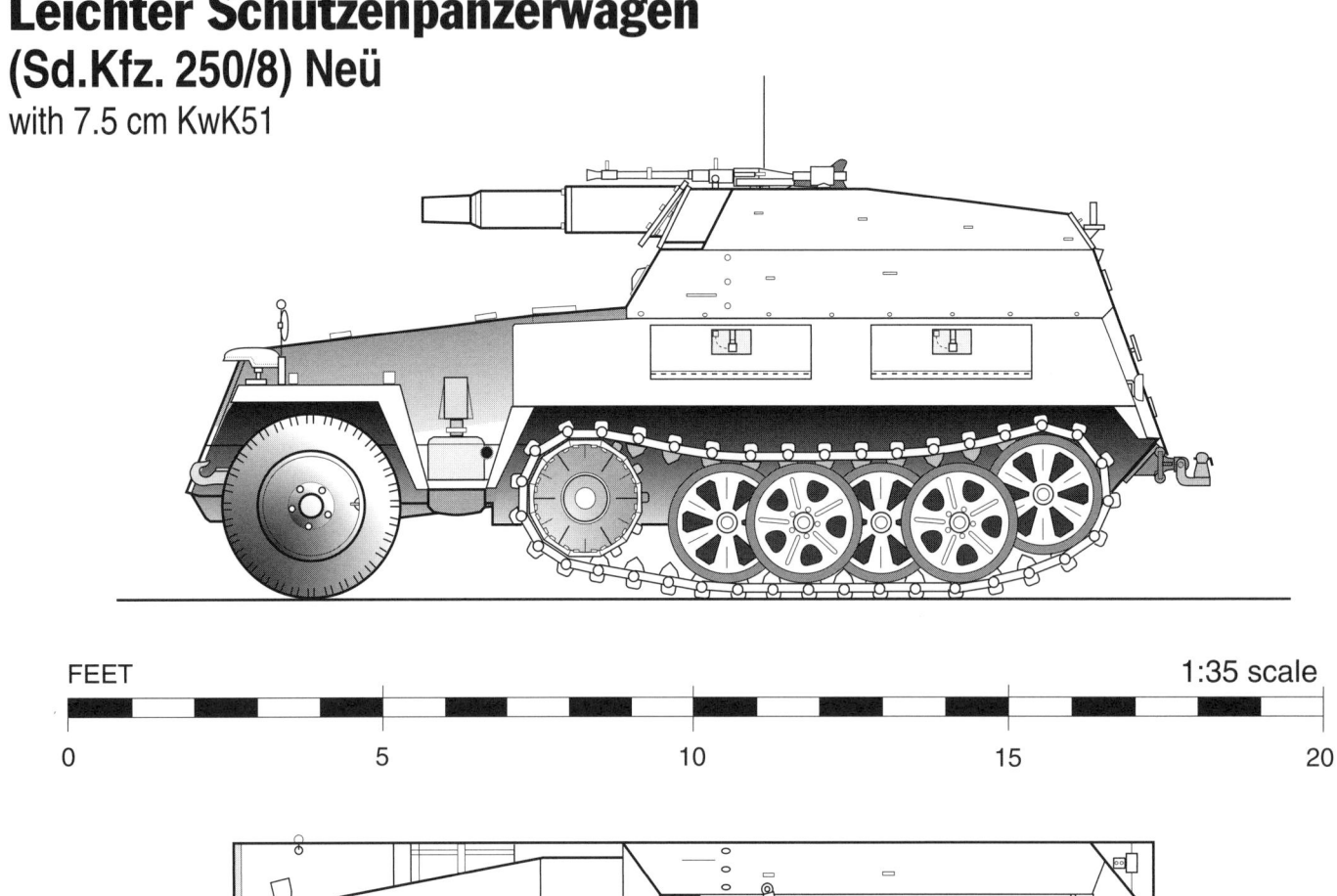

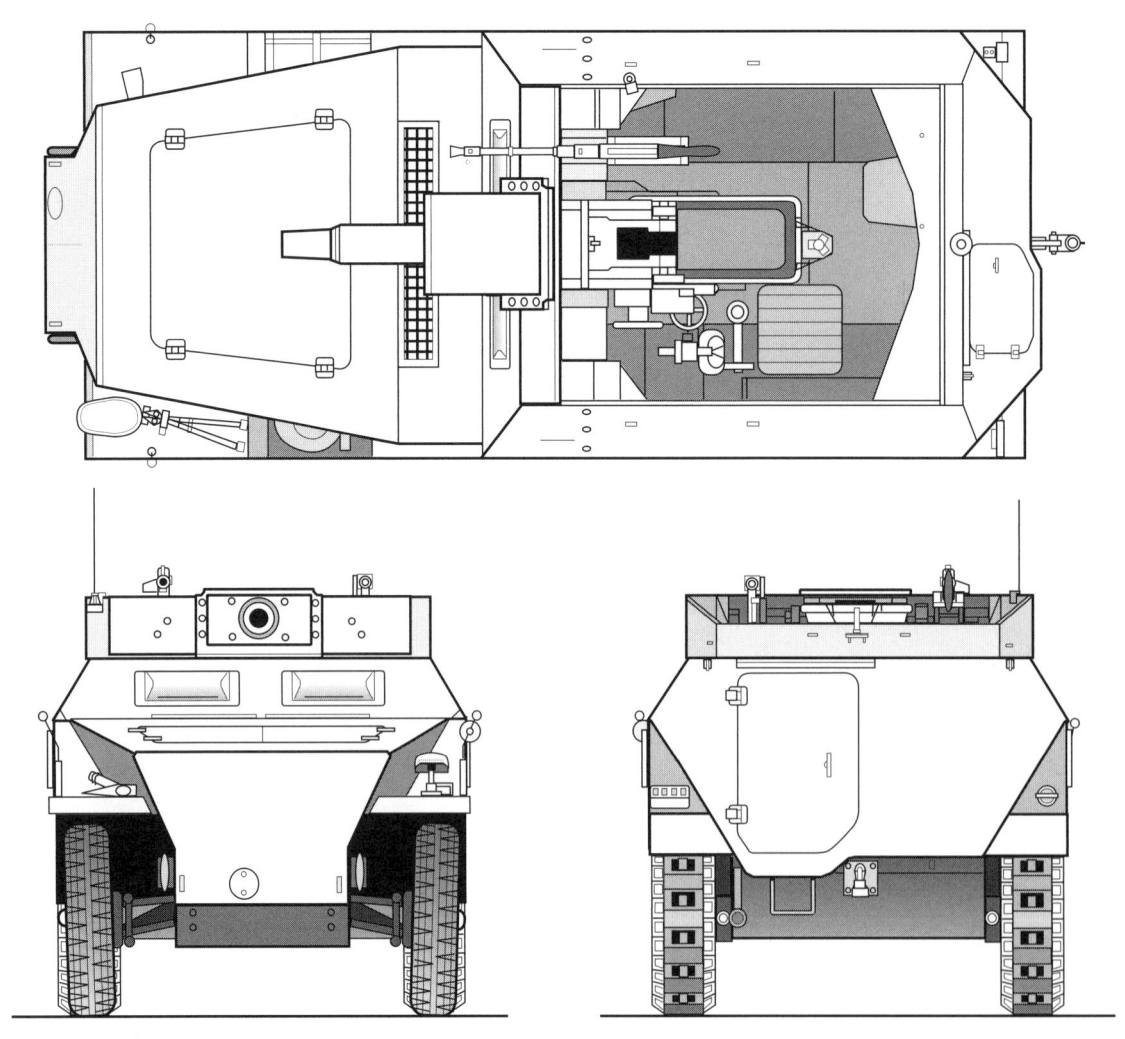

FEET
0 5 10 15 20
1:35 scale

40   German Late War Armored Fighting Vehicles

Panzer IV/70(V) (Sd.Kfz. 162/1)
Vomag final production design

The need to mount the long 75mm 42 L/70 gun on the Panzer IV chassis was first achieved with the interim Panzer IV/70 (A), and finally with the Panzer IV/70 (V). From August 1944, Vomag built 930 of this production vehicle.

Due to the increased 80mm frontal armor and the heavier gun with long overhang, the front portion of the suspension was overtaxed. Steel roadwheels were used in the first two stations to help alleviate the problem.

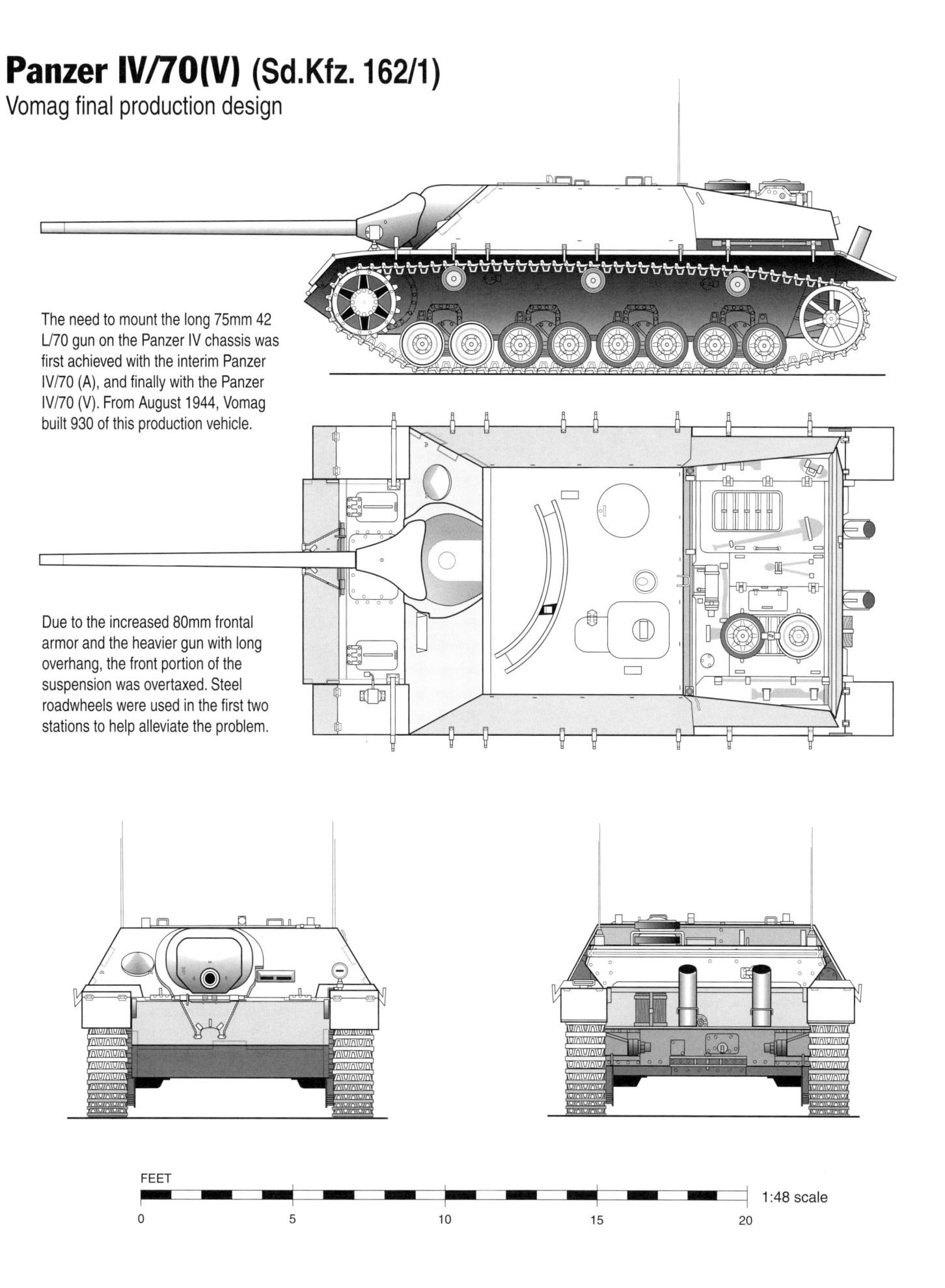

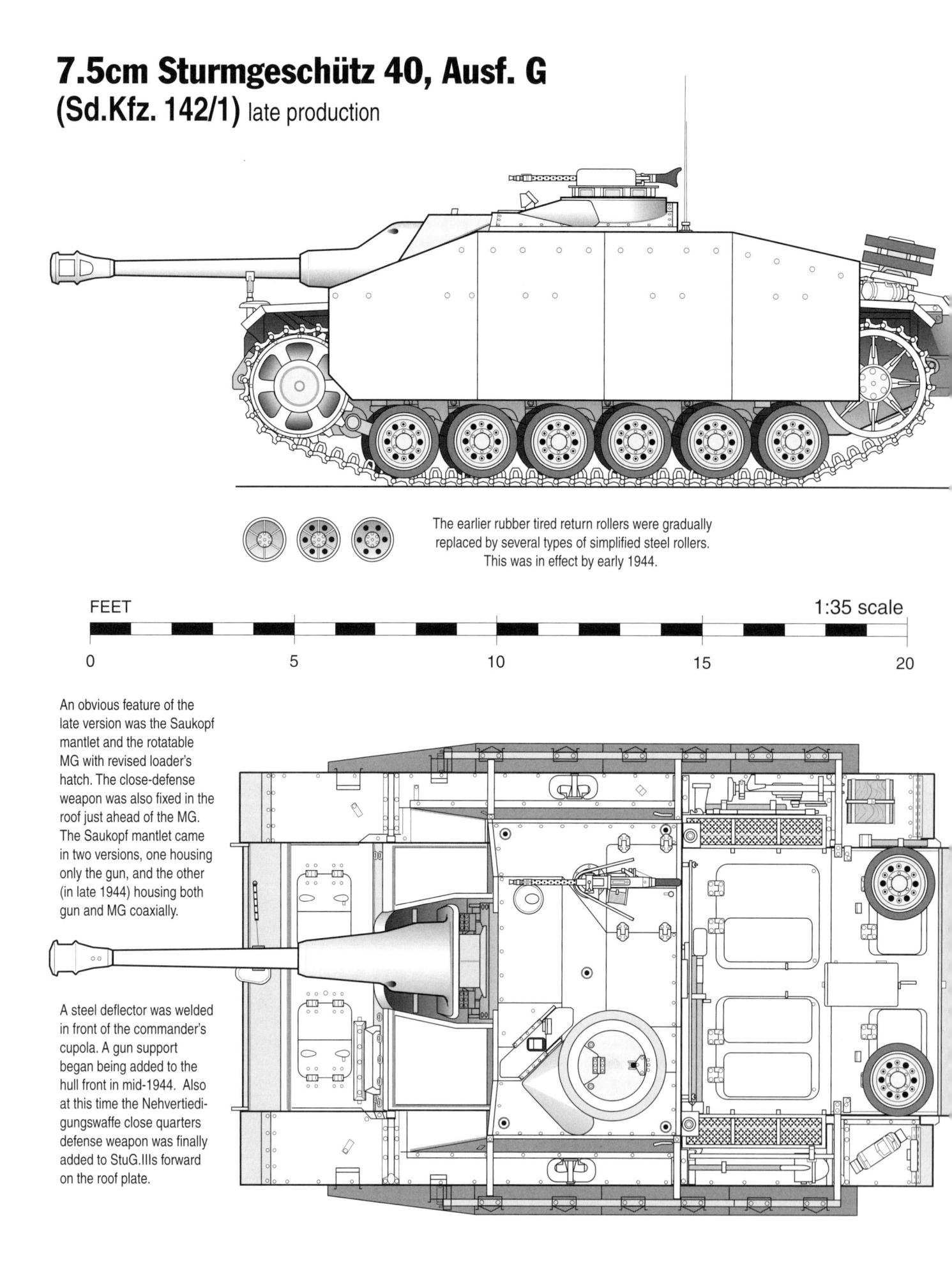

7.5cm Sturmgeschütz 40, Ausf. G
(Sd.Kfz. 142/1) late production

The earlier rubber tired return rollers were gradually replaced by several types of simplified steel rollers. This was in effect by early 1944.

FEET   1:35 scale
0   5   10   15   20

An obvious feature of the late version was the Saukopf mantlet and the rotatable MG with revised loader's hatch. The close-defense weapon was also fixed in the roof just ahead of the MG. The Saukopf mantlet came in two versions, one housing only the gun, and the other (in late 1944) housing both gun and MG coaxially.

A steel deflector was welded in front of the commander's cupola. A gun support began being added to the hull front in mid-1944. Also at this time the Nehvertiedigungswaffe close quarters defense weapon was finally added to StuG.IIIs forward on the roof plate.

42   German Late War Armored Fighting Vehicles

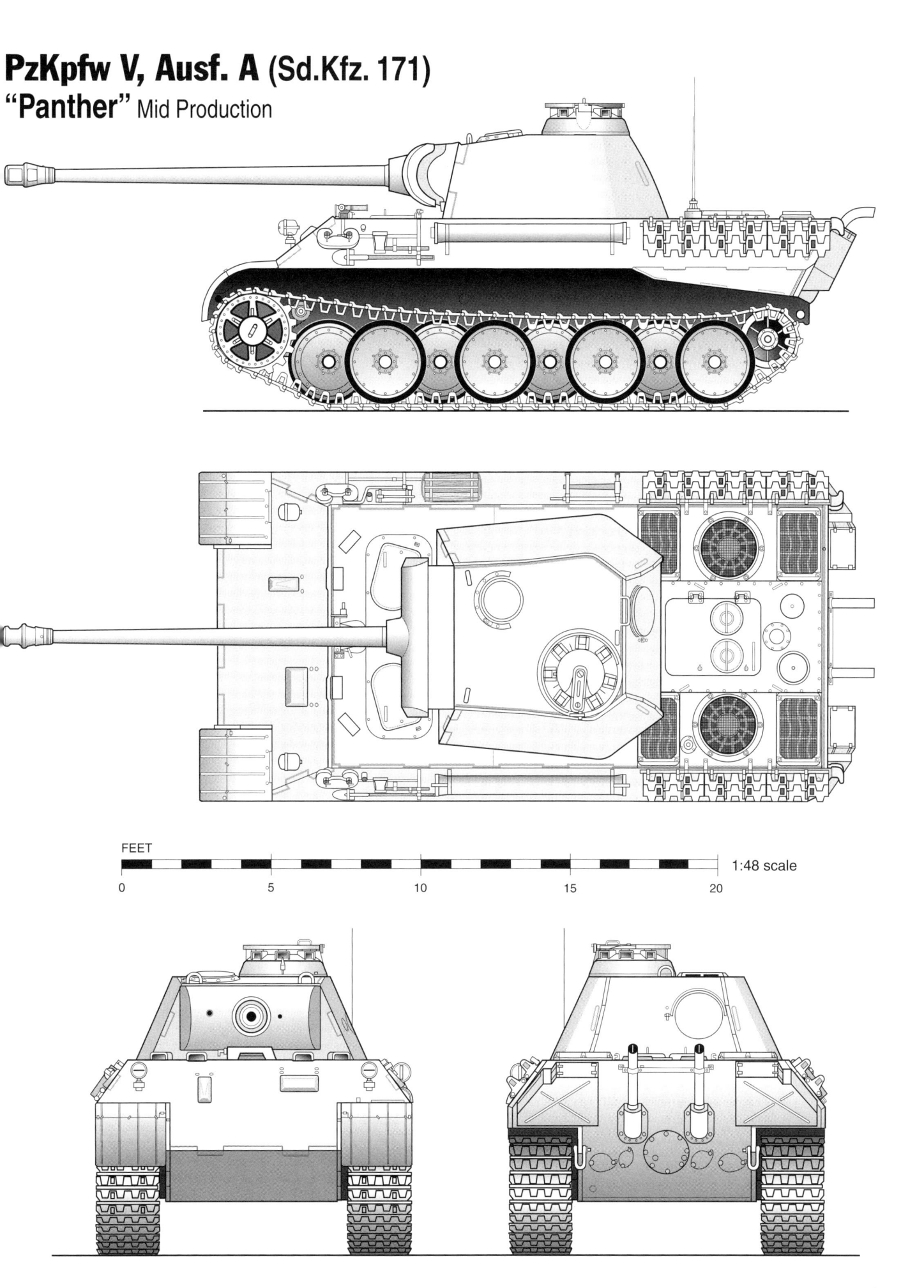

PzKpfw V, Ausf. A (Sd.Kfz. 171)
"Panther" Mid Production

1:48 scale

German Late War Armored Fighting Vehicles

Bergepanther
Ausf. A (Sd.Kfz. 179)
Late version

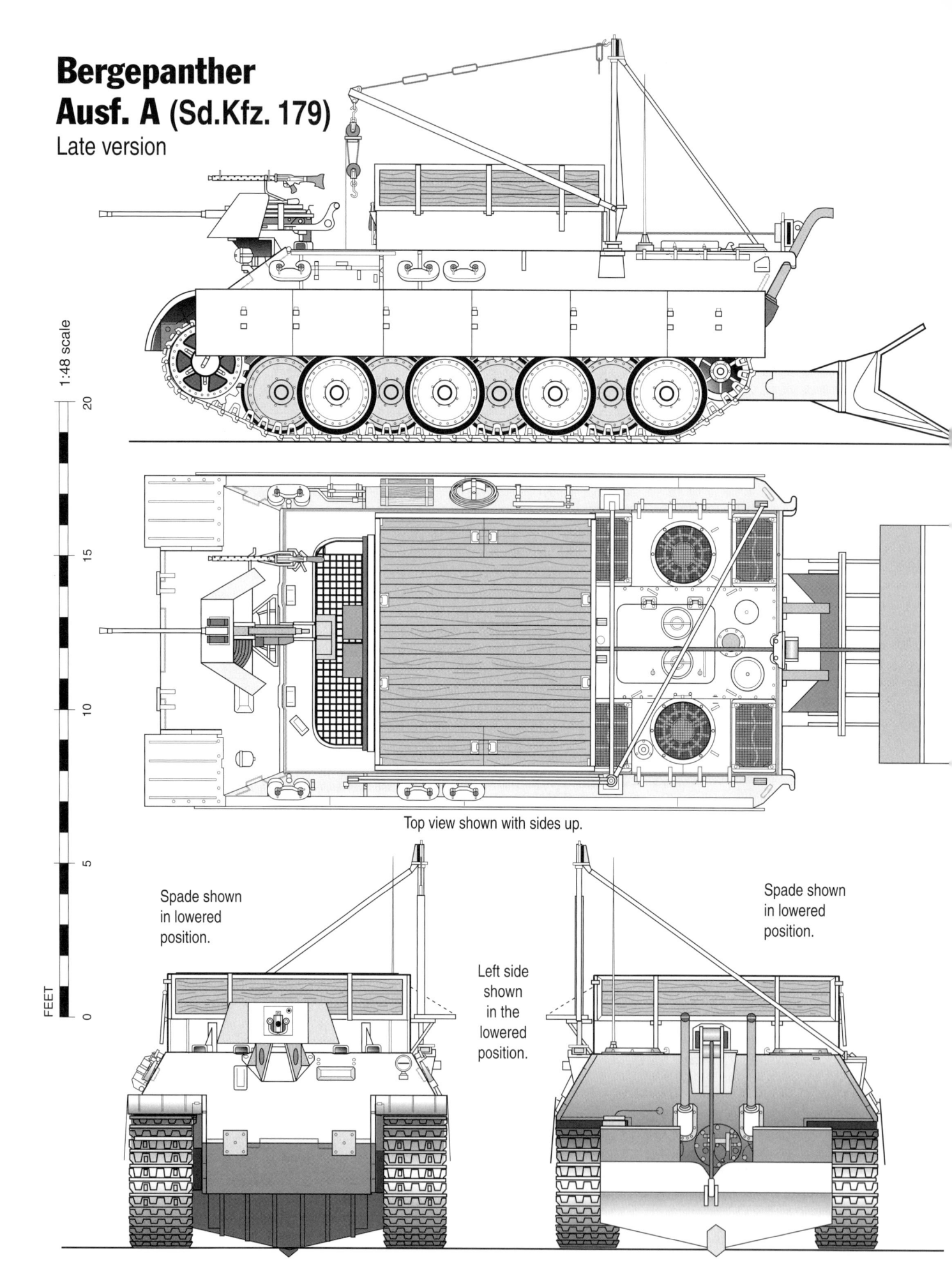

1:48 scale

Top view shown with sides up.

Spade shown in lowered position.

Left side shown in the lowered position.

Spade shown in lowered position.

44 German Late War Armored Fighting Vehicles

A rear view of the Bergepanther with the anchor spade in the lowered position.

A fine overall view of the Bergepanther Ausf. D with spade raised and crew compartment open.

German Late War Armored Fighting Vehicles 45

15cm sIG 33/1 auf Sf 38(t) Ausf. M
Grille (Sd.Kfz. 138/1)

FEET 0 5 10 15 1:35 scale 20

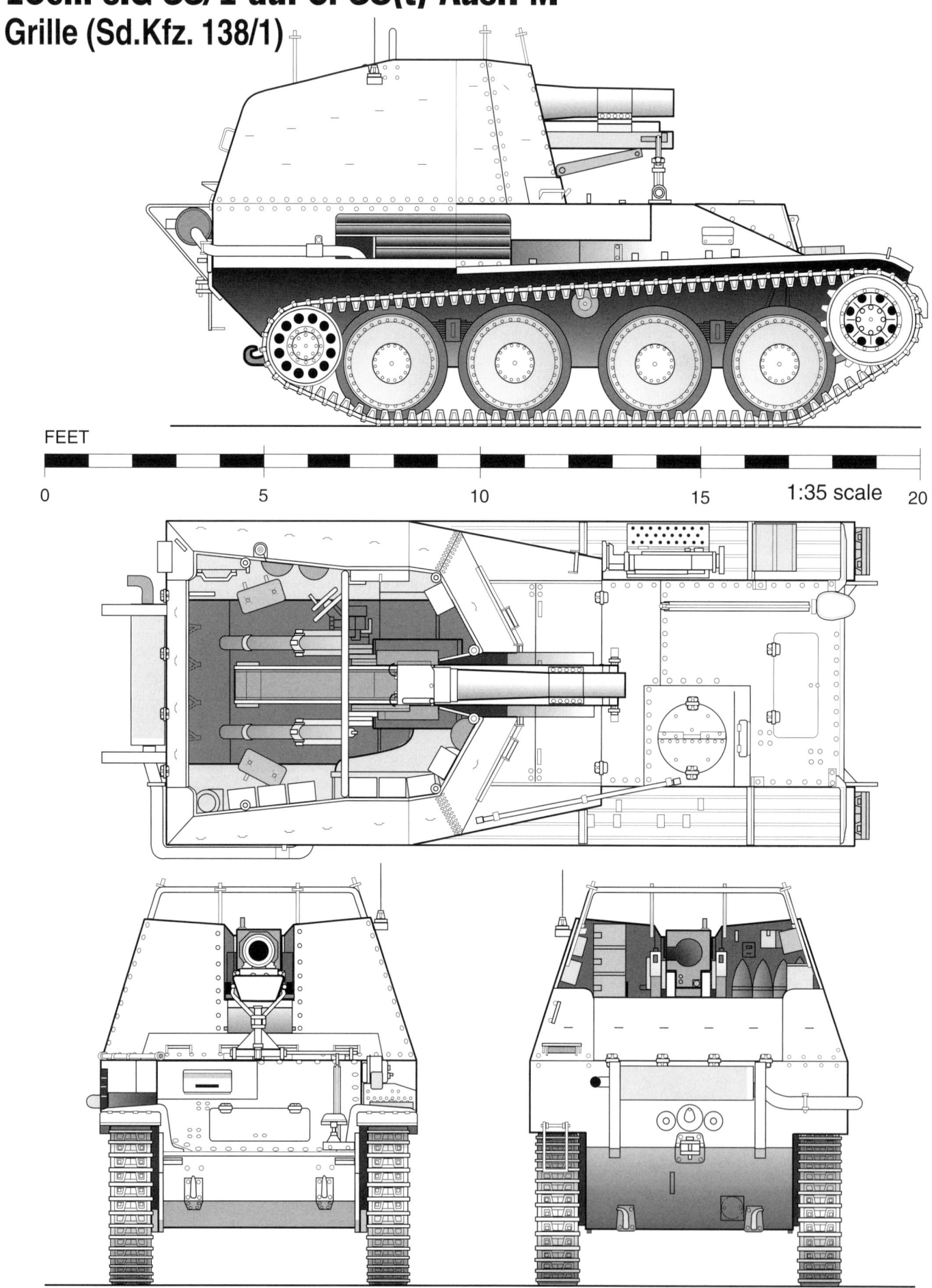

46 German Late War Armored Fighting Vehicles

Mittlerer Schützenpanzerwagen
Ausf. D (Sd Kfz 251/1)

FEET
1:35 scale

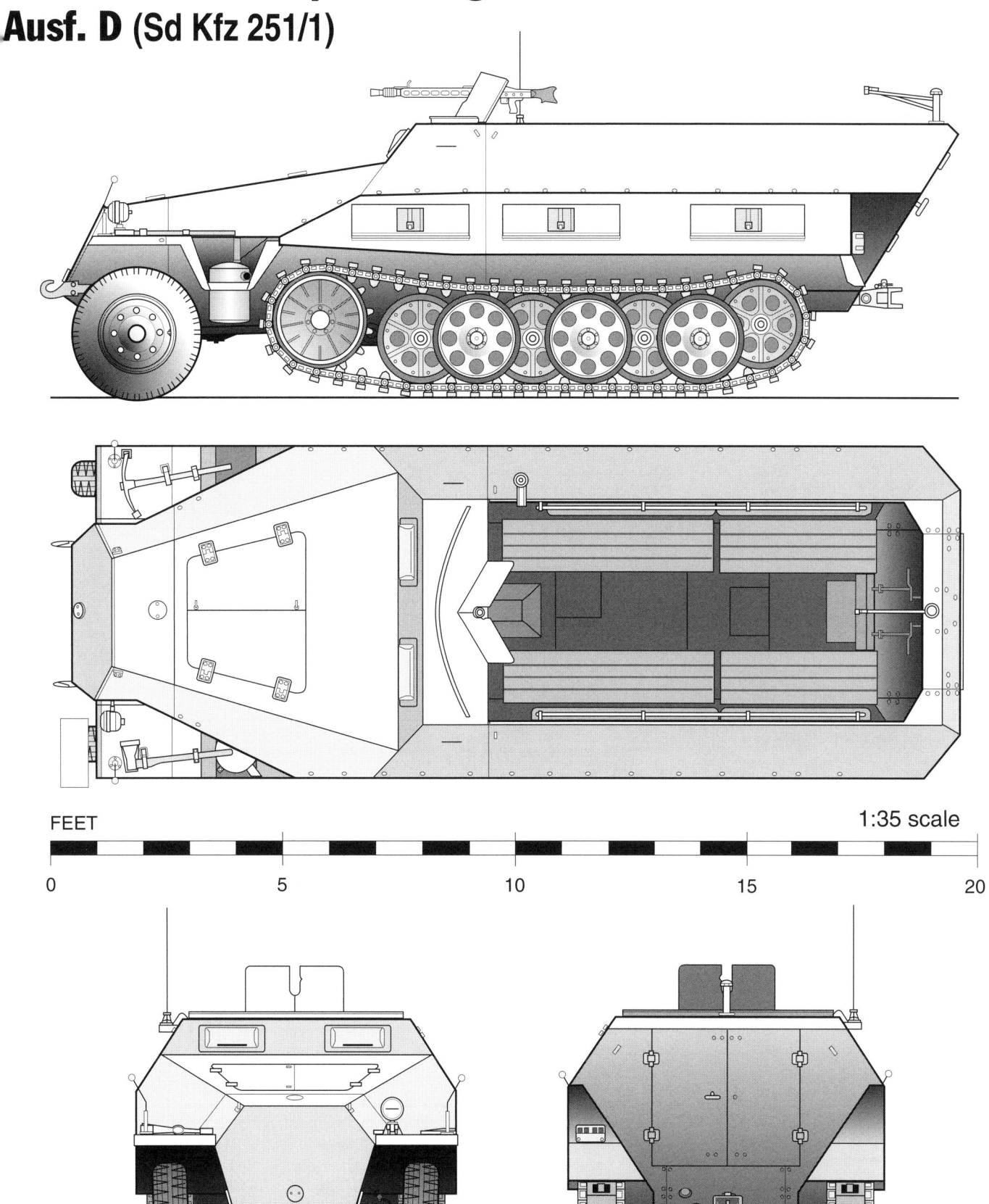

German Late War Armored Fighting Vehicles

Panzerjäger Tiger (P) mit 8.8 Pak 43.2 (L/71)
"Elefant" (Sd.Kfz. 184)

The original Panzerjäger Tiger (P) "Ferdinand" made its debut in 1943 during the "Zitadelle" attacks against the Kursk salient. Like the new Panthers, they too had difficulties, but also learned some vital lessons.

After heavy fighting and the losses at Kursk, and in order to correct the problems and improve its defensive characteristics, the Ferdinands were withdrawn in December 1943 for a complete overhaul at the Nibelungenwerk in Austria. At the same time, the name was officially changed to "Elefant", but the crews still continued to refer to them as Ferdinands. The overhaul was extensive and some of the visible features follow: new tracks, radio operator's MG, armored grates over the radiators, new commander's Stug.III style cupola, shrapnel guard in front of the reversed ball mount, jack and tools stored at rear, and rain gutters added to front and later to rear, also.

By the end of February 1944 most of the Elefants were ready for action again, and 11 of them, plus a Berge-Ferdinand, outfitted the 1.Kompanie, sPzJägAbt.653 for an attack on the Allied bridgehead at Nettuno, Italy. The main units to receive the Ferdinand/Elefant were the two schwere Panzerjäger-Abteilungen 653 and 654, of s.Pz.Jäg.Rgt.656.

These vehicles never quite lived up to the hopes for them, and more times than enough they were either bogged down on the Eastern Front or falling through the wooden bridges.

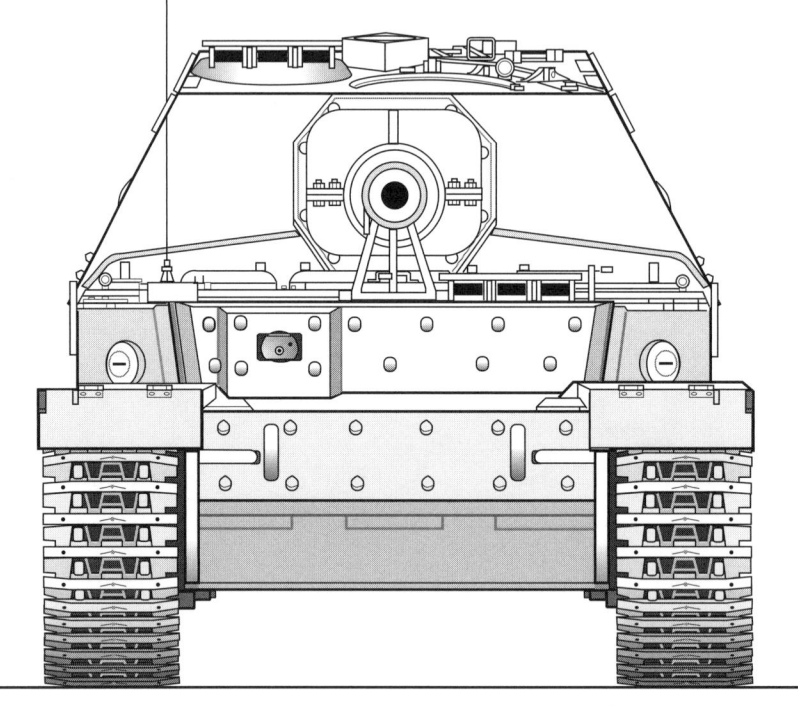

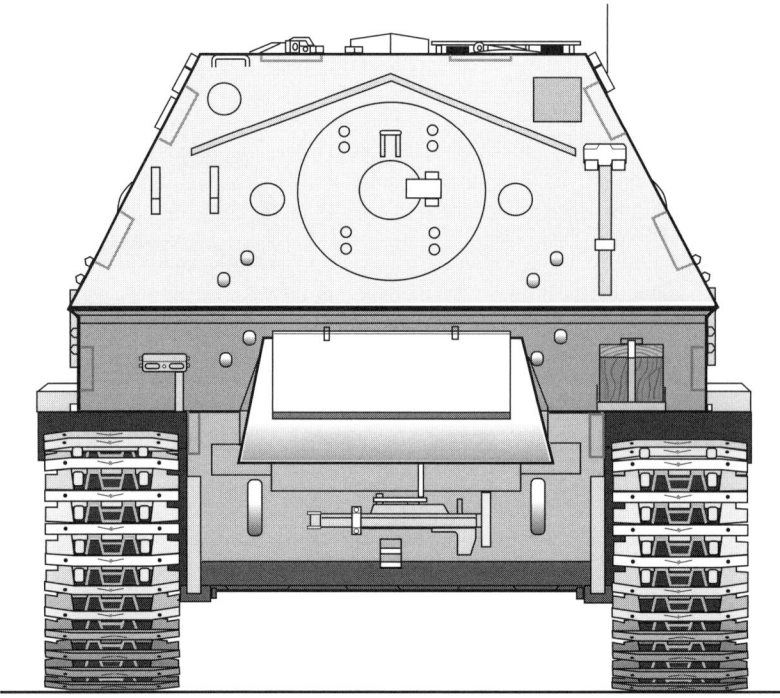

An interesting in-field upgrade made to the "Elefant" in the spring of 1944 was a rebuild of the rear access door. This large circular hatch was held in place by 8 bolts fastened to interior plates. The only part that opened readily was the smaller shell ejection & loading port in the center. To permit simpler access through the rear hatch it was replaced by split rear doors, hinged to the outside, but still with the smaller round service port hinged to the right half of the split door. This rebuild appears to have been done to only 4 of the Pz.Jag.Abt.653 vehicles in Italy, and was seen in service by July 1944.

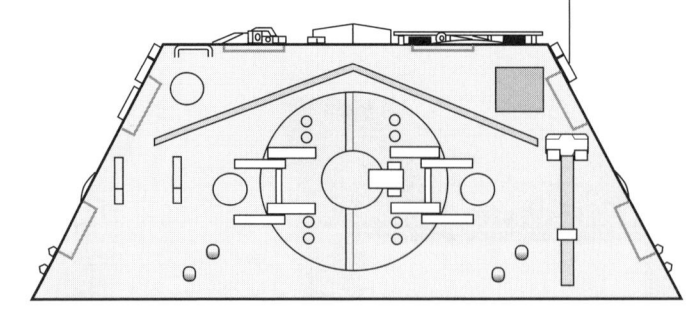

48 German Late War Armored Fighting Vehicles

German Late War Armored Fighting Vehicles 49

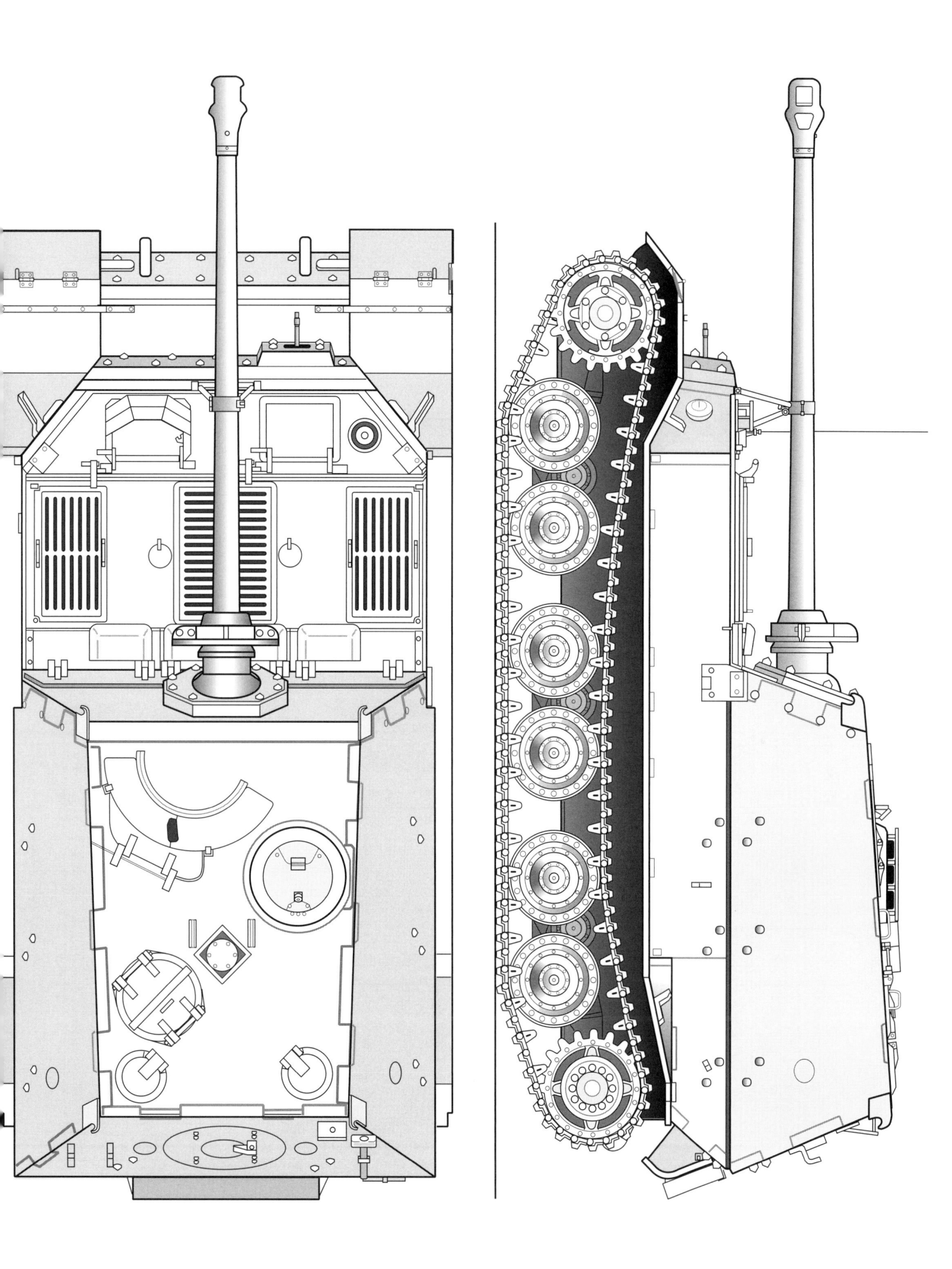

Sturmgeschütz IV
(Sd.Kfz. 167) mid production

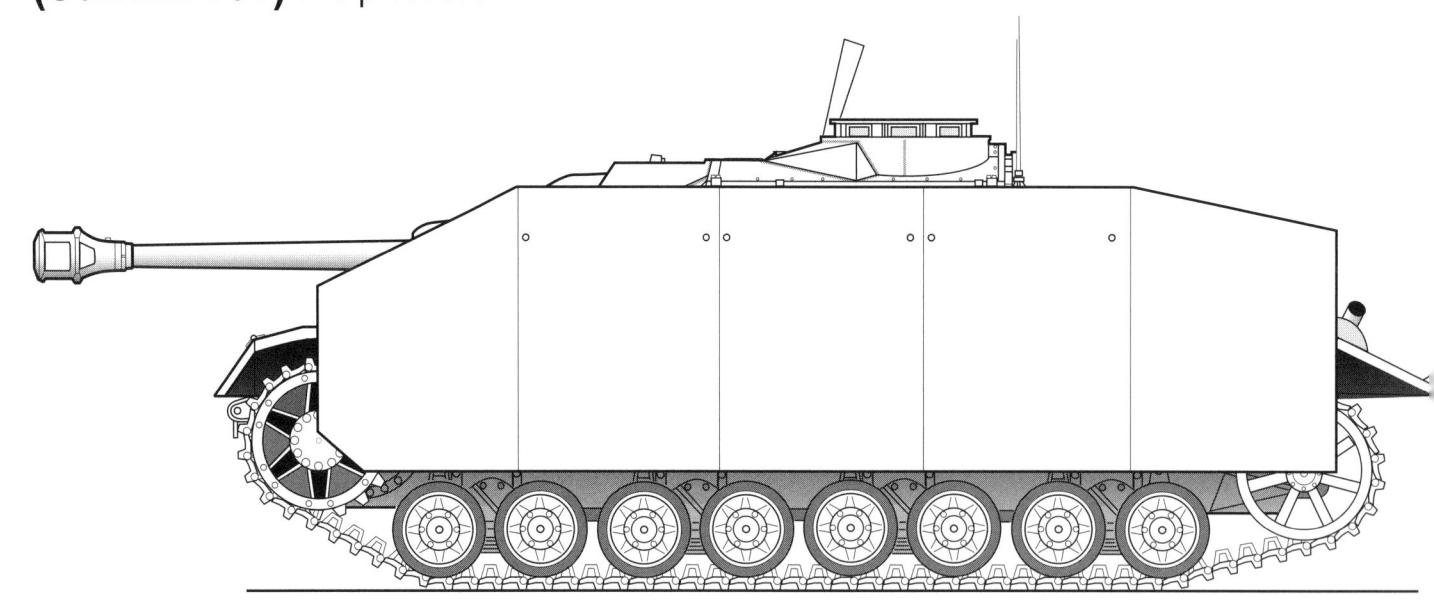

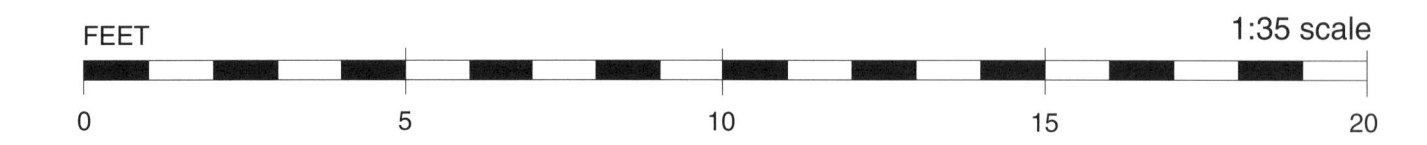

FEET   1:35 scale
0   5   10   15   20

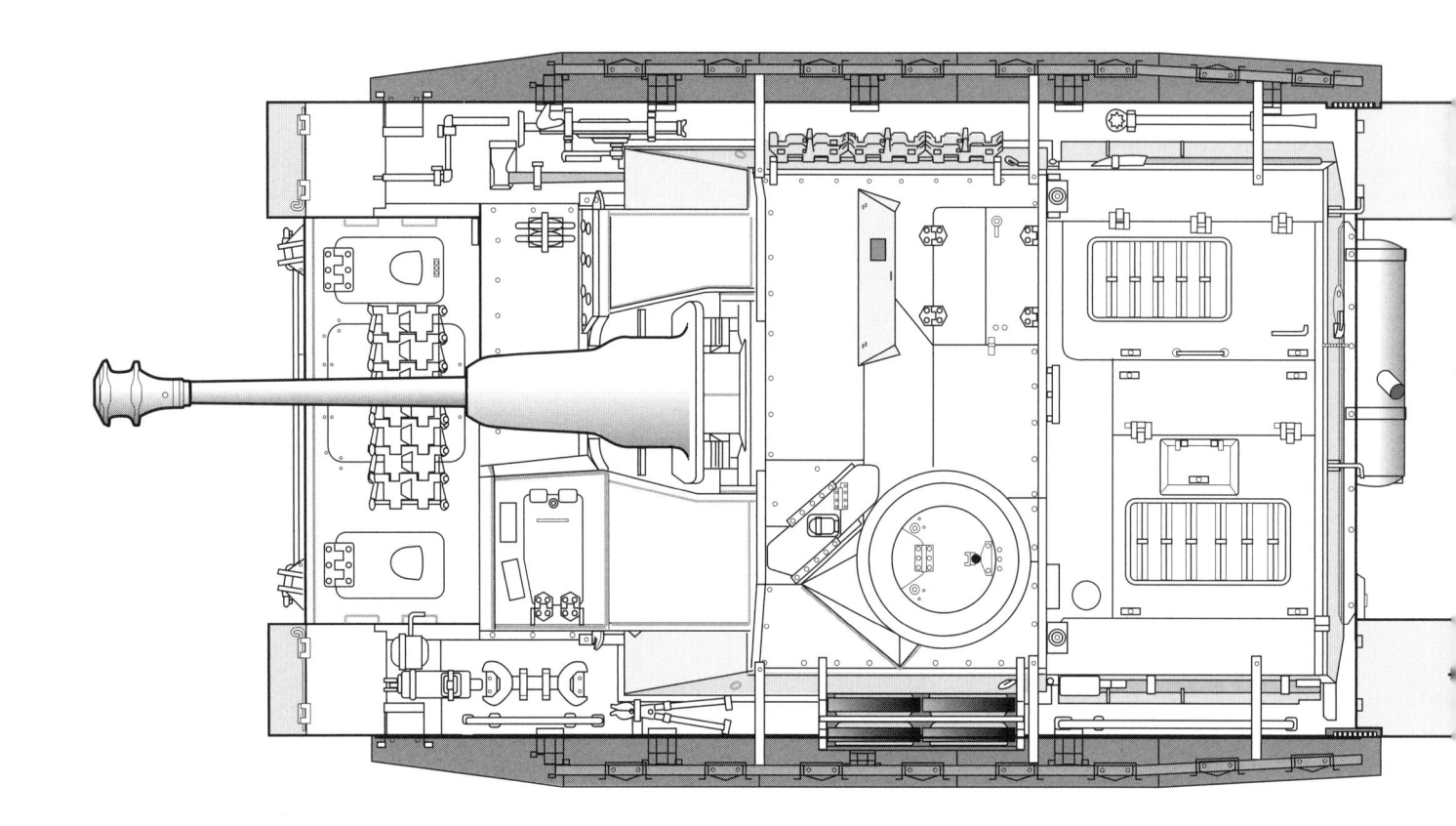

Sturmgeschütz IV
(Sd.Kfz. 167) mid production

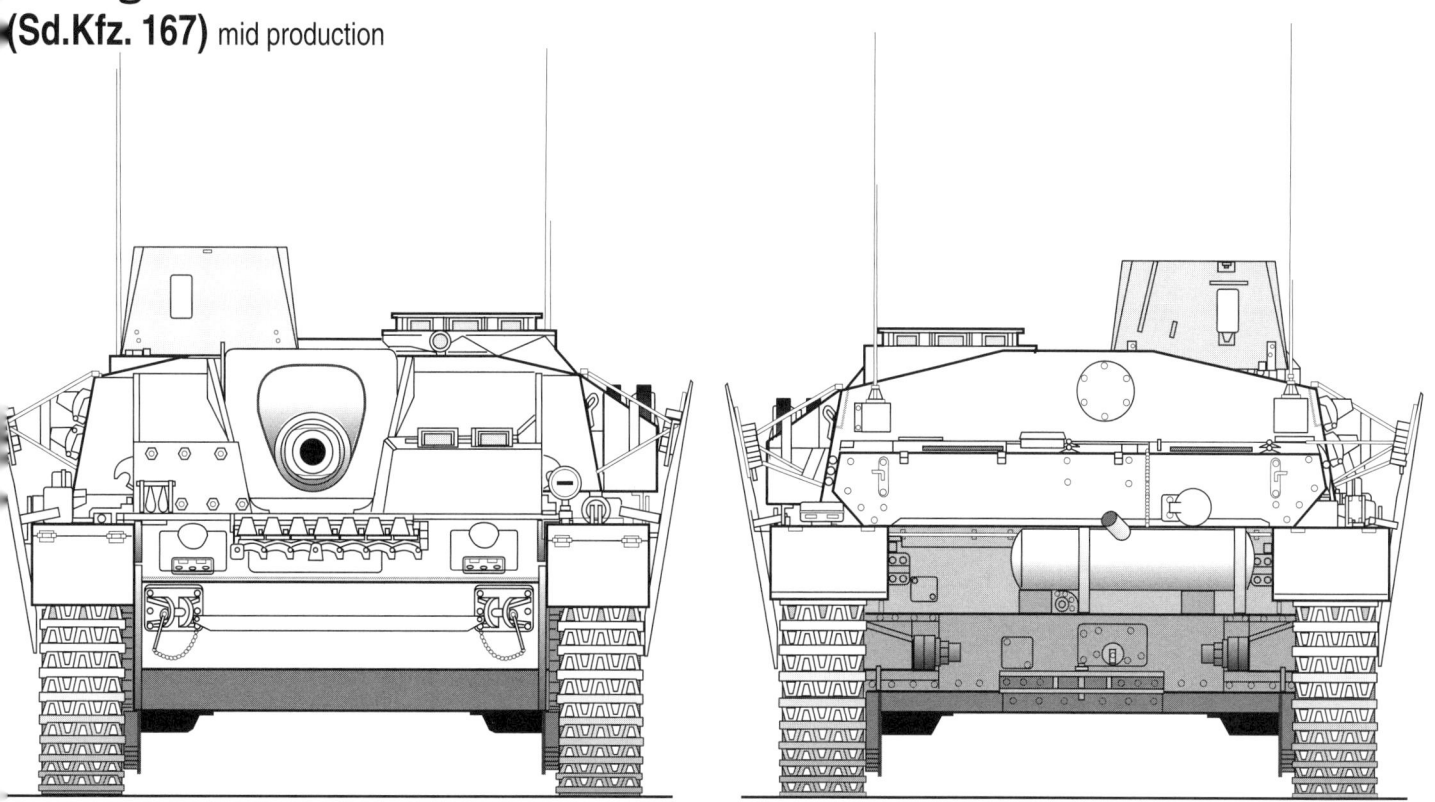

Canadian troops pass a German StuG. IV knocked out between Pignataro and Pontecorvo, Italy, May 19, 1944.

German Late War Armored Fighting Vehicles **51**

Panzerbeobachtungswagen
Panther Prototype

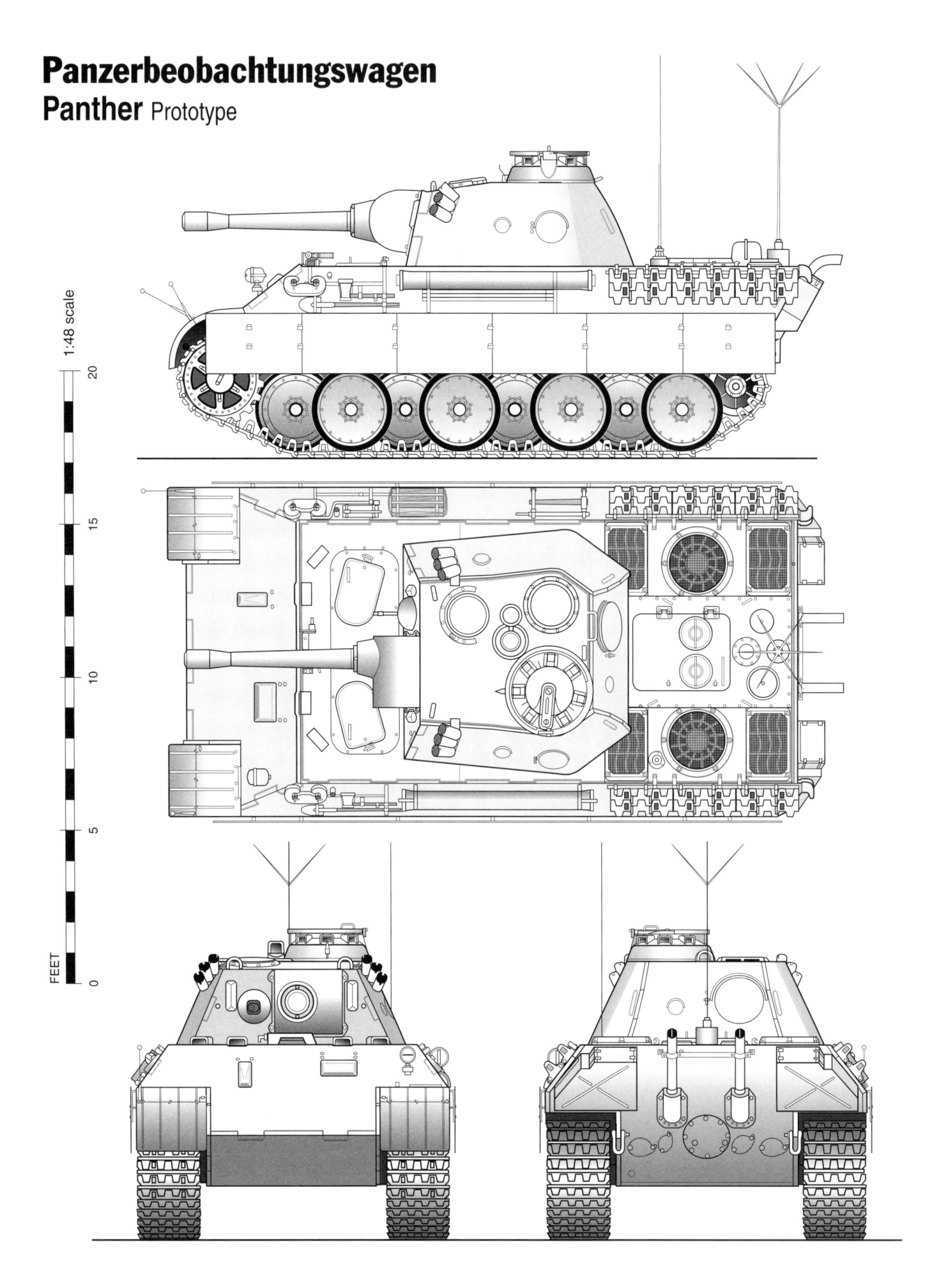

Jagdpanzer 38(t) "Hetzer"
(Late production)

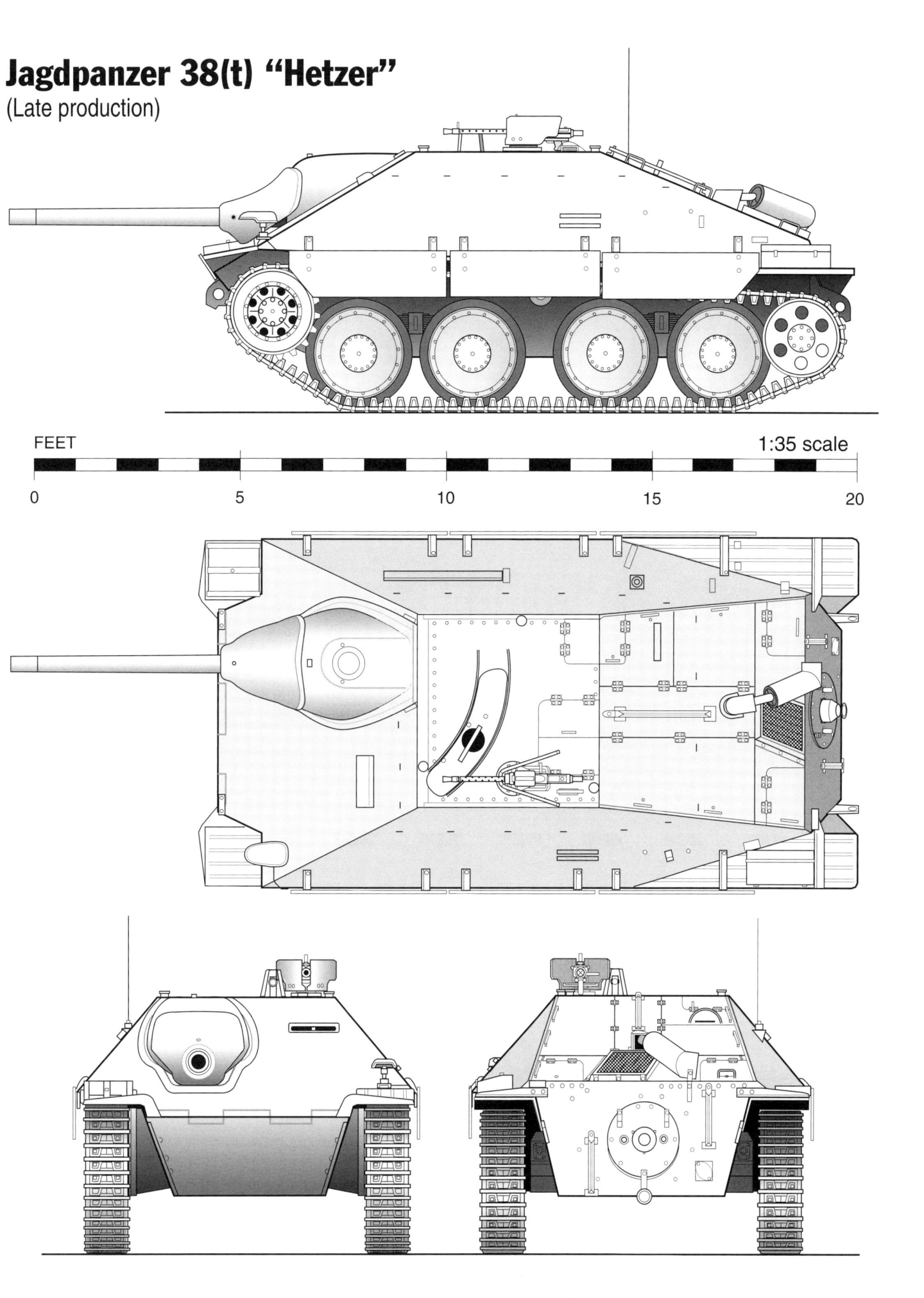

FEET 1:35 scale
0 5 10 15 20

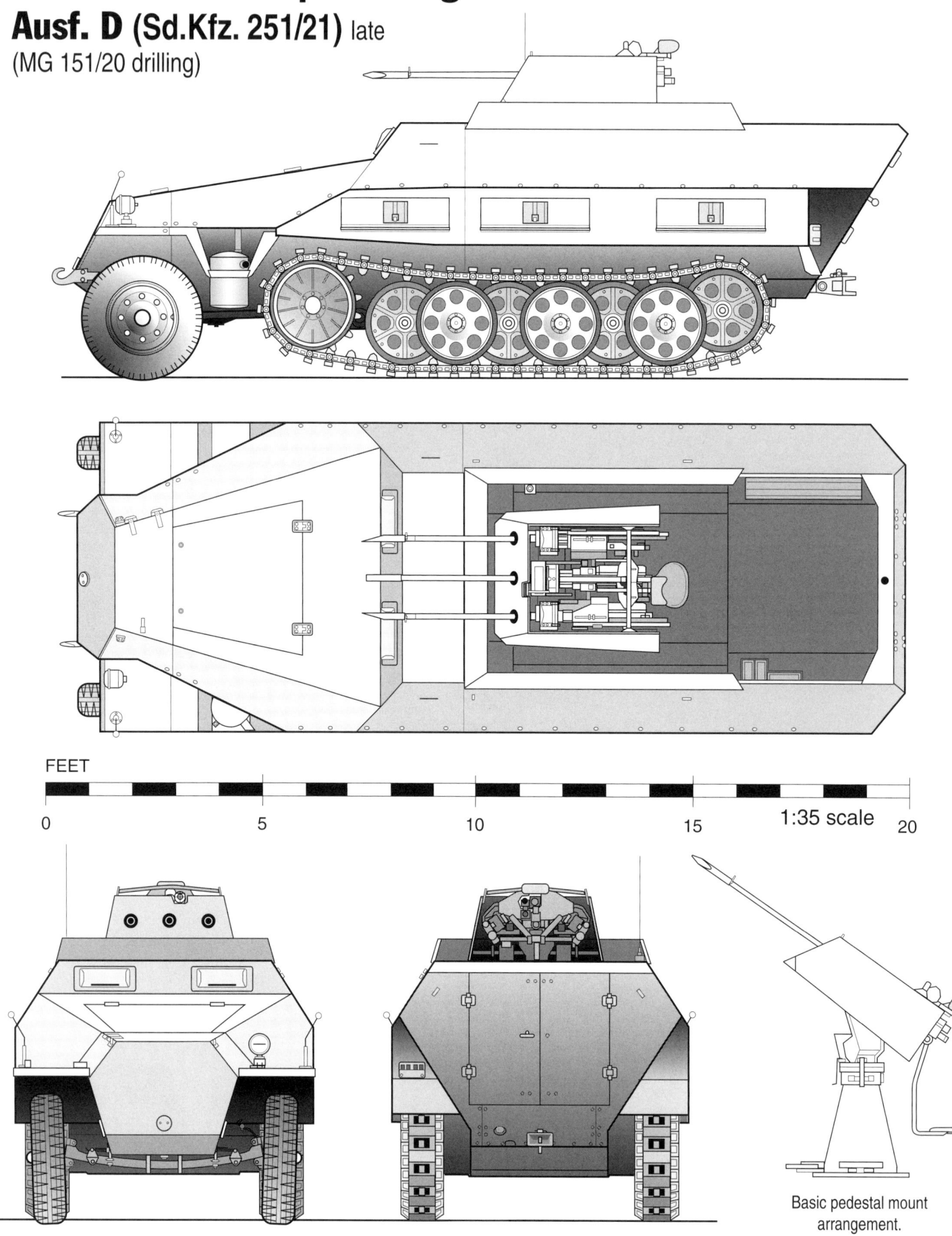

Mittlerer Schützenpanzerwagen
Ausf. D (Sd.Kfz. 251/21) late
(MG 151/20 drilling)

FEET

1:35 scale

Basic pedestal mount arrangement.

54   German Late War Armored Fighting Vehicles

Mittlerer Schützenpanzerwagen
Ausf. D (Sd.Kfz. 251/22)
(7.5cm PaK40)

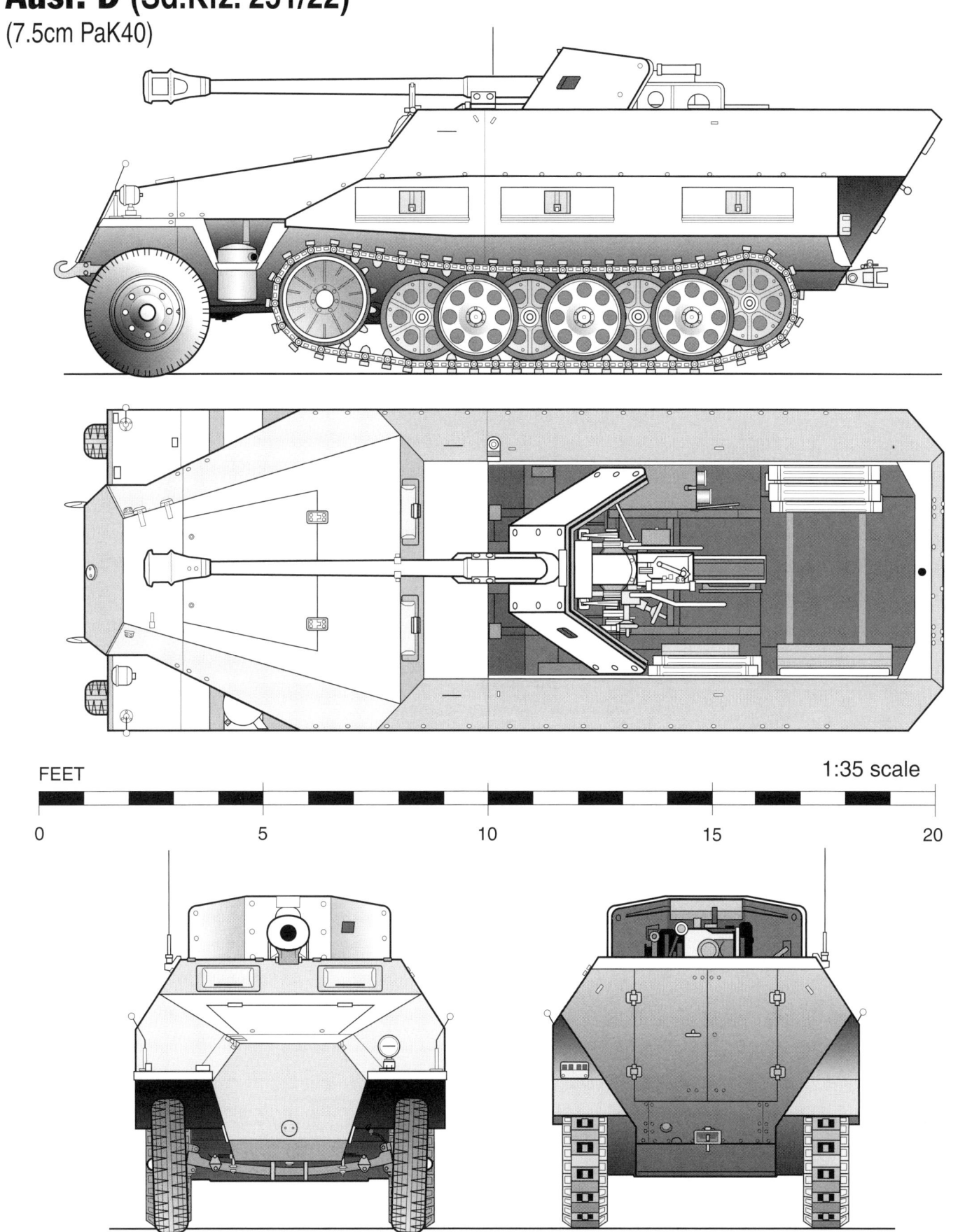

FEET

1:35 scale

0   5   10   15   20

German Late War Armored Fighting Vehicles

Befehls-Panther Ausf. A
(Sd.Kfz. 171) Command model

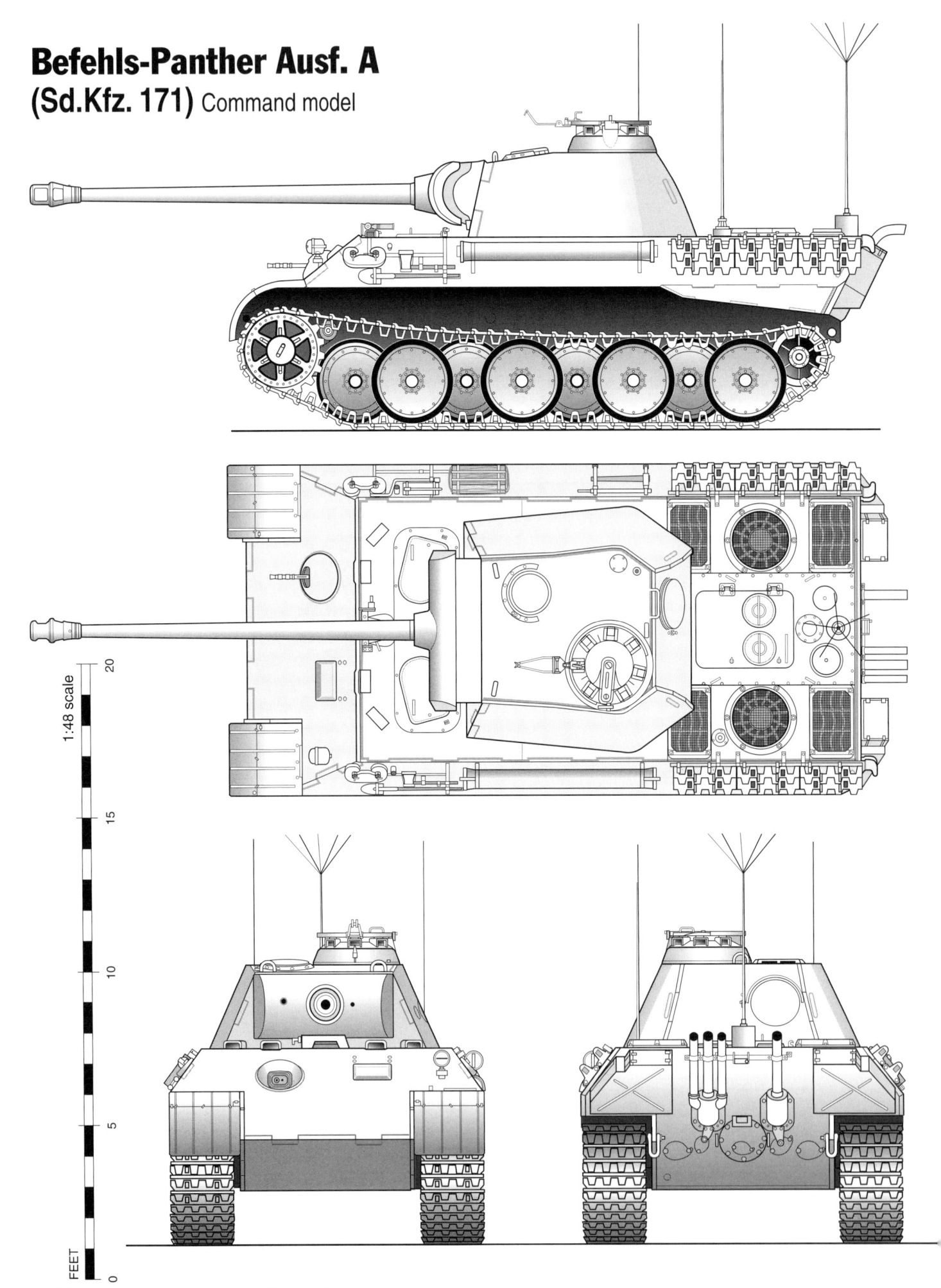

1:48 scale

56   German Late War Armored Fighting Vehicles

On the night of June 8–9, 1944, the Canadian Regina Rifles used PIATs and grenades to knock out this 12th SS Pz.Div. (Hitler Jugend) Panther in the small French town of Bretteville-l'Orgueilleuse.

British troops drive past one of nine Panthers knocked out along the Uedem-Xanten road in Holland. This one is an Ausf. G with the obvious chinned gun mantlet.

German Late War Armored Fighting Vehicles 57

Pz.Kpfw. V Panther Ausf. G

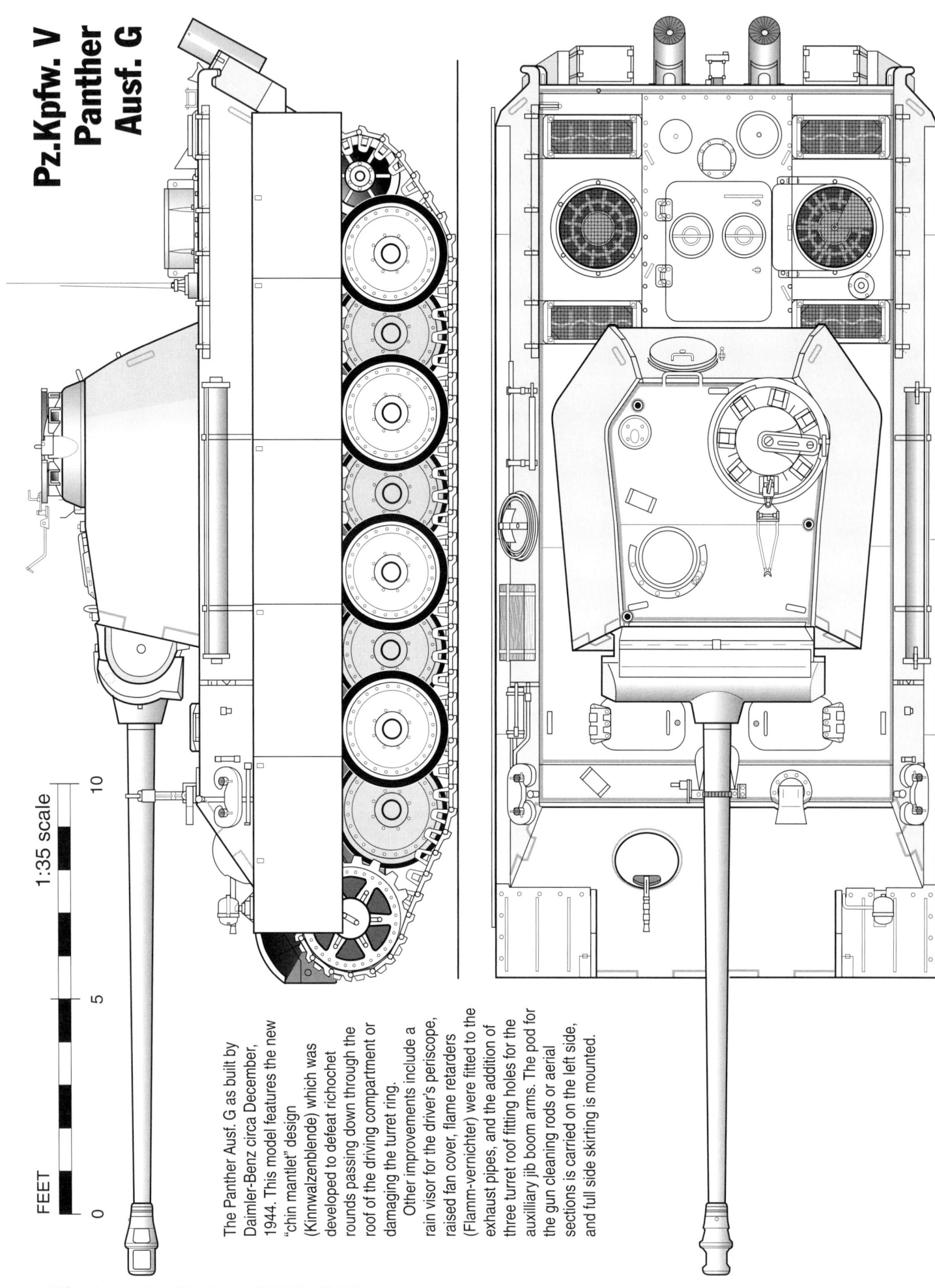

The Panther Ausf. G as built by Daimler-Benz circa December, 1944. This model features the new "chin mantlet" design (Kinnwalzenblende) which was developed to defeat richochet rounds passing down through the roof of the driving compartment or damaging the turret ring.

Other improvements include a rain visor for the driver's periscope, raised fan cover, flame retarders (Flamm-vernichter) were fitted to the exhaust pipes, and the addition of three turret roof fitting holes for the auxilliary jib boom arms. The pod for the gun cleaning rods or aerial sections is carried on the left side, and full side skirting is mounted.

FEET 1:35 scale

58   German Late War Armored Fighting Vehicles

Pz.Kpfw. V, Ausf. G
Panther

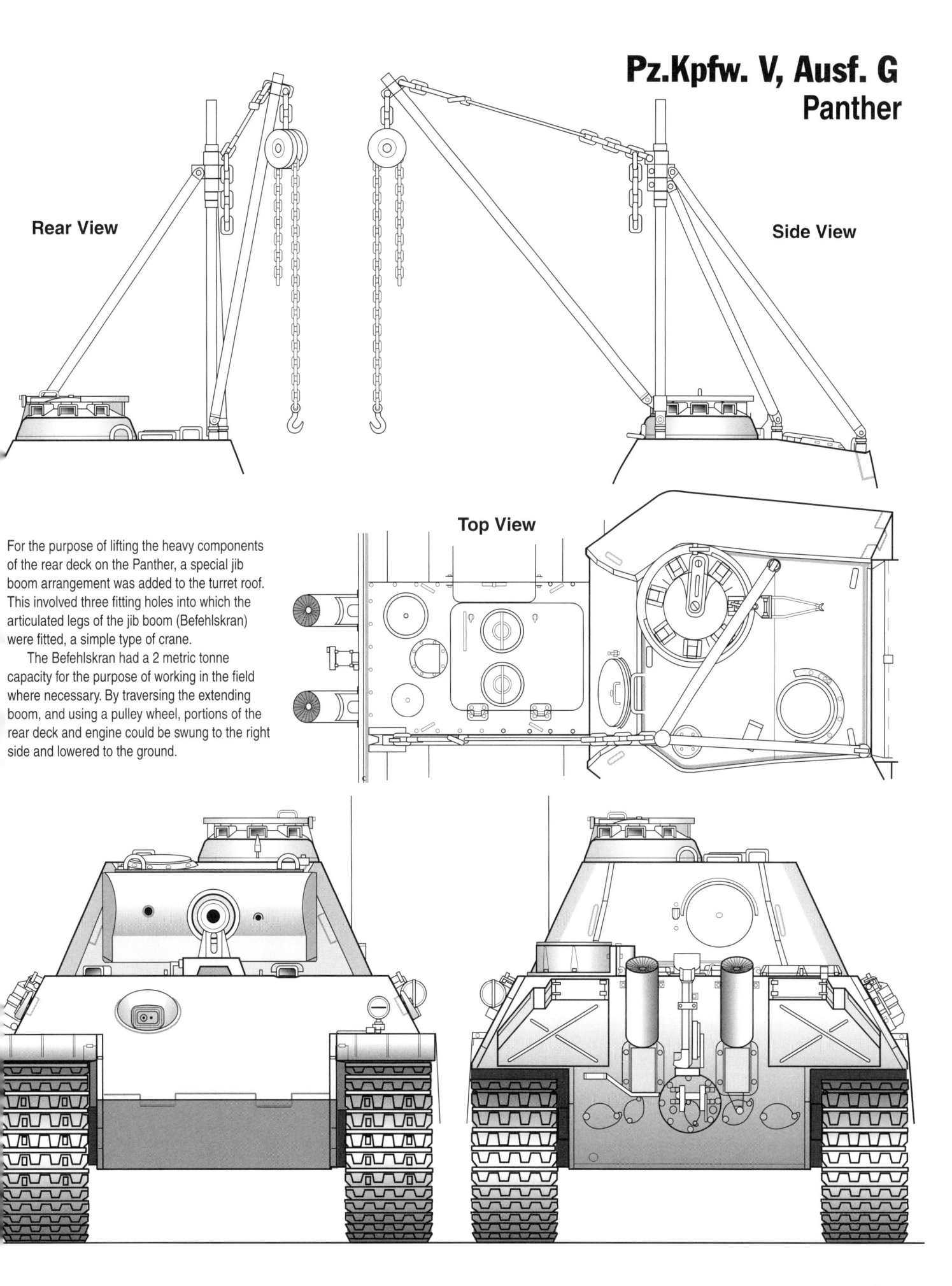

Rear View

Side View

Top View

For the purpose of lifting the heavy components of the rear deck on the Panther, a special jib boom arrangement was added to the turret roof. This involved three fitting holes into which the articulated legs of the jib boom (Befehlskran) were fitted, a simple type of crane.

The Befehlskran had a 2 metric tonne capacity for the purpose of working in the field where necessary. By traversing the extending boom, and using a pulley wheel, portions of the rear deck and engine could be swung to the right side and lowered to the ground.

German Late War Armored Fighting Vehicles 59

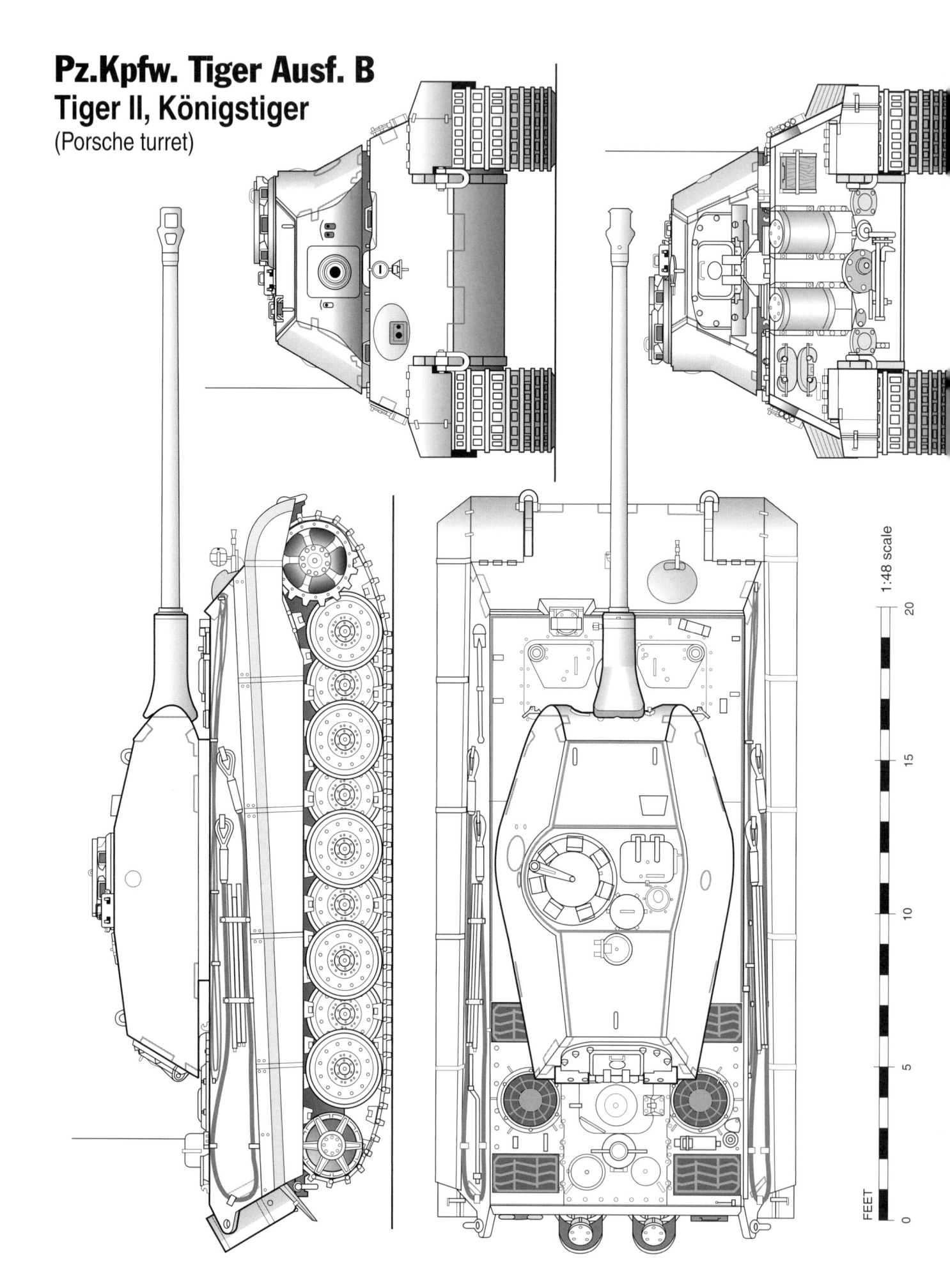

Pz.Kpfw. Tiger Ausf. B
Tiger II, Königstiger
(Porsche turret)

1:48 scale

60 German Late War Armored Fighting Vehicles

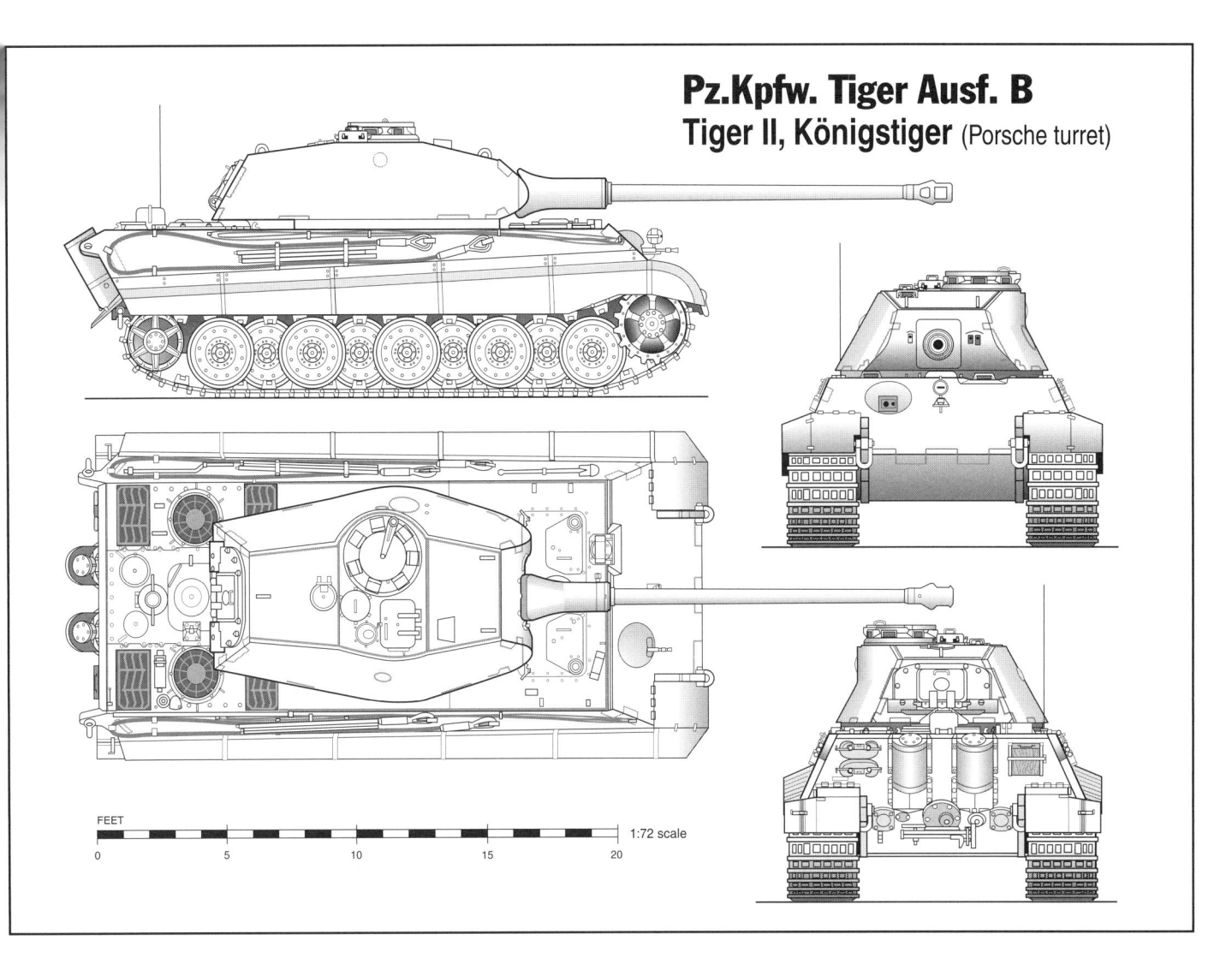

Pz.Kpfw. Tiger Ausf. B
Tiger II, Königstiger (Porsche turret)

FEET 1:72 scale

British soldiers inspect a destroyed Tiger Ausf. B with dislodged Porsche-style turret. This heavy tank was also referred to as Tiger II, Royal Tiger, Königstiger, VK4503, and Pz.Kpfw.VI Ausf. B.

German Late War Armored Fighting Vehicles

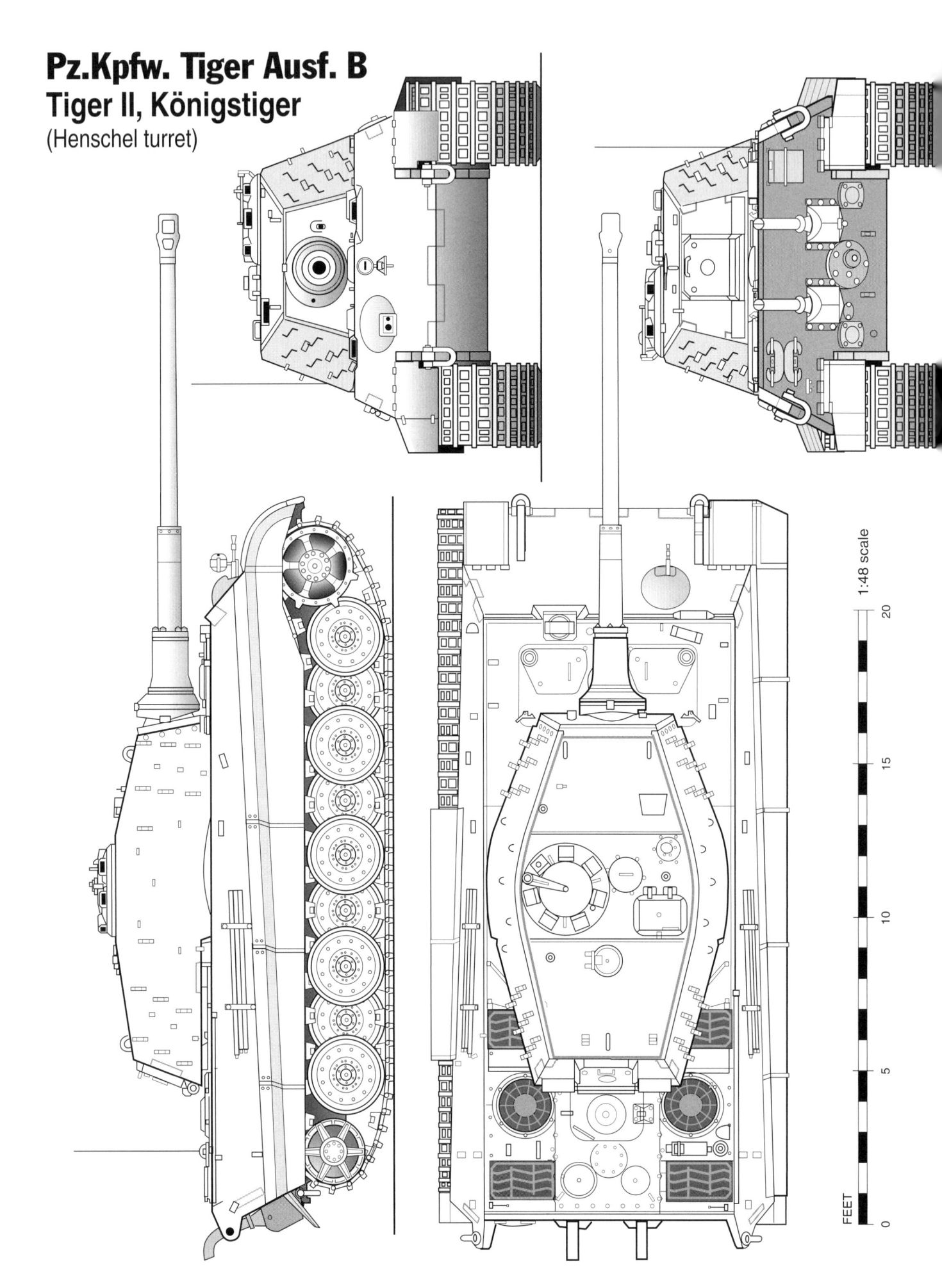

Pz.Kpfw. Tiger Ausf. B
Tiger II, Königstiger
(Henschel turret)

1:48 scale

FEET

62 German Late War Armored Fighting Vehicles

Jagdpanther (Sd.Kfz. 173) (early production)

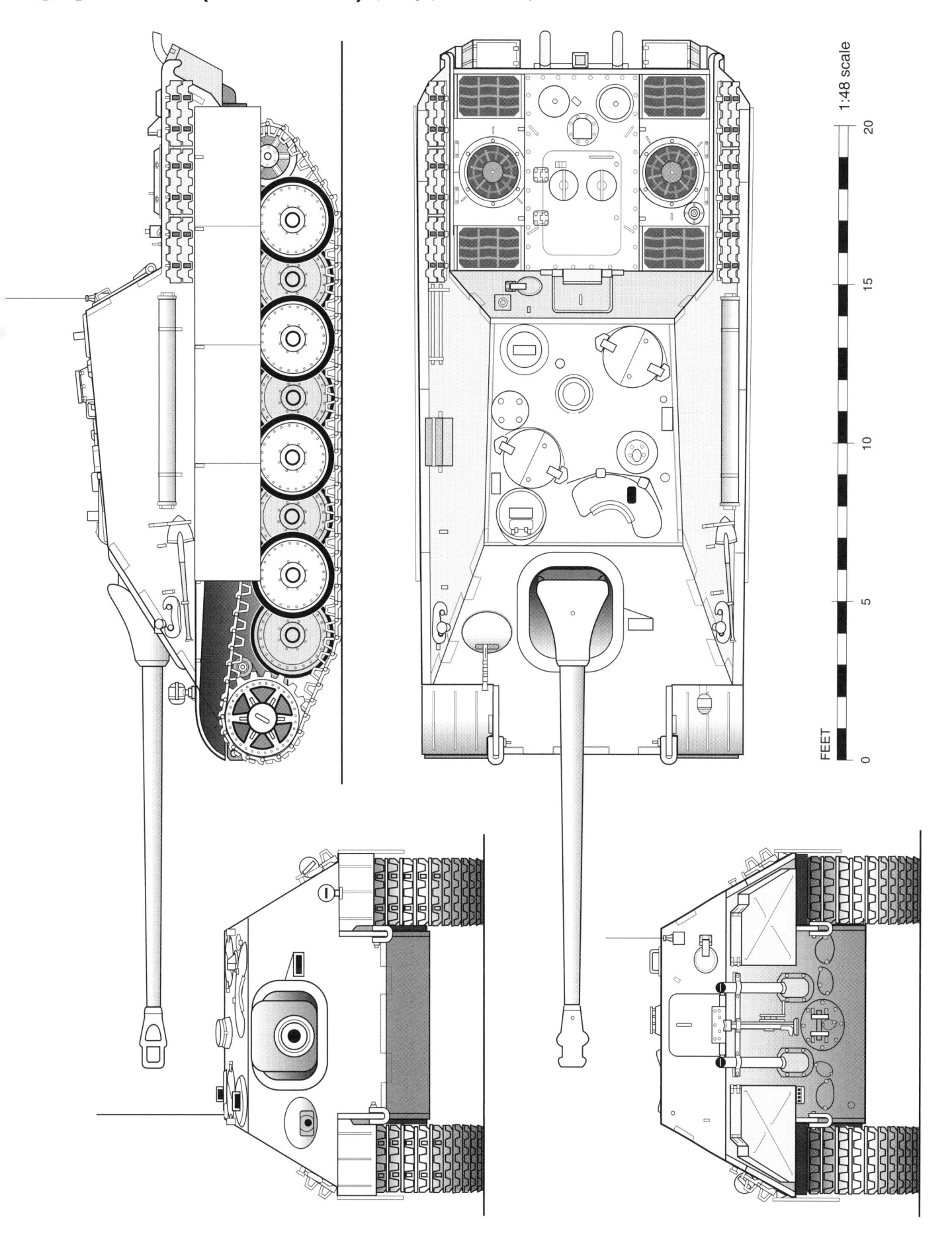

1:48 scale

German Late War Armored Fighting Vehicles

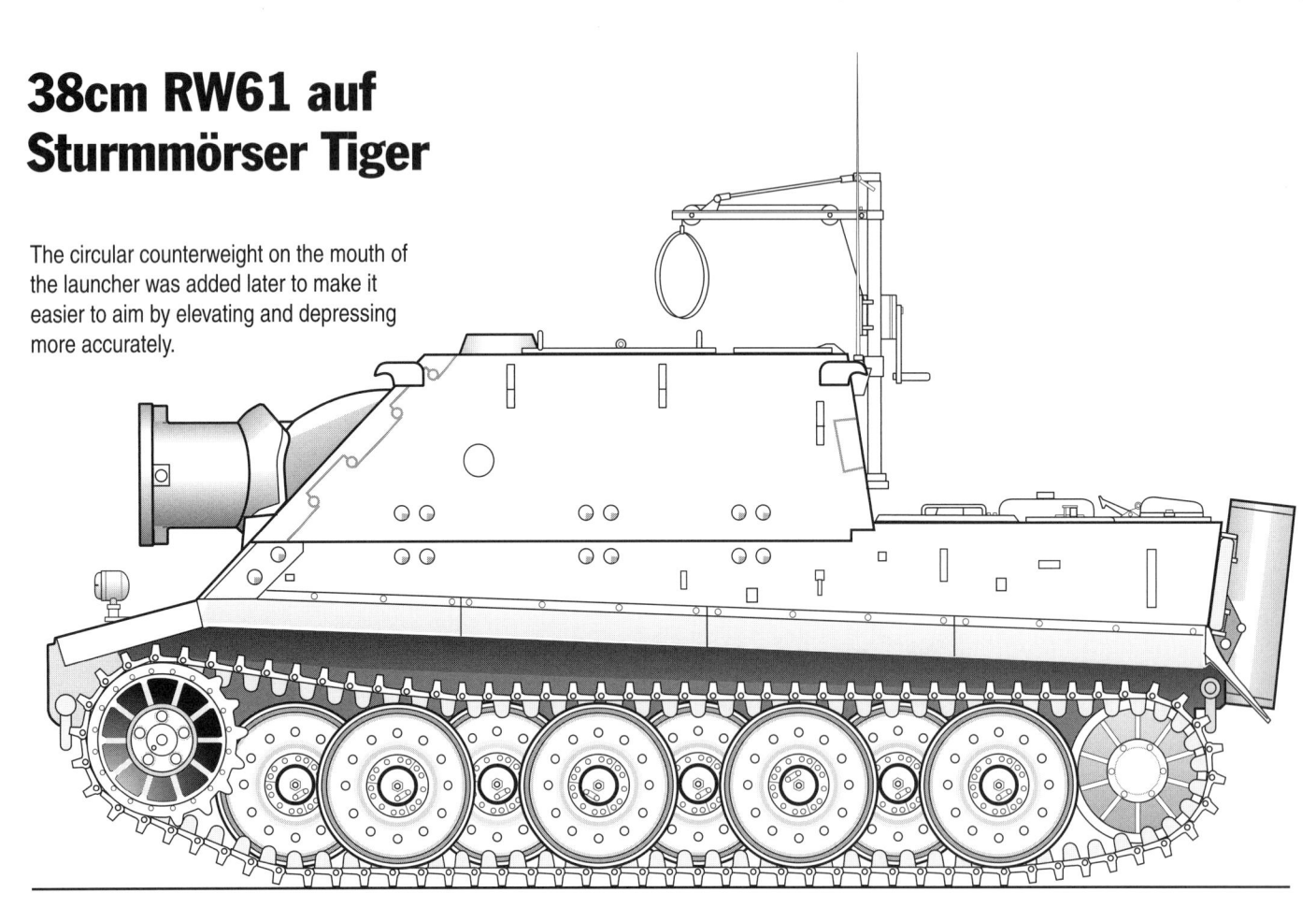

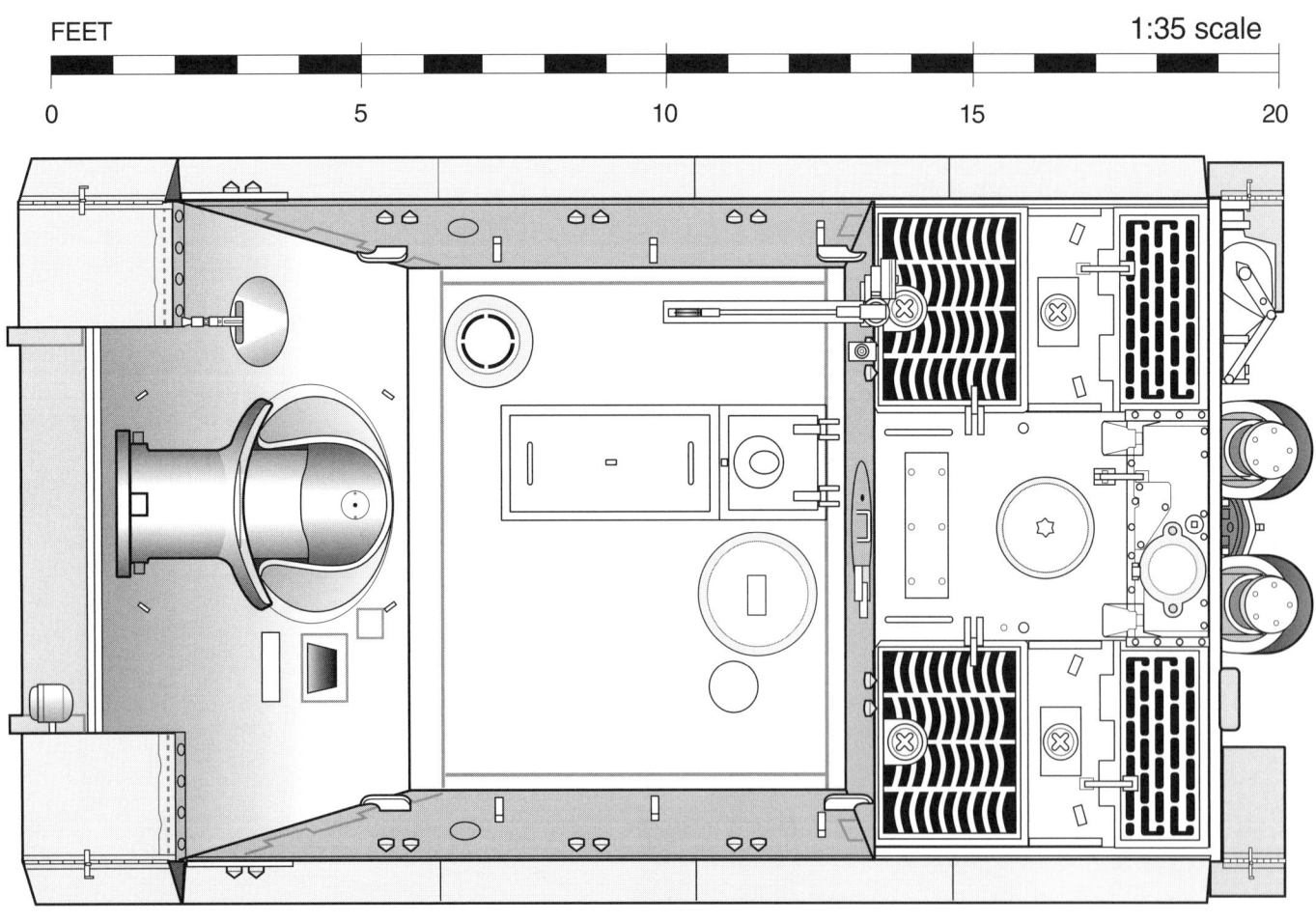

38cm RW61 auf Sturmmörser Tiger

The circular counterweight on the mouth of the launcher was added later to make it easier to aim by elevating and depressing more accurately.

FEET

1:35 scale

0   5   10   15   20

64 German Late War Armored Fighting Vehicles

38cm RW61 auf Sturmmörser Tiger

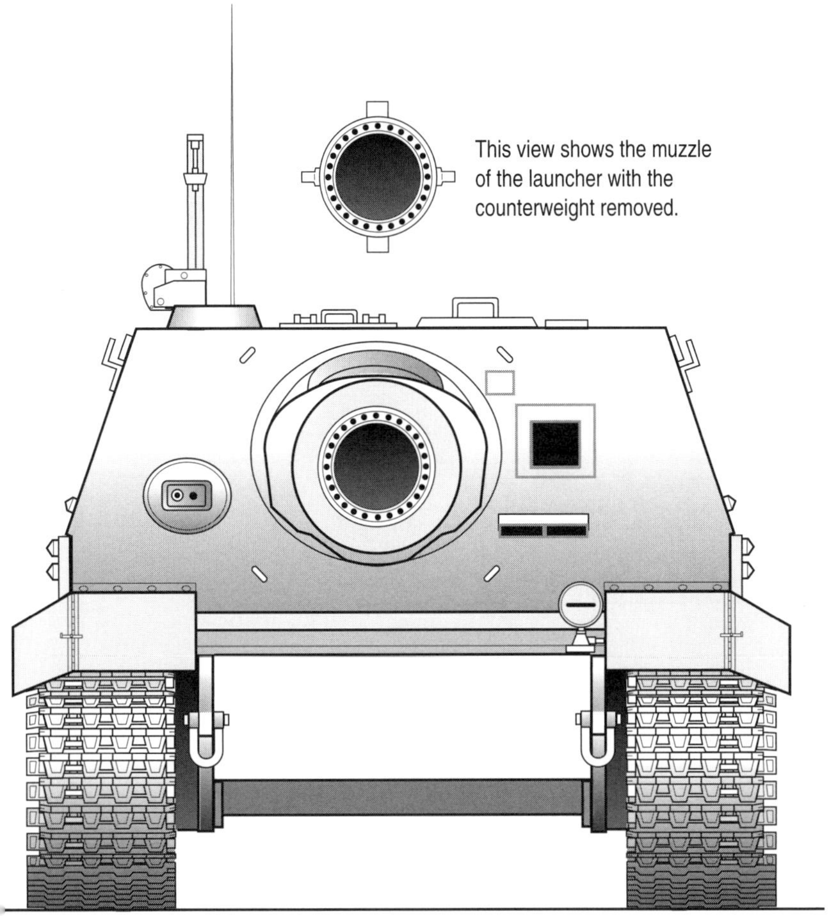

There were only eighteen Sturmtigers produced, and these were built on the Tiger I chassis, both new and on Tigers returned for repairs. These conversions took place from August 1944 until the end of that year.

They were issued to three companies: 1000, 1001 and 1002 Sturmmörser Companies. The 1000 and 1001 each had a roster strength of four Sturmtigers and saw service in the Ardennes, in November 1944. The 1000th was deployed west of Trier in December 1944, but mechanical problems allowed only one vehicle to be committed on the Alsatian border. The 1001st, under Hauptmann von Gottberg, went into action in the western Eifel region near Gemund in November 1944. Then in January 45 they were shifted to the Duren – Euskirchen front. Here the 1001st bombarded Allied tanks caught in several villages. Under pressure of Allied advances, three of them were ferried across the Rhine at Bonn, and engaged in combat just east of the city. After expending their remaining ammunition the three Sturmtigers were destroyed by their crews.

Company 1002 was commanded by Oberleutnant Zippel and fielded six Sturmtigers. This unit fought in the Reichwald region. In March 1945 they retreated across the Rhine and took up positions around Rheinberg. There they fought near Dorsten and Kirchhellen. Later the 1002nd fought retreating actions to the east, moving through Polsum, Marl and Dattein. In Datteln the crews destroyed their Sturmtigers after they had run out of ammunition. The crews were eventually captured near Minden in the Sauerland.

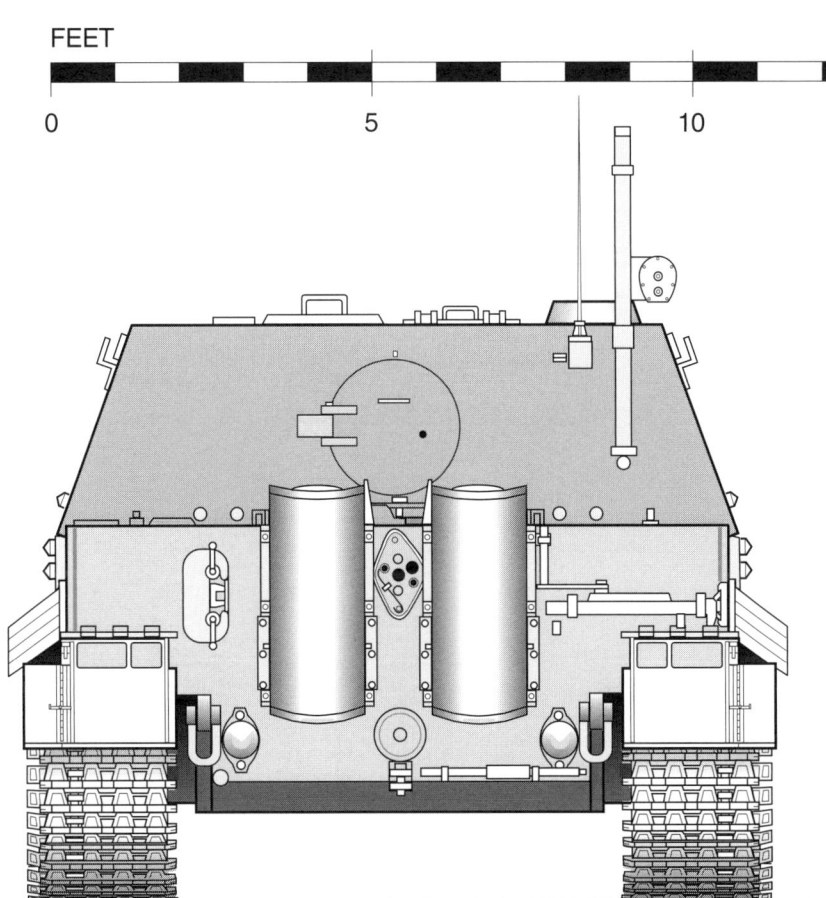

This view shows the muzzle of the launcher with the counterweight removed.

FEET   1:35 scale

The 38cm RW61 mortar launched a rocket propelled projectile to a maximum range of 5500 metres. The rocket gases were blocked from entering the fighting compartment and rerouted out through the holes around the muzzle. The vehicle was able to carry 13 rounds, and plans for a Tiger I chassis carrying an additional 40 rounds was in the works.

The onboard winch was used for raising and lowering the huge projectiles. The winch could be swung to the offside right where the cable was was hooked to the band around the round and raised by a crank on the the rear of the winch. The roof hatch was in two parts, the forward portion simply lifted off with two handles, and the rear portion was hinged back and featured the close-in defense weapon. With these hatches open the round could be lowered into the fighting compartment and positioned in racks.

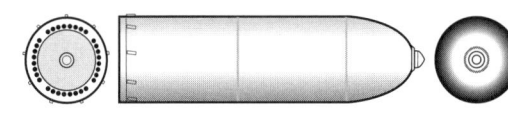

German Late War Armored Fighting Vehicles

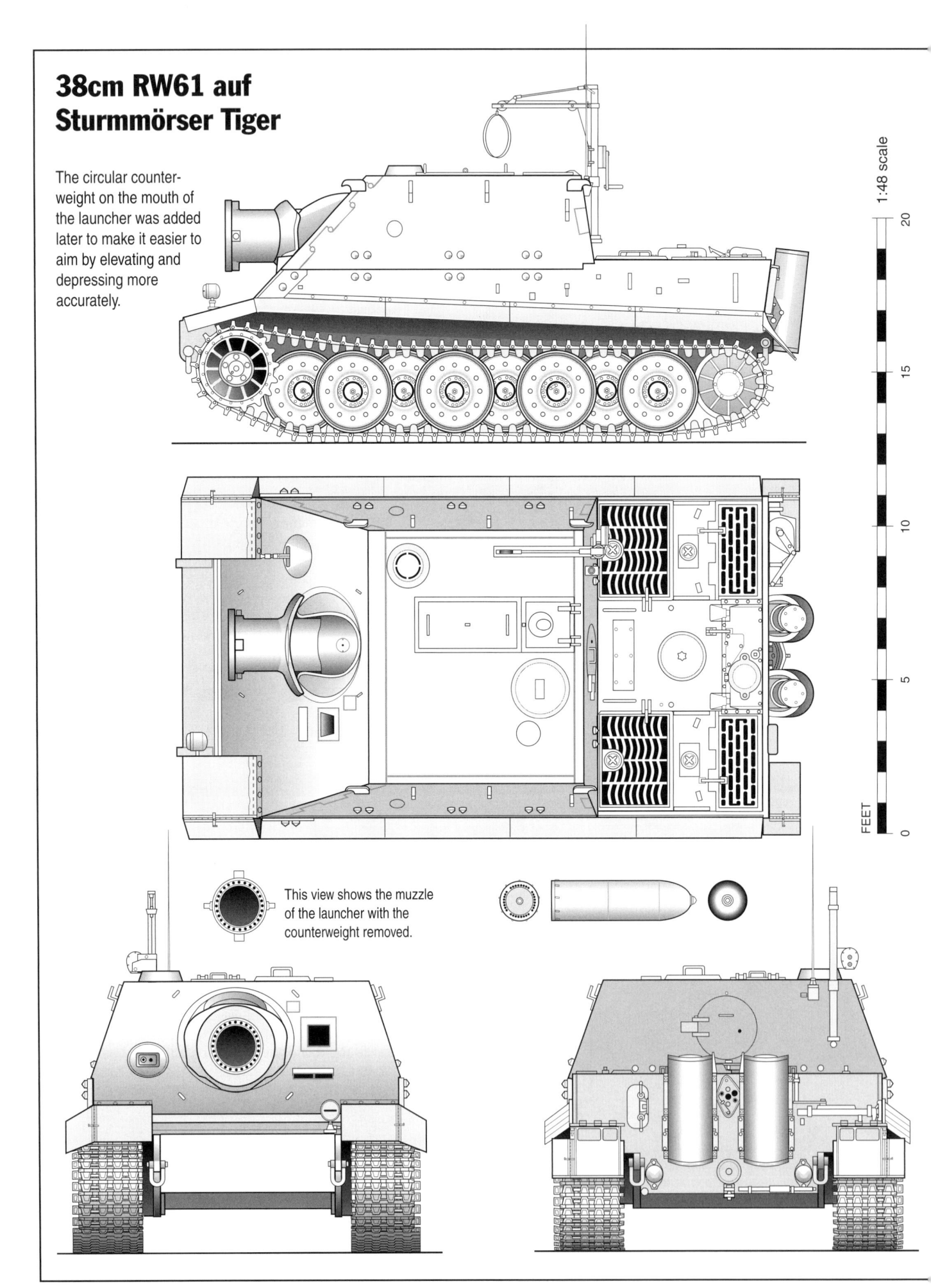

38cm RW61 auf Sturmmörser Tiger

The circular counterweight on the mouth of the launcher was added later to make it easier to aim by elevating and depressing more accurately.

This view shows the muzzle of the launcher with the counterweight removed.

Two good views of the Sturmmörser Tiger showing its massive size and thick armor. Both vehicles were abandoned by their crews, the lower one after throwing its right track.

Jagdtiger (Sd.Kfz. 186)
Henschel Suspension

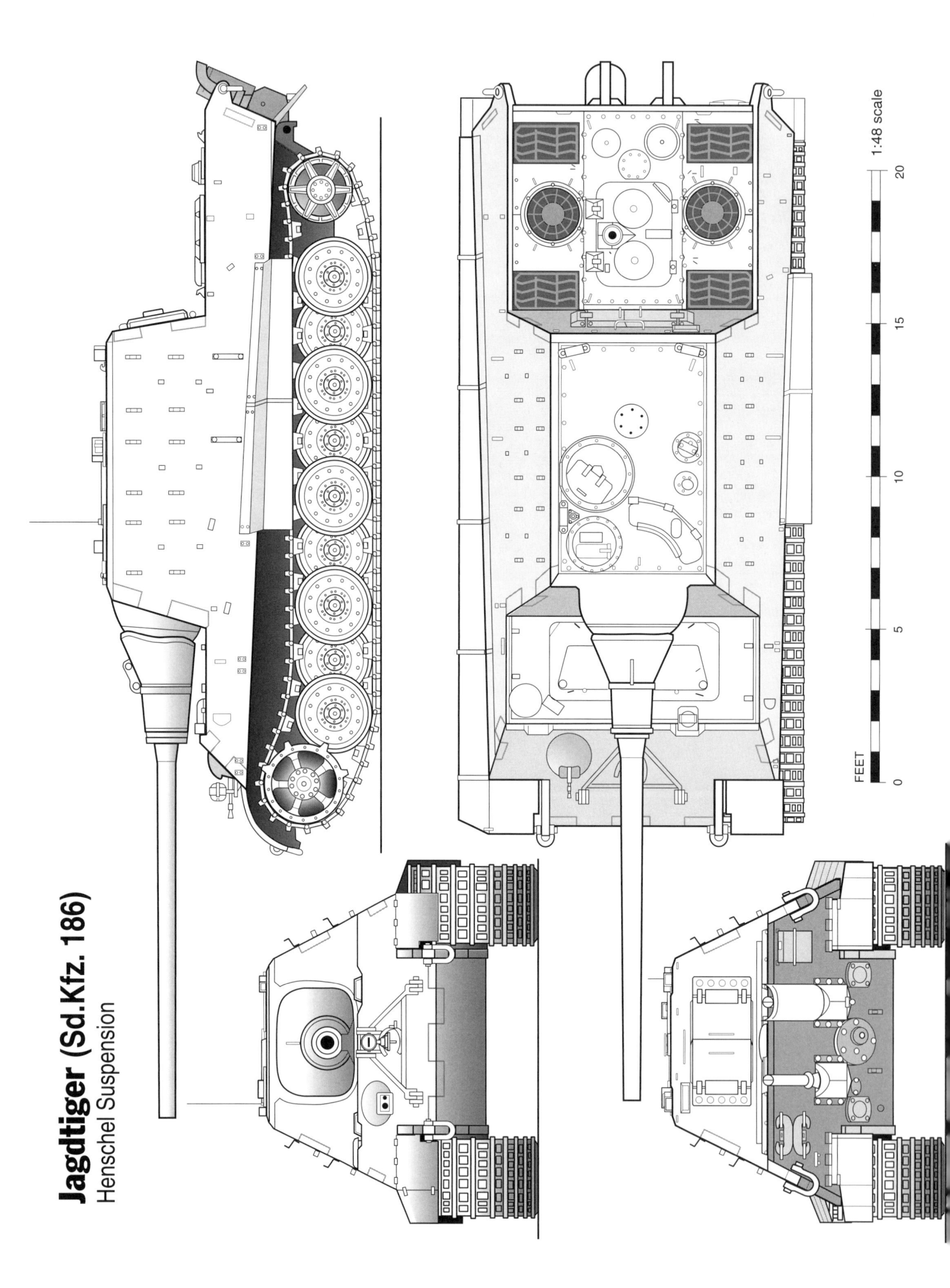

1:48 scale

FEET

68 German Late War Armored Fighting Vehicles

Jagdtiger (Sd.Kfz. 186)
Porsche Suspension

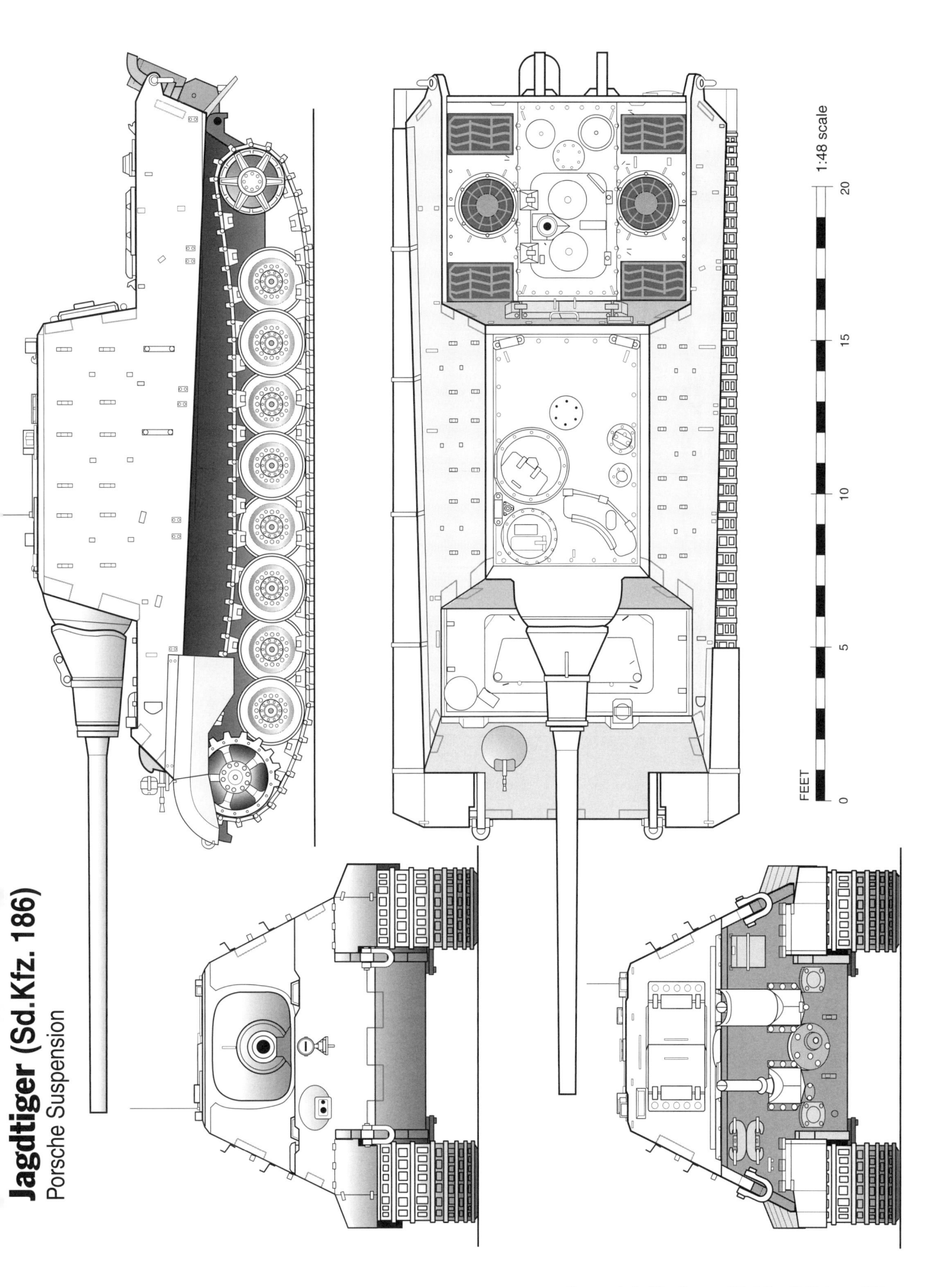

German Late War Armored Fighting Vehicles

Feürleitpanzerfahrzeug für V-2 Raketen auf Zugkraftwagen 8t

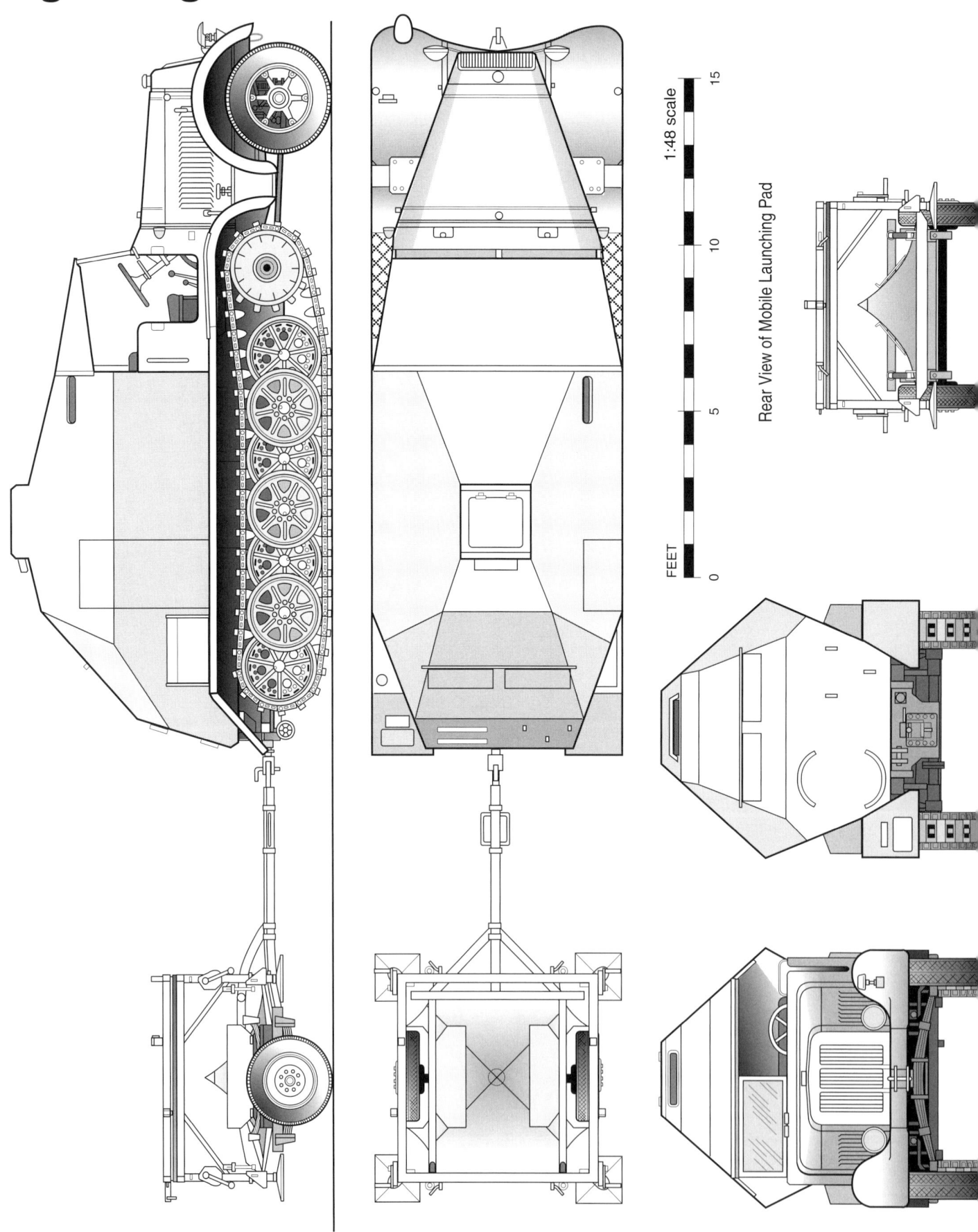

1:48 scale

Rear View of Mobile Launching Pad

Flakpanzer IV 3.7cm Flak
Ostwind I

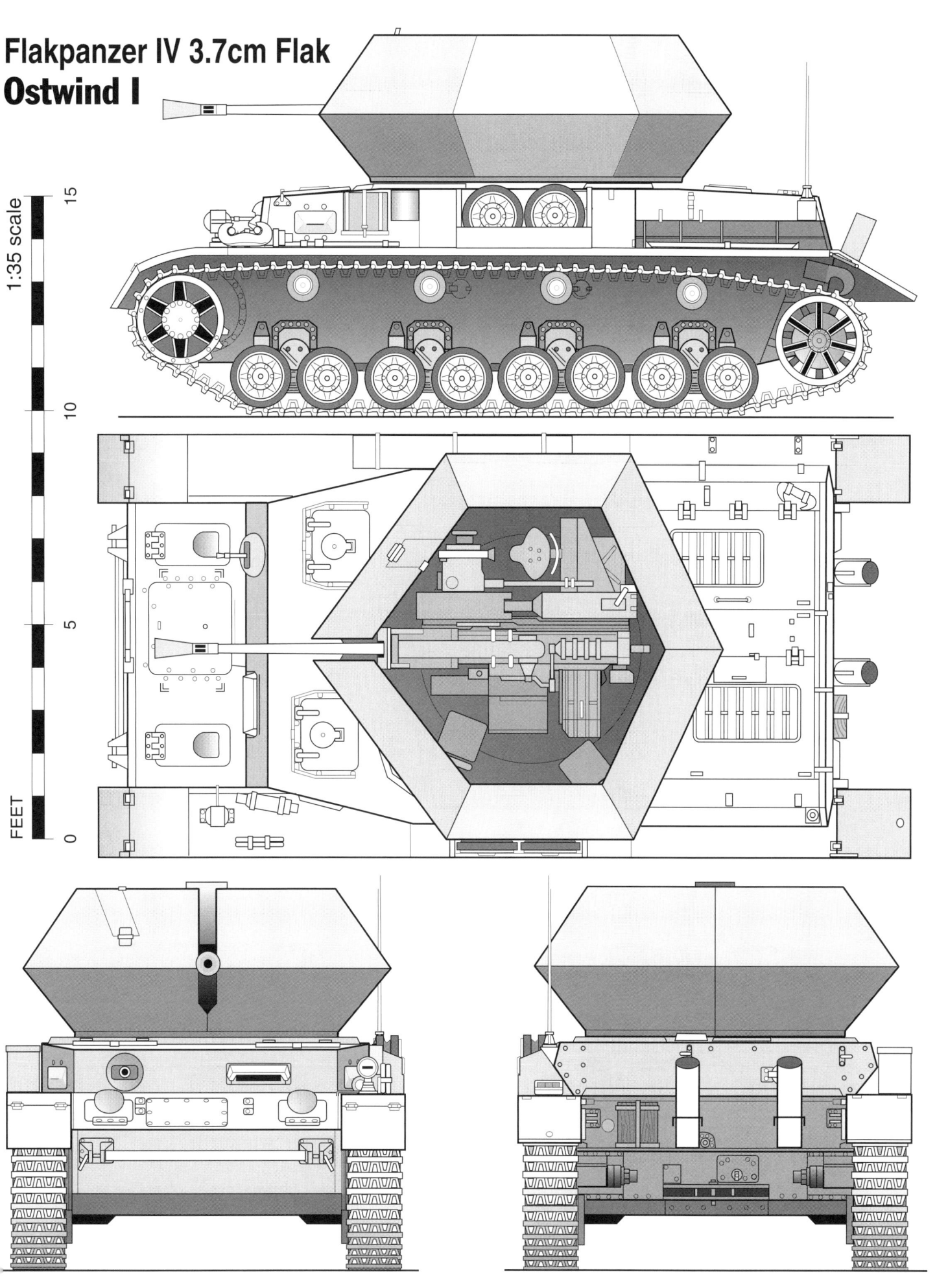

1:35 scale

FEET

Panzerjäger Tiger (P) mit 8.8 Pak 43.2 (L/71)
(Sd.Kfz.184) "Elefant"

FEET　　　　　　　　　　　　　　　　　1:48 scale
0　　　5　　　10　　　15　　　20

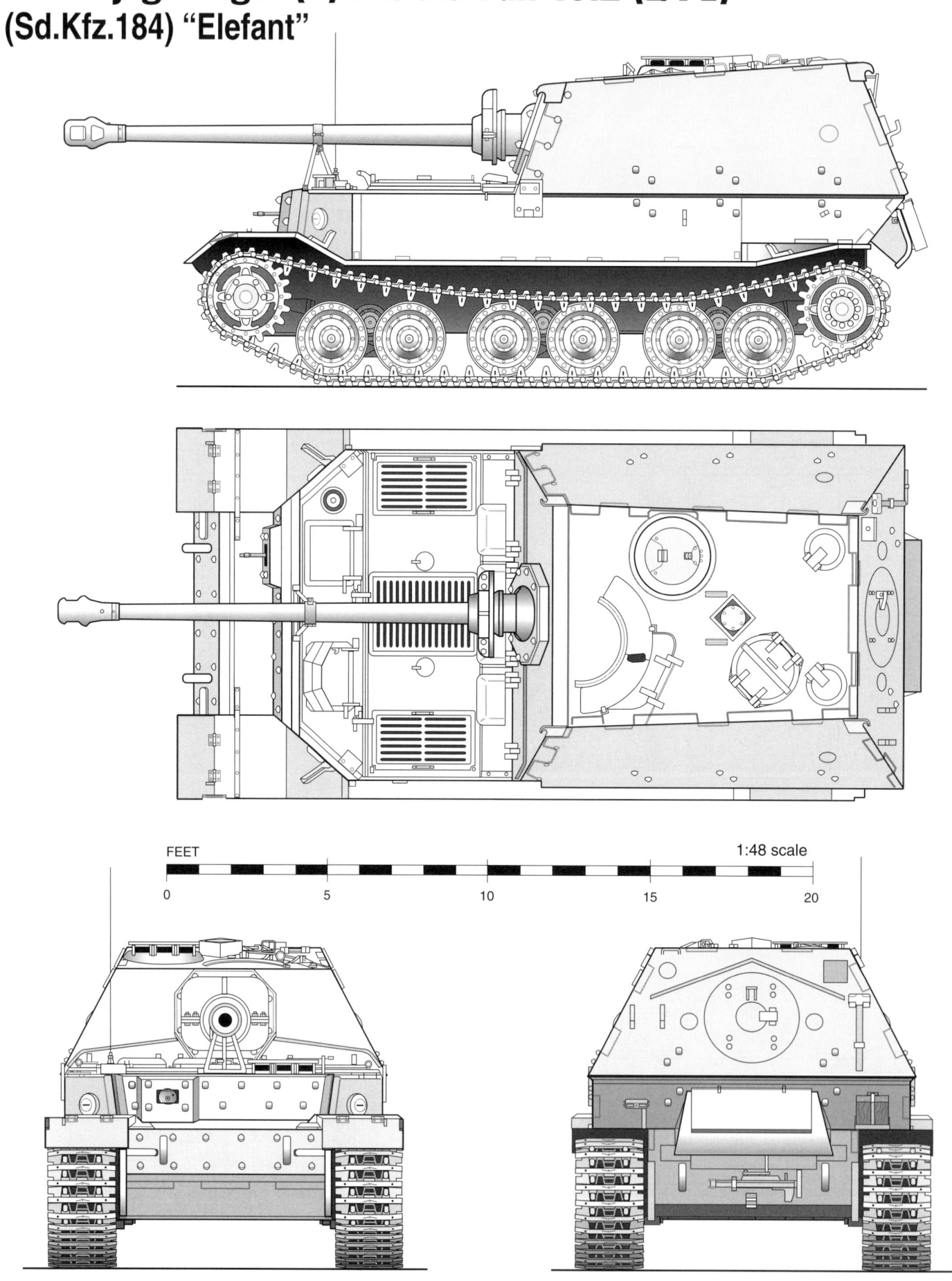

72　German Late War Armored Fighting Vehicles

Pz.Kpfw. Tiger Ausf. E,
(Sd.Kfz. 181) late production

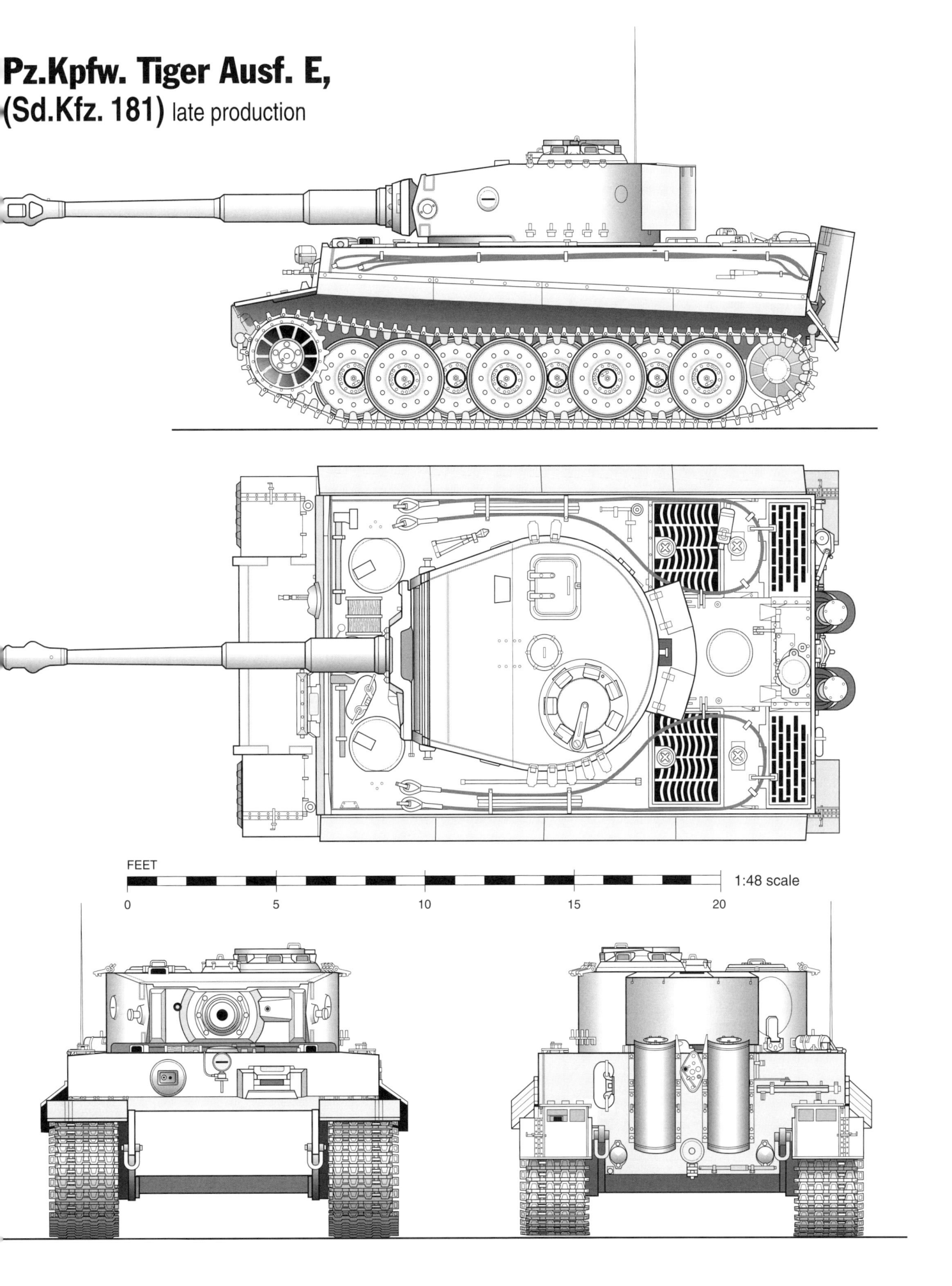

1:48 scale

German Late War Armored Fighting Vehicles 73

BMM/CKD 15cm sIG 33/2 (Sf) auf Jagdpanzer 38(t)
SP Heavy Infantry Gun on Hetzer chassis

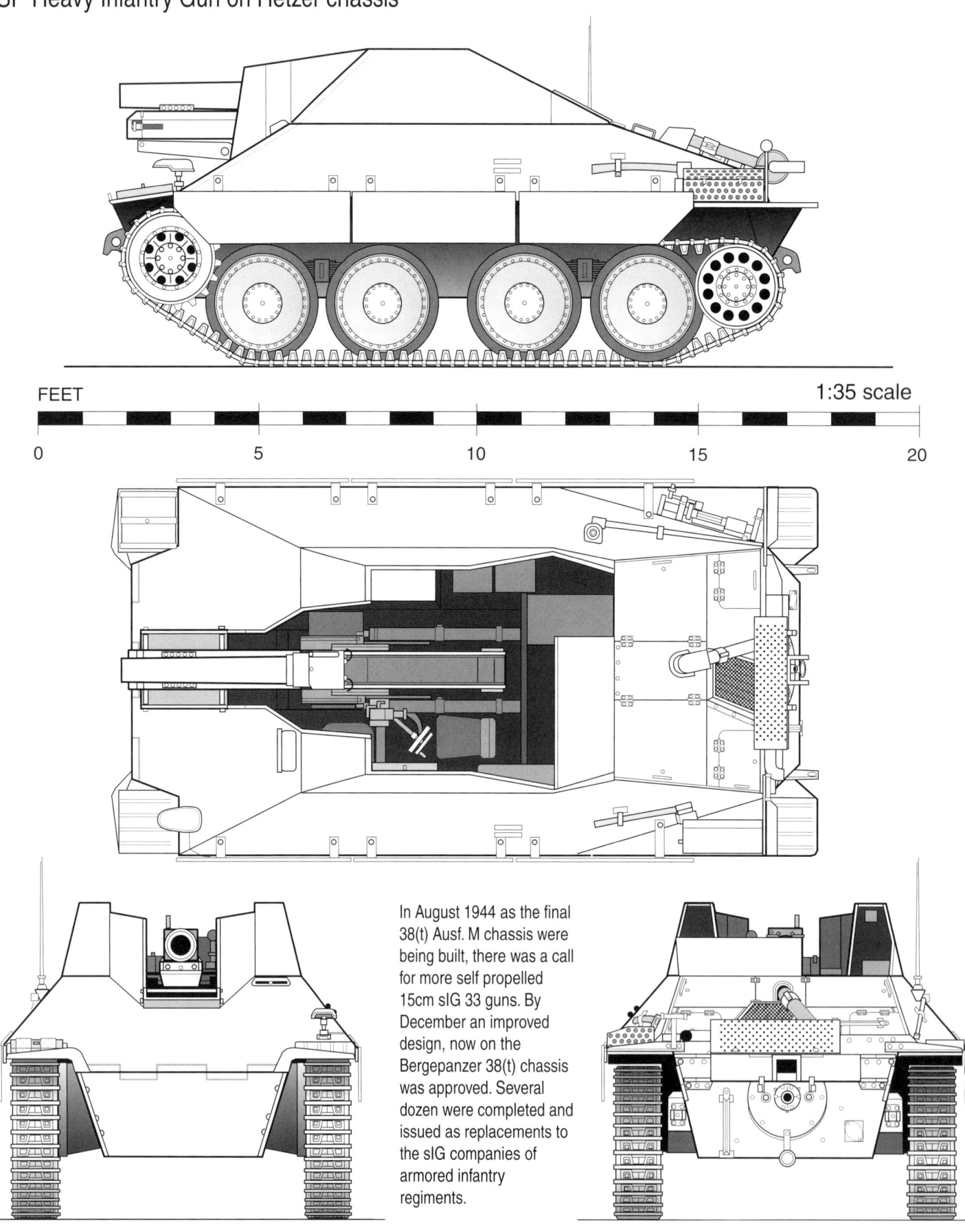

FEET 1:35 scale

In August 1944 as the final 38(t) Ausf. M chassis were being built, there was a call for more self propelled 15cm sIG 33 guns. By December an improved design, now on the Bergepanzer 38(t) chassis was approved. Several dozen were completed and issued as replacements to the sIG companies of armored infantry regiments.

74 German Late War Armored Fighting Vehicles

Flakpanzer IV Wirbelwind (Sd.Kfz. 161/4)

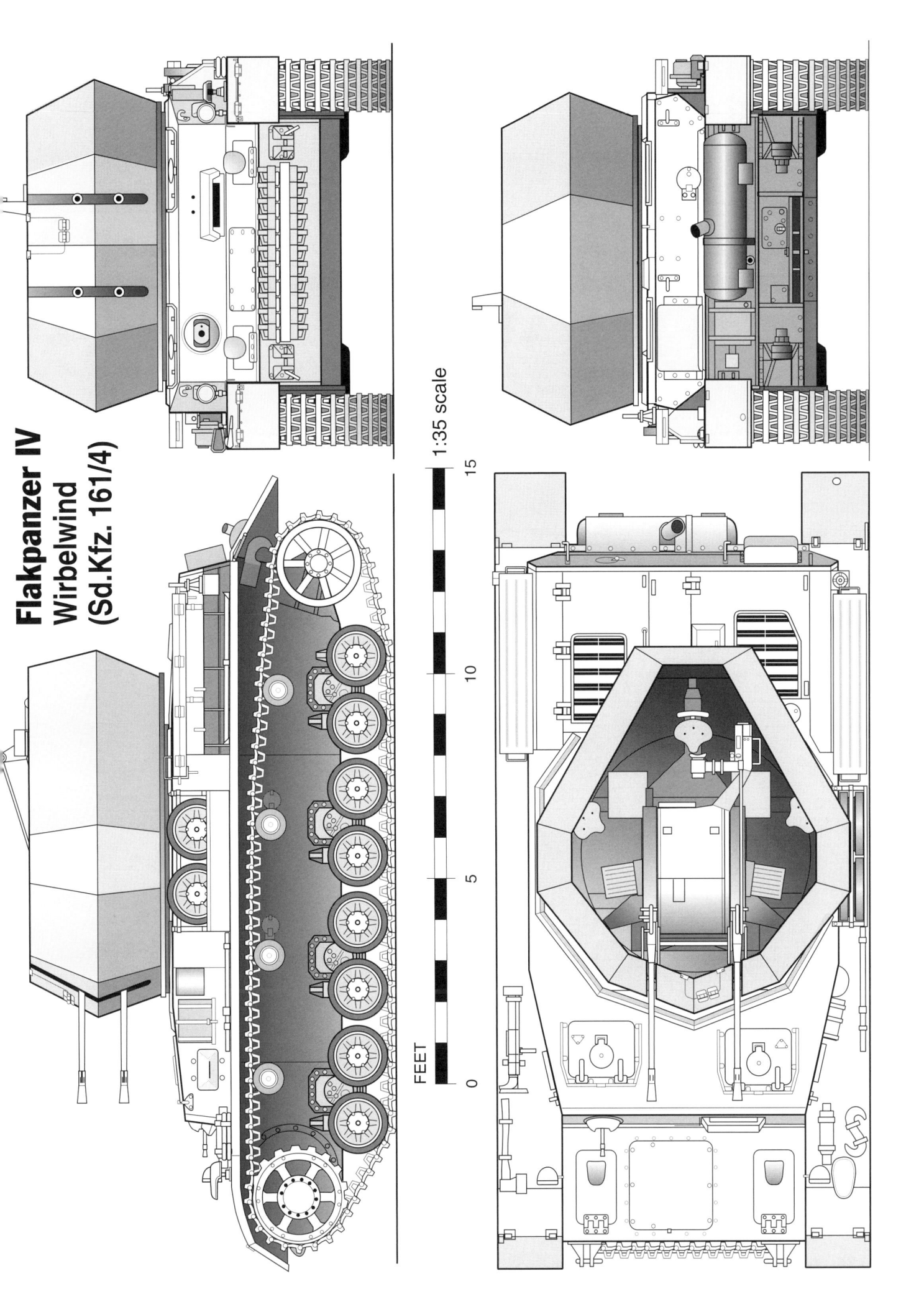

1:35 scale

FEET 0 5 10 15

15cm Panzerwerfer 42 (Zehnling) auf sWS

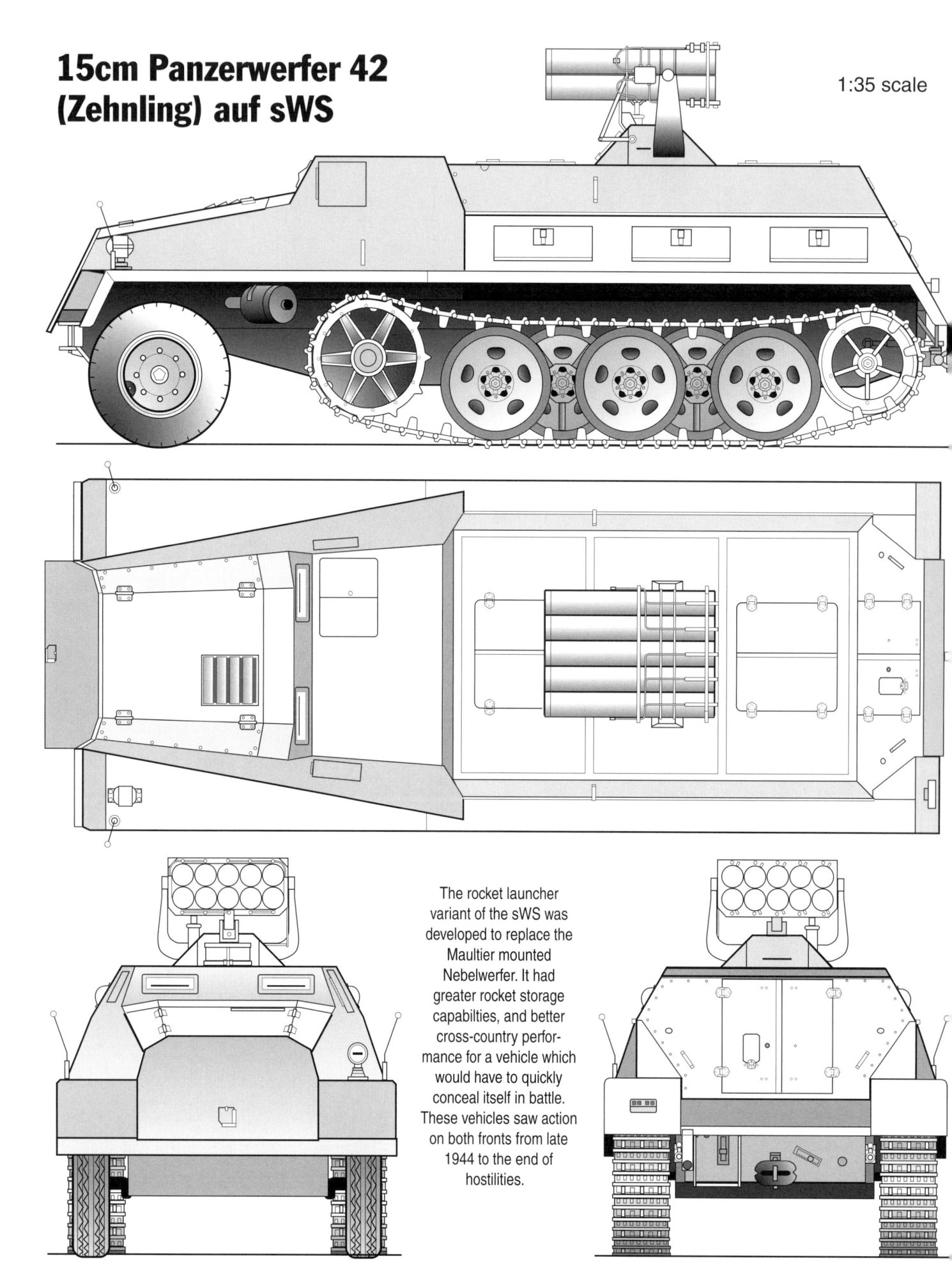

1:35 scale

The rocket launcher variant of the sWS was developed to replace the Maultier mounted Nebelwerfer. It had greater rocket storage capabilties, and better cross-country performance for a vehicle which would have to quickly conceal itself in battle. These vehicles saw action on both fronts from late 1944 to the end of hostilities.

76 German Late War Armored Fighting Vehicles

Jagdpanther (Sd.Kfz. 173) (final production version)

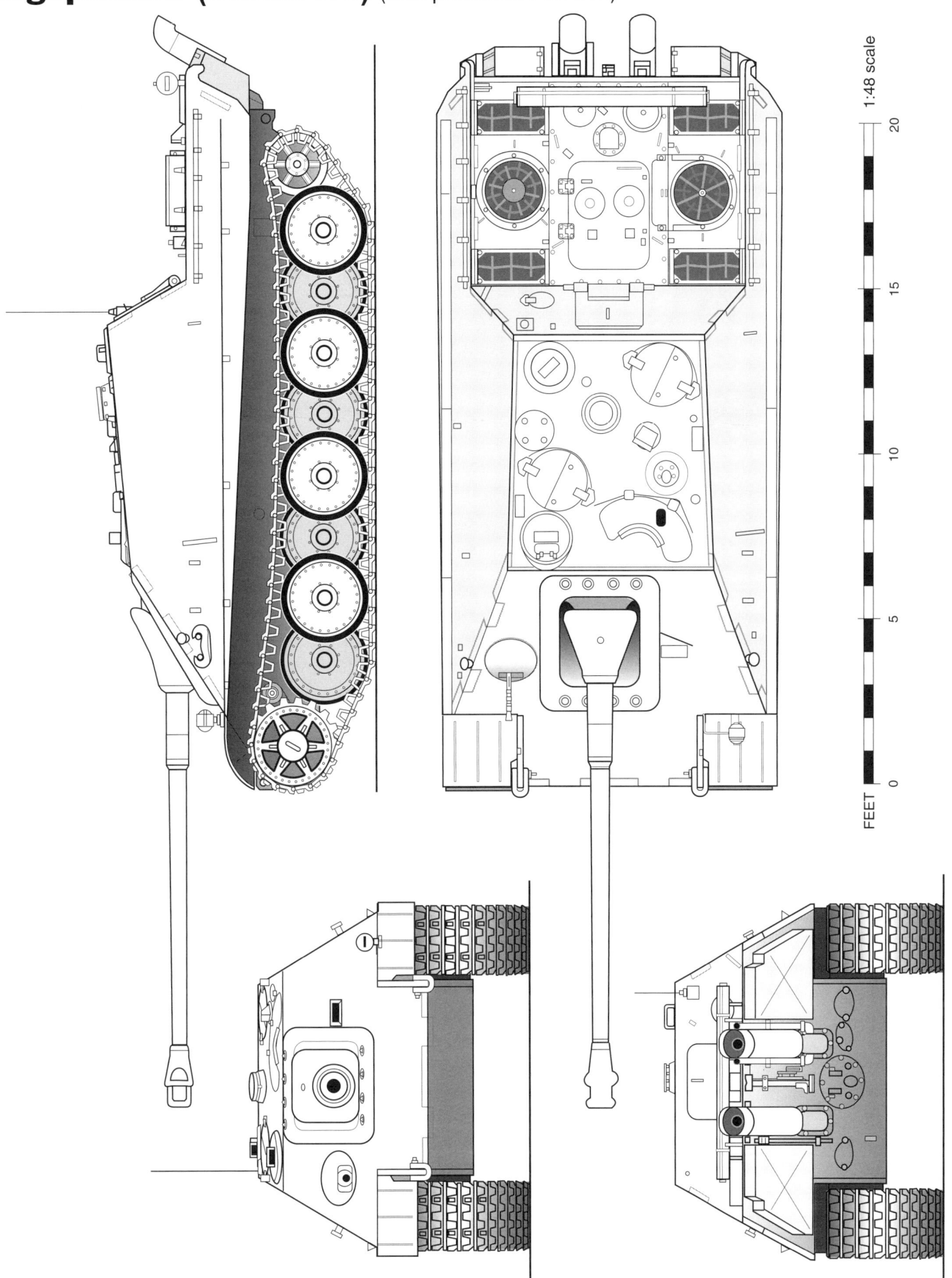

1:48 scale

German Late War Armored Fighting Vehicles

A Canadian officer stands atop a late version Jagdpanther shown here in a captured vehicle park under Allied control after hostilities ceased in that area of Western Europe.

Mittlerer Ladungsträger Sd.Kfz. 304
NSU "Springer"

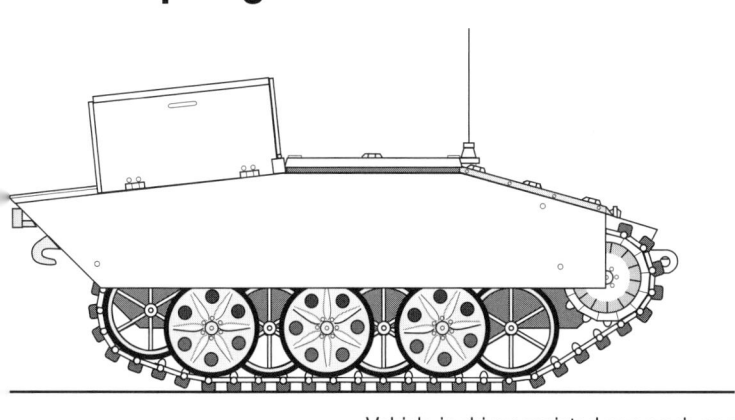

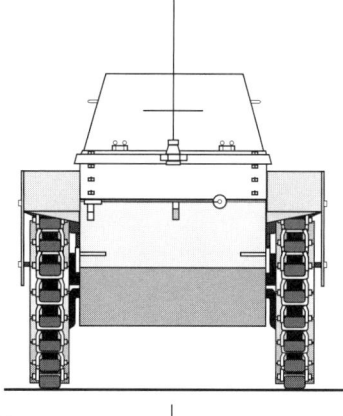

Vehicle in driver assisted approach configuration

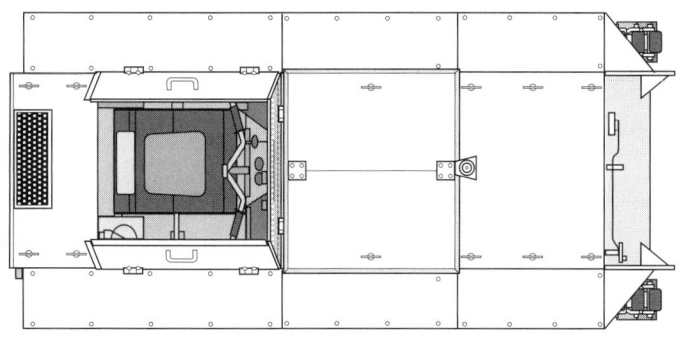

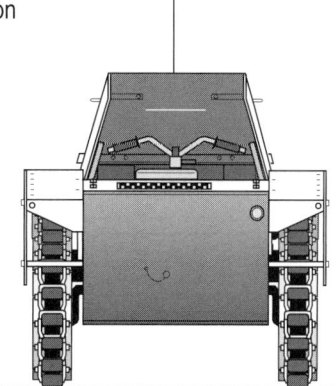

FEET   1:35 scale
0   5   10   15   20

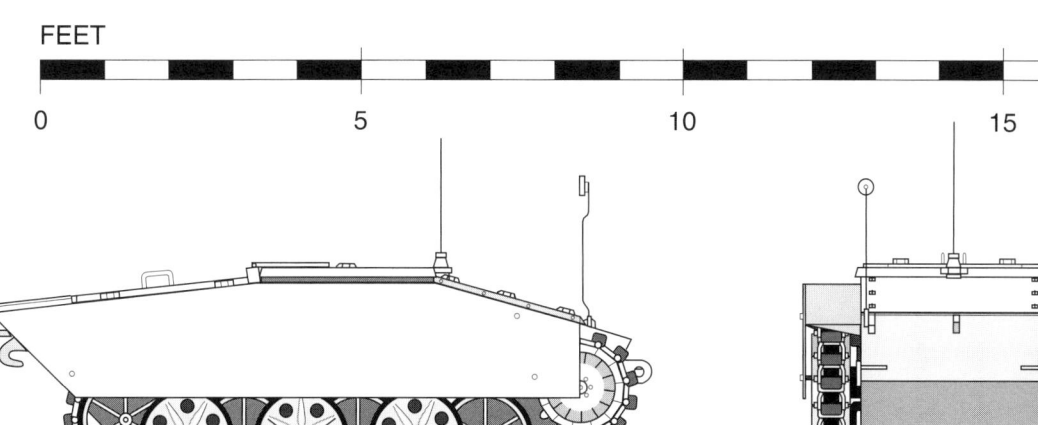

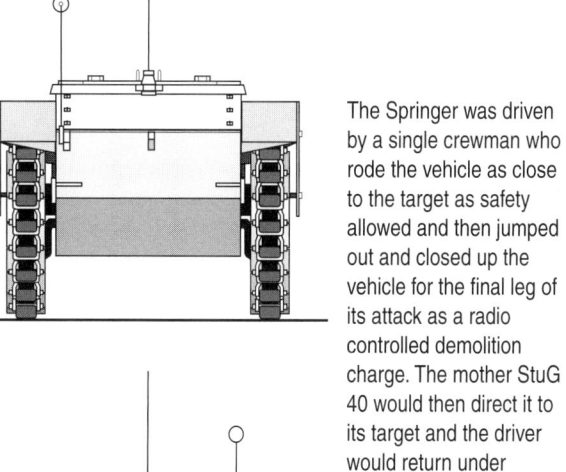

Vehicle in final radio control attack configuration

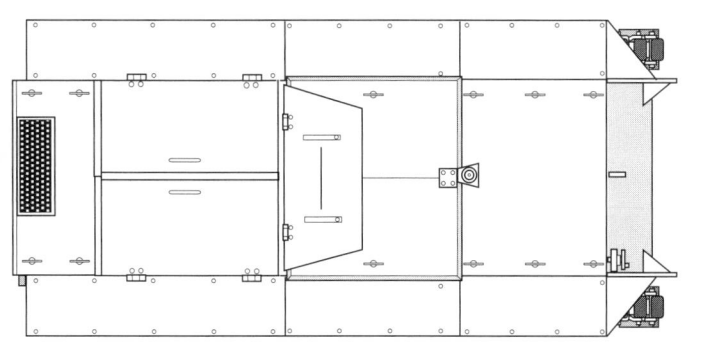

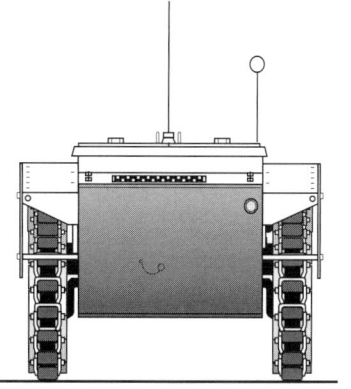

The Springer was deemed a middle-of-the-road, cost-effective replacement for the earlier Goliath and B IV demolition charge layers. They were issued to StuG 40 Ausf. G companies fitted for radio control operations. Each R/C Zug consisted of four vehicles, a command StuG 49 plus three StuG 40, each with three Springers.

The Springer replaced the NSU Kettenkrad on their assembly but probably no more than fifty were completed before the war ended.

The Springer was driven by a single crewman who rode the vehicle as close to the target as safety allowed and then jumped out and closed up the vehicle for the final leg of its attack as a radio controlled demolition charge. The mother StuG 40 would then direct it to its target and the driver would return under covering fire if need be.

The vehicle carried a 330Kg load of explosives and could move at about 40 Km/hr.

German Late War Armored Fighting Vehicles   79

Schwerer Wehrmachtschlepper (Gepanzerter Ausführung)
Armored Forward Area Supply Vehicle

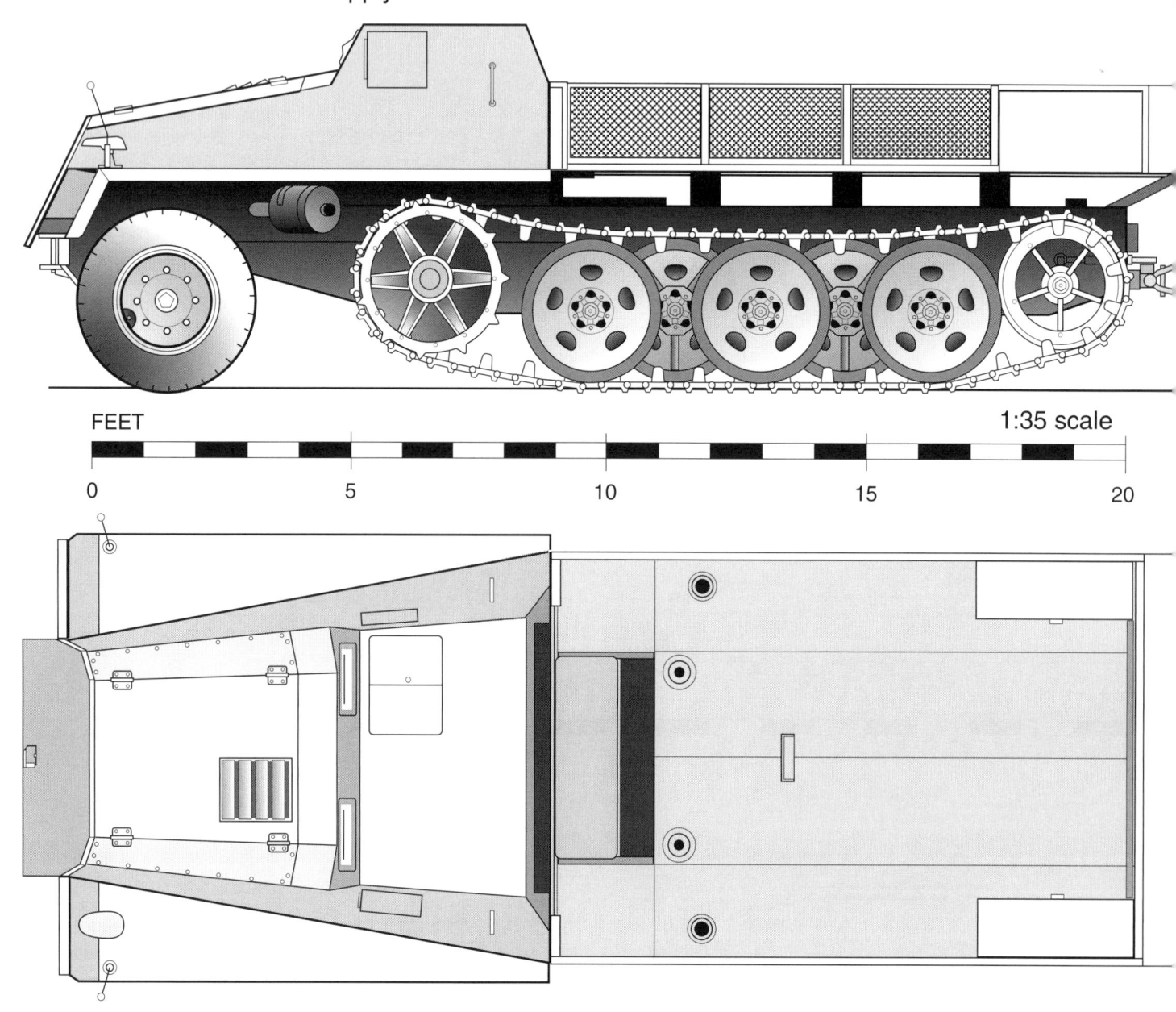

FEET   1:35 scale
0   5   10   15   20

This late version of the sWS depicts the armored version in its load carrier configuration. It also served as the chassis for the 3.7cm Flak 43 auf sWS and the 15cm Panzerwerfer 42 (Zehnling) auf sWS, among other things. The softskin version began appearing in 1943, and a total of 825 went into service before production was halted in favor of the simpler and cheaper Maultier. The armored cab was introduced in mid-1944, replacing the makeshift armor kits applied to the softskin version.

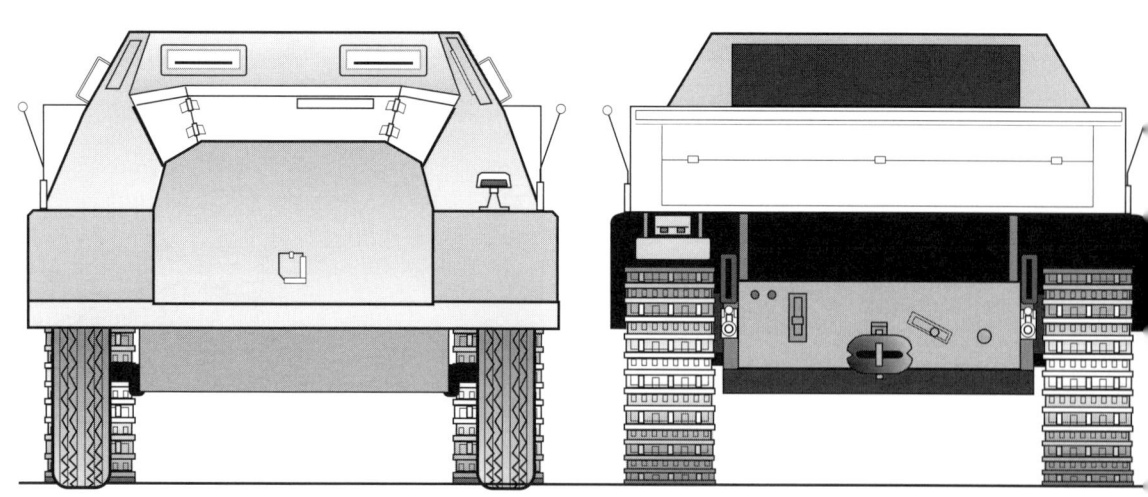

80   German Late War Armored Fighting Vehicles

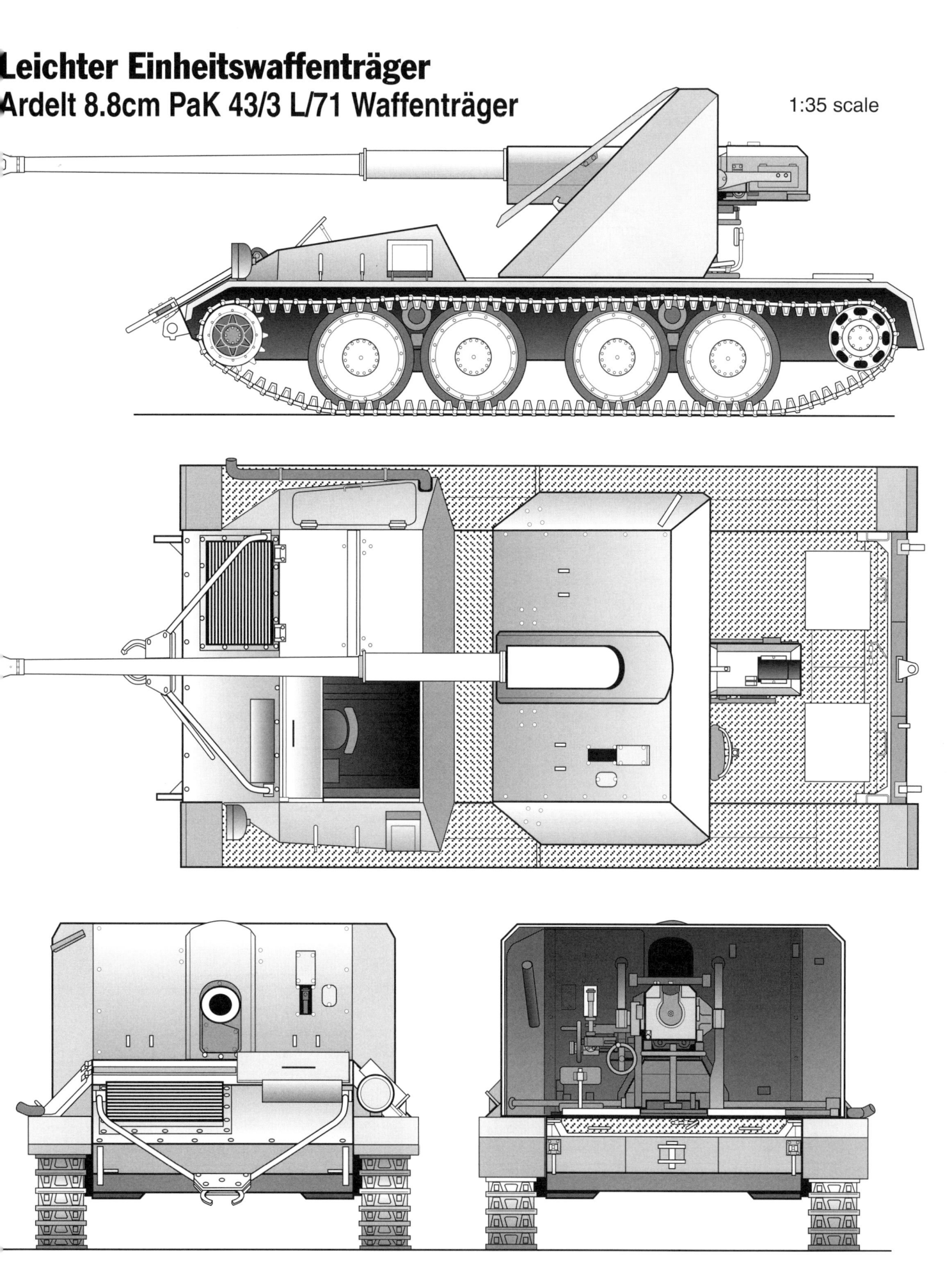

Leichter Einheitswaffenträger
Ardelt 8.8cm PaK 43/3 L/71 Waffenträger

1:35 scale

German Late War Armored Fighting Vehicles 81

Jagdpanzer 38(t) "Starr"
(prototype)

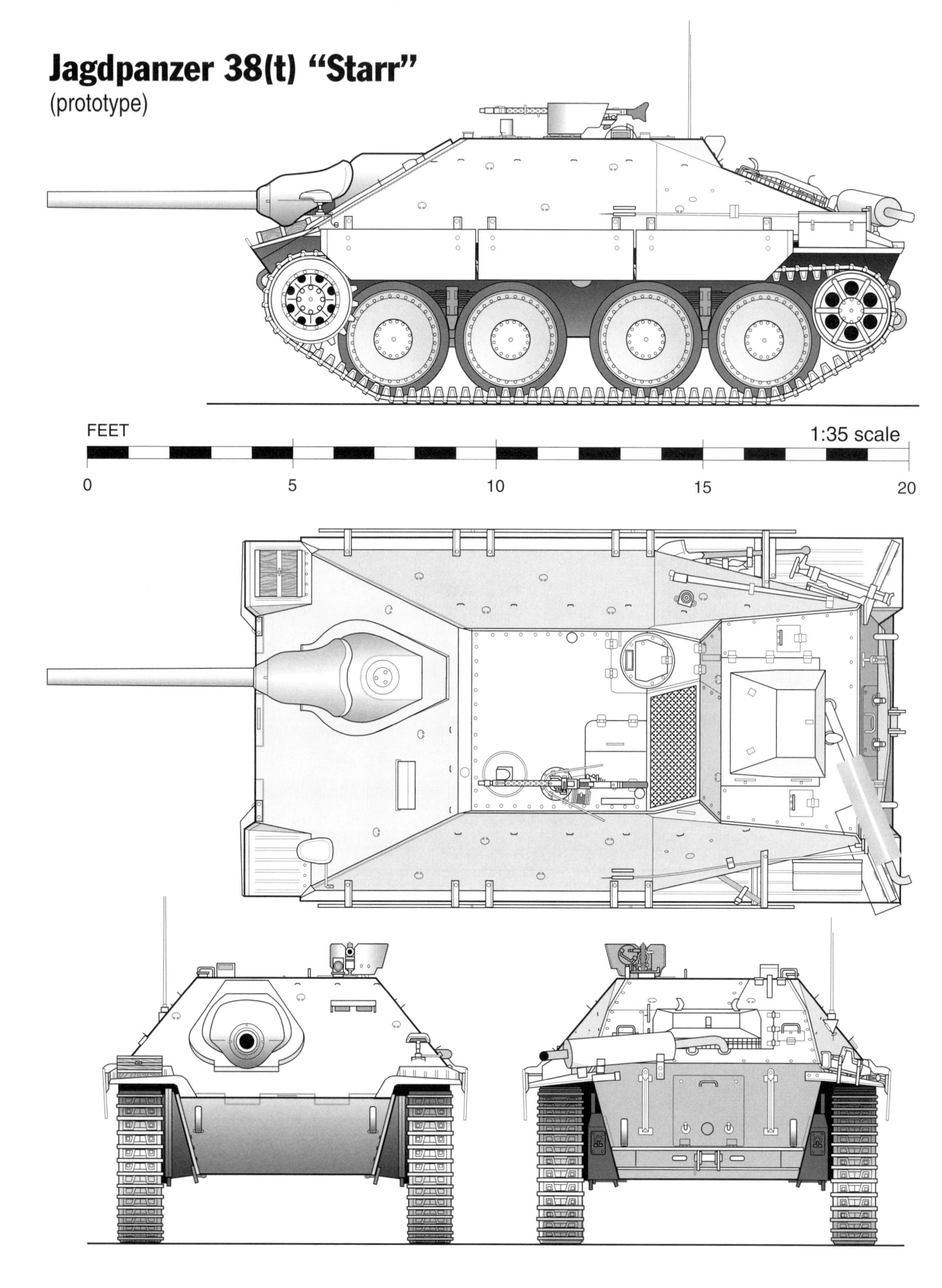

FEET   1:35 scale
0   5   10   15   20

82 German Late War Armored Fighting Vehicles

Panzerkampfwagen Maus

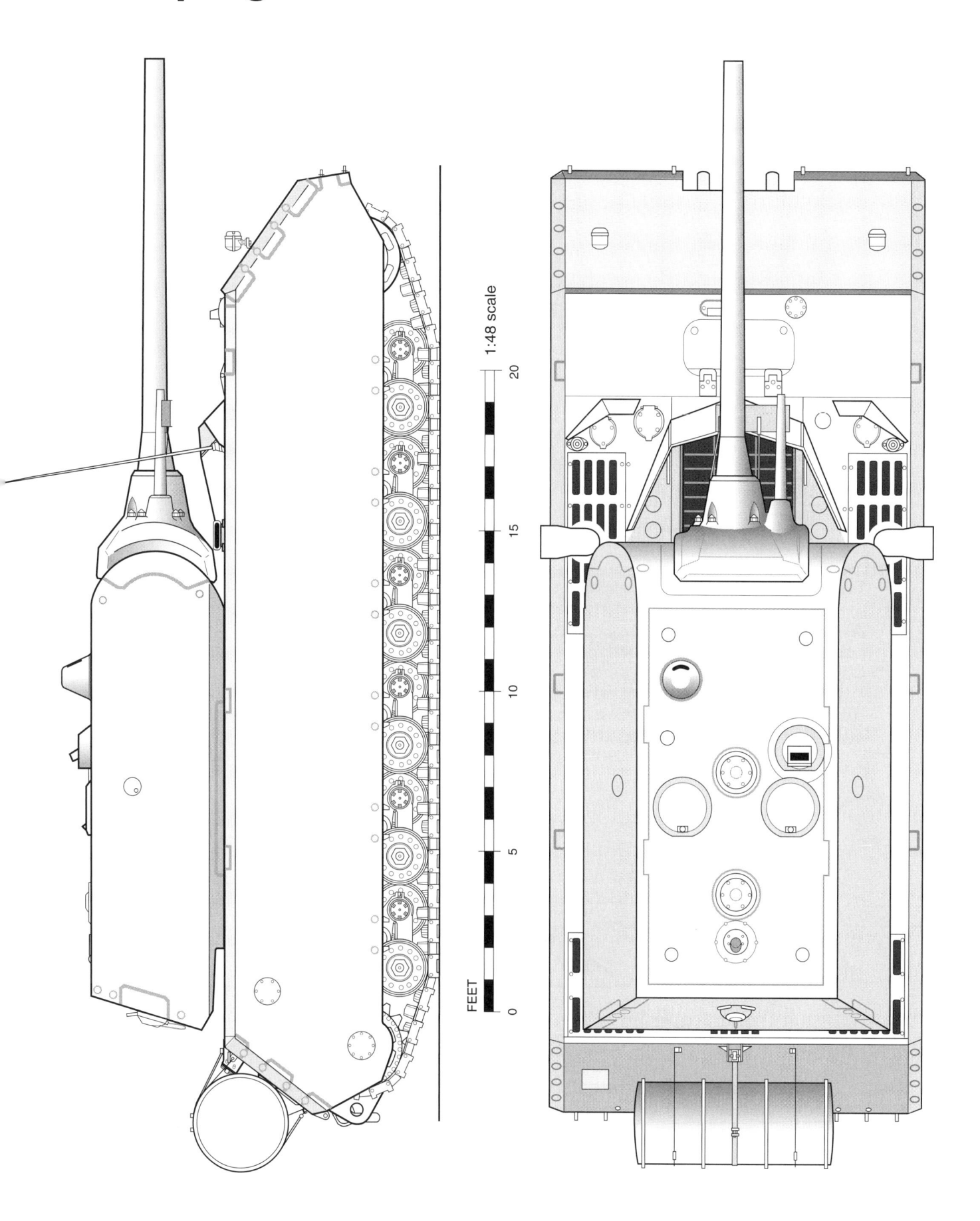

German Late War Armored Fighting Vehicles

Panzerkampfwagen Maus

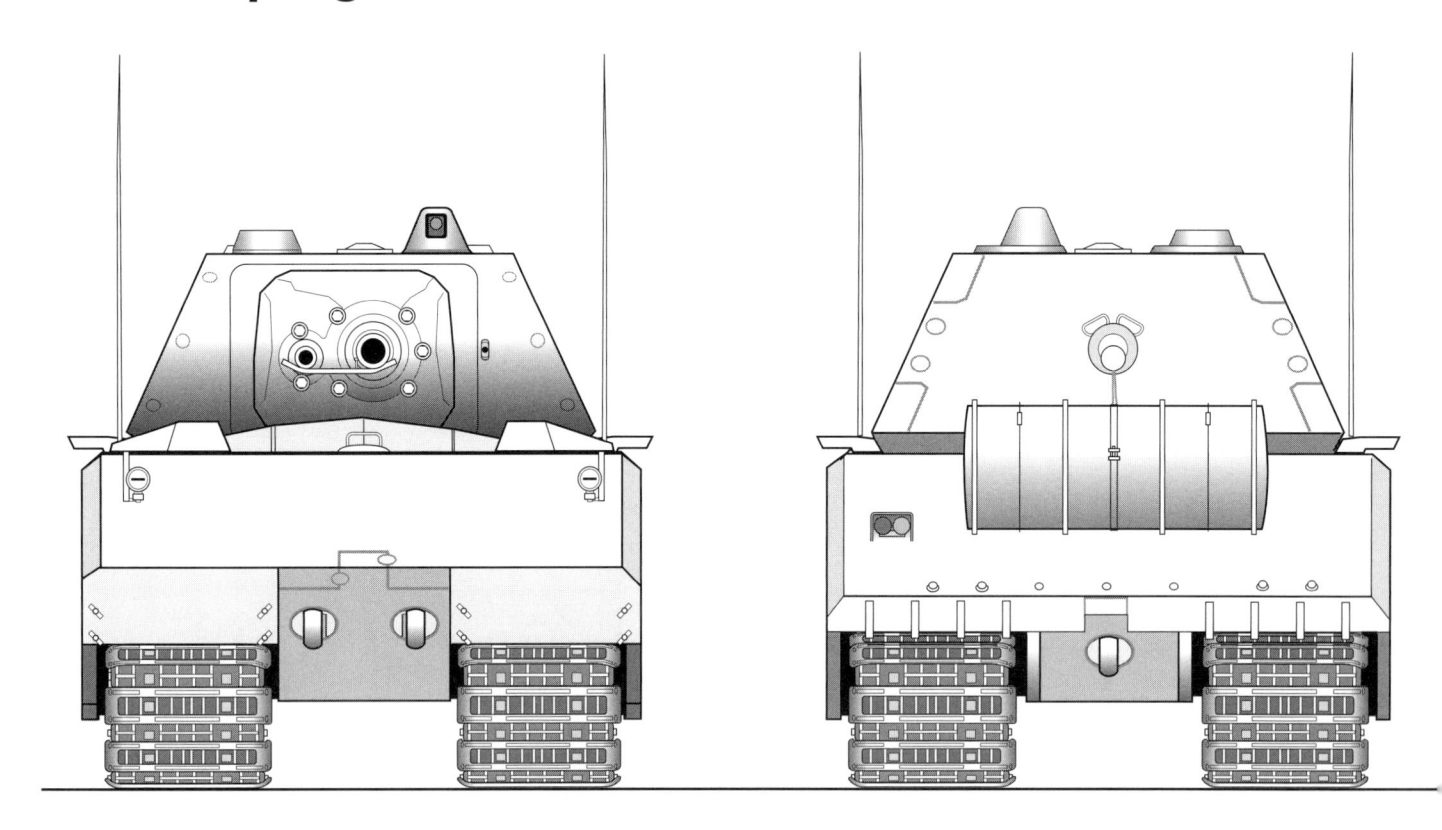

These drawings are based on the composite Maus on display at the Kubinka Museum in Russia. There were two Maus vehicles completed, designated as 1.Fahrzeug and 2.Fahrzeug. Both vehicles were blown up by the Germans at the end of the war, but the Russians managed to salvage the 2.Fahrzeug turret and the 1.Fahrzeug chassis to produce a reasonable example. The original completed 2.Fahrzeug chassis detail differed in a number of ways from the 1.Fahzeug, and I have attempted to incorporate some of these details.

The Maus superheavy tank concept was never to see fruition, and how the Germans ever expected to find the materials and maintain the facities to produce them in any number is unknown. Most sources agree that the project simply ate up manpower and materials, with little chance of changing the direction of the war.

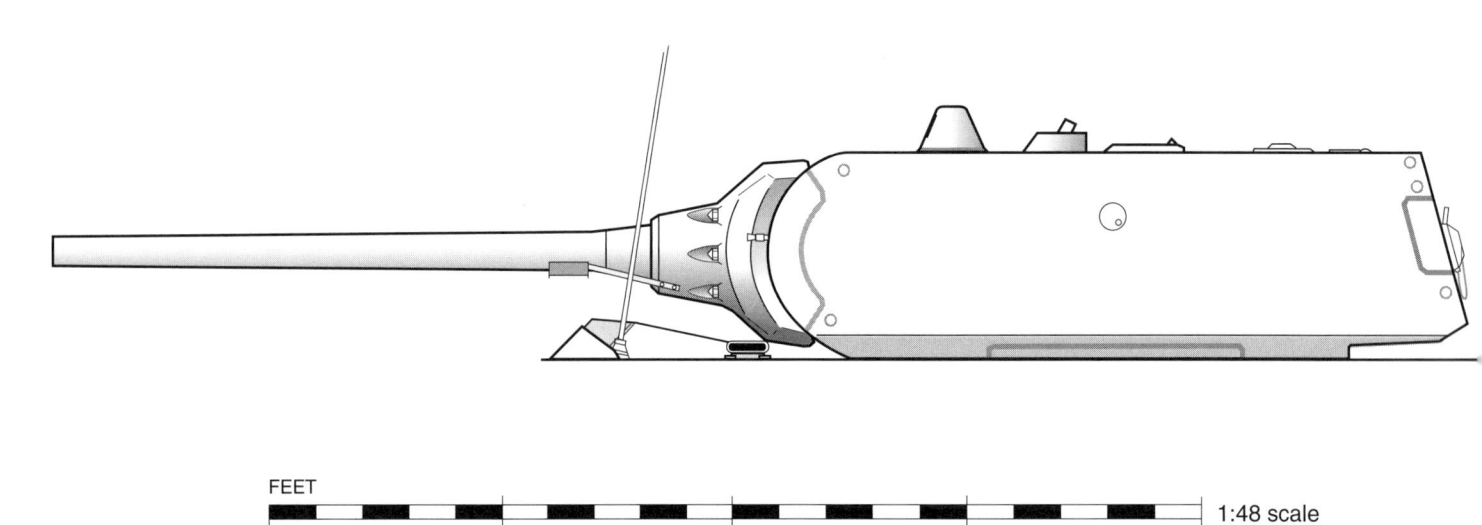

84 German Late War Armored Fighting Vehicles

Leichter Flakpanzer IV
"Kugelblitz"

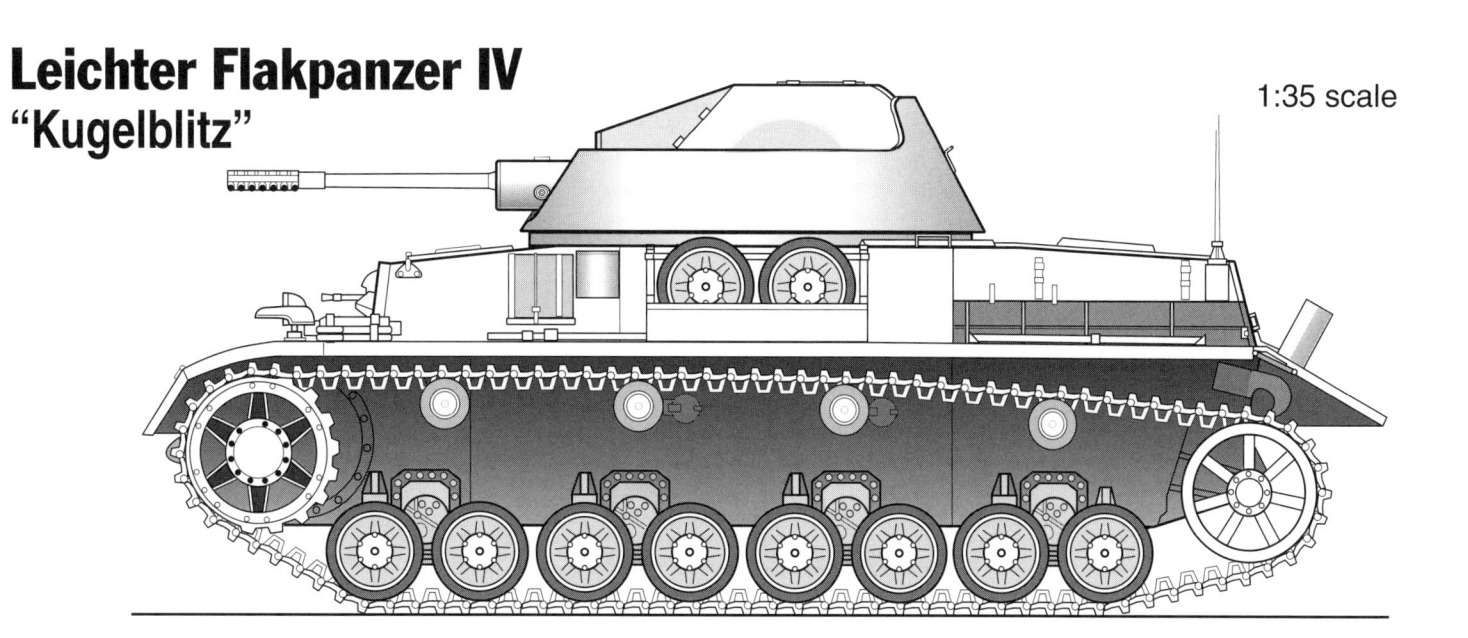

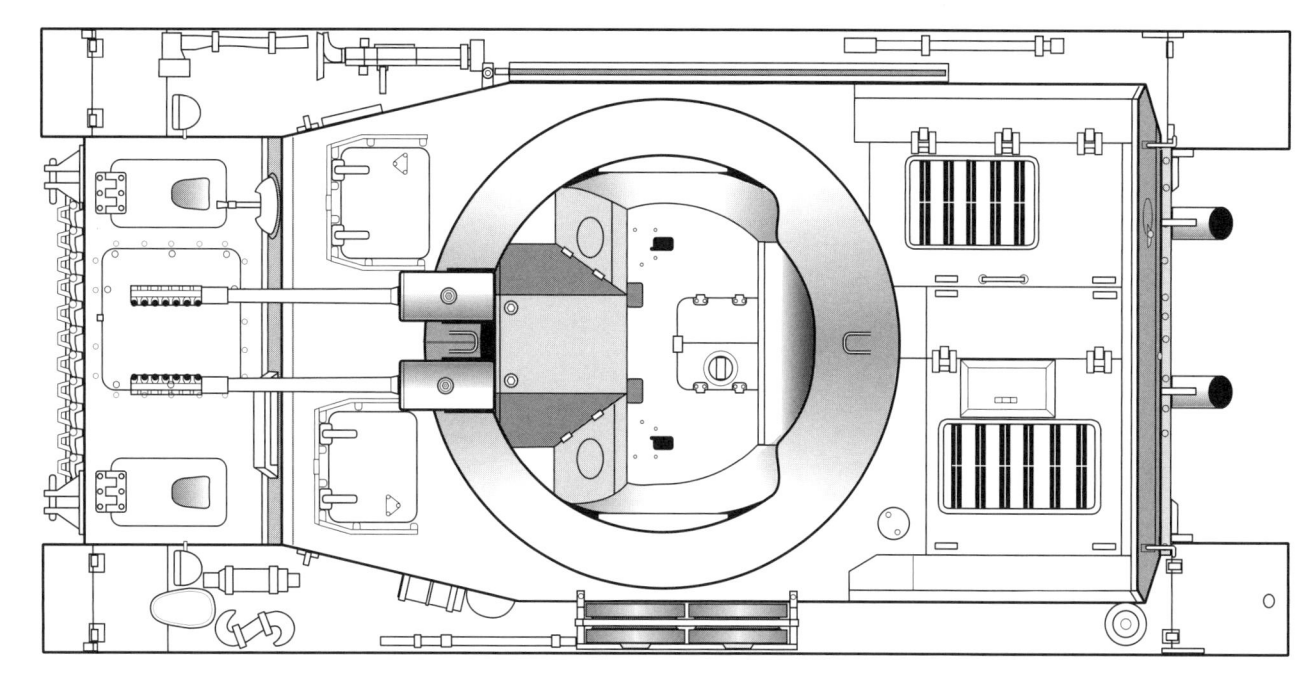

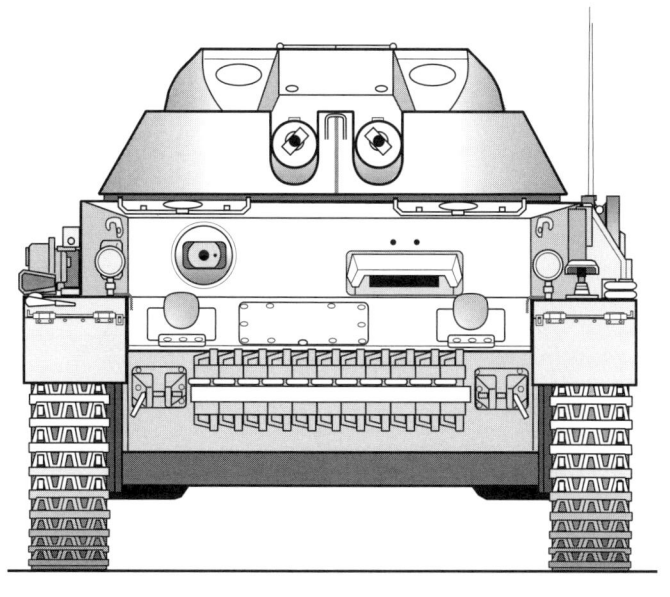

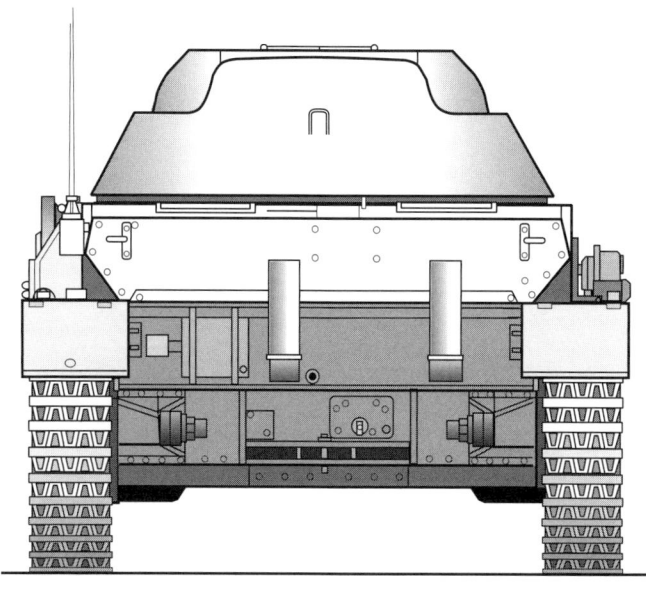

1:35 scale

German Late War Armored Fighting Vehicles 85

5.5cm FlakPz. Panther
paper prototype

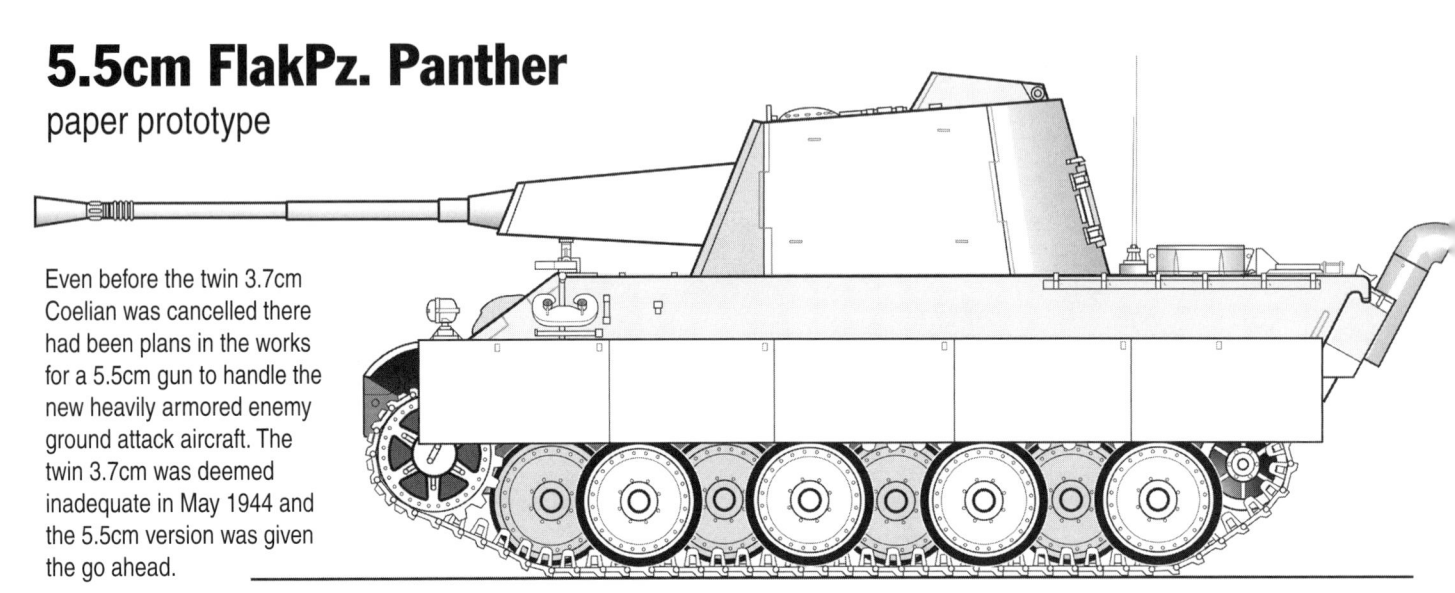

Even before the twin 3.7cm Coelian was cancelled there had been plans in the works for a 5.5cm gun to handle the new heavily armored enemy ground attack aircraft. The twin 3.7cm was deemed inadequate in May 1944 and the 5.5cm version was given the go ahead.

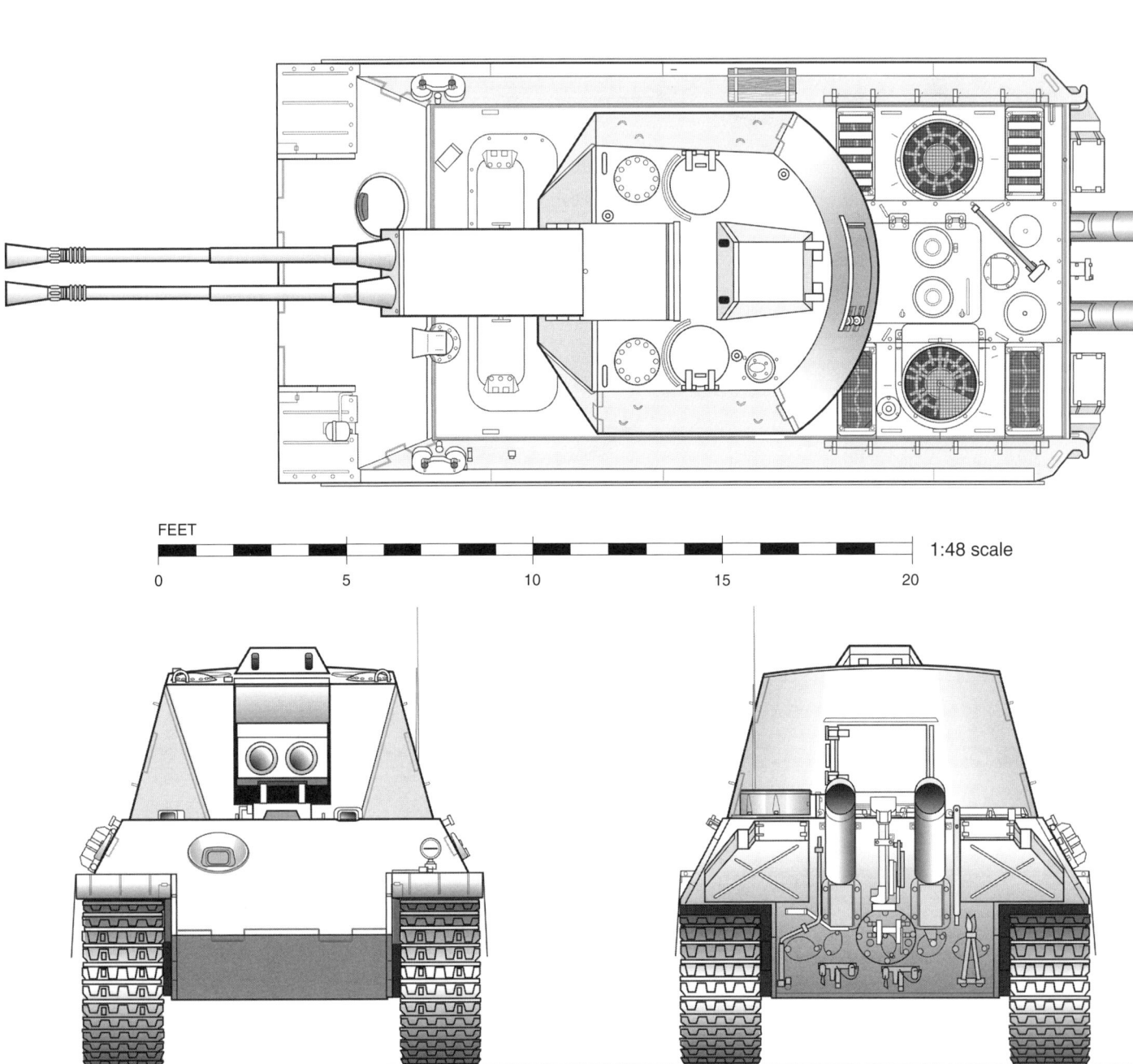

FEET 1:48 scale

86   German Late War Armored Fighting Vehicles

Pz.Kpfw. V, Ausf. F (Sd.Kfz. 171)
"Panther"

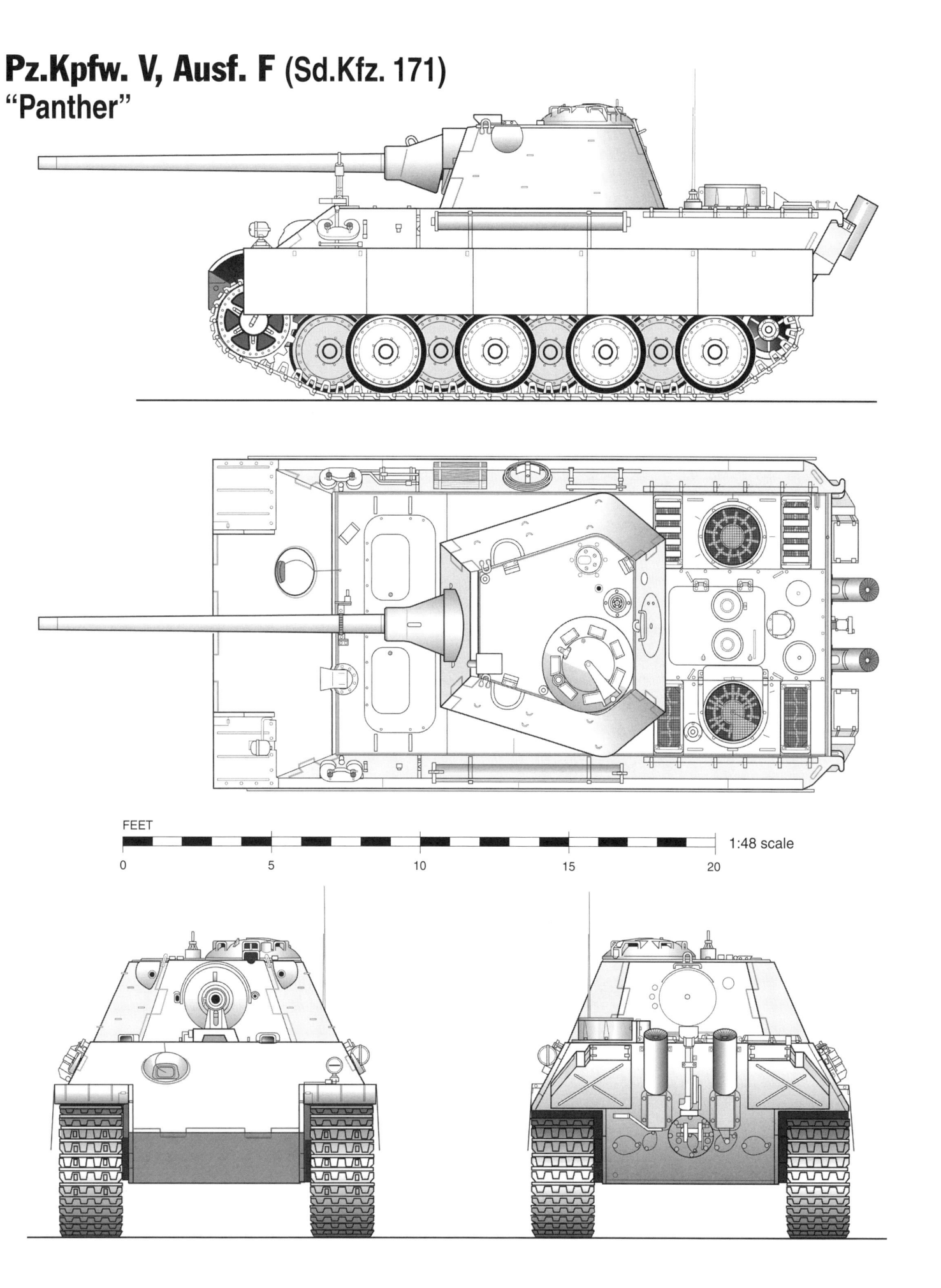

FEET

1:48 scale

German Late War Armored Fighting Vehicles 87

Pz.Kpfw. E-100

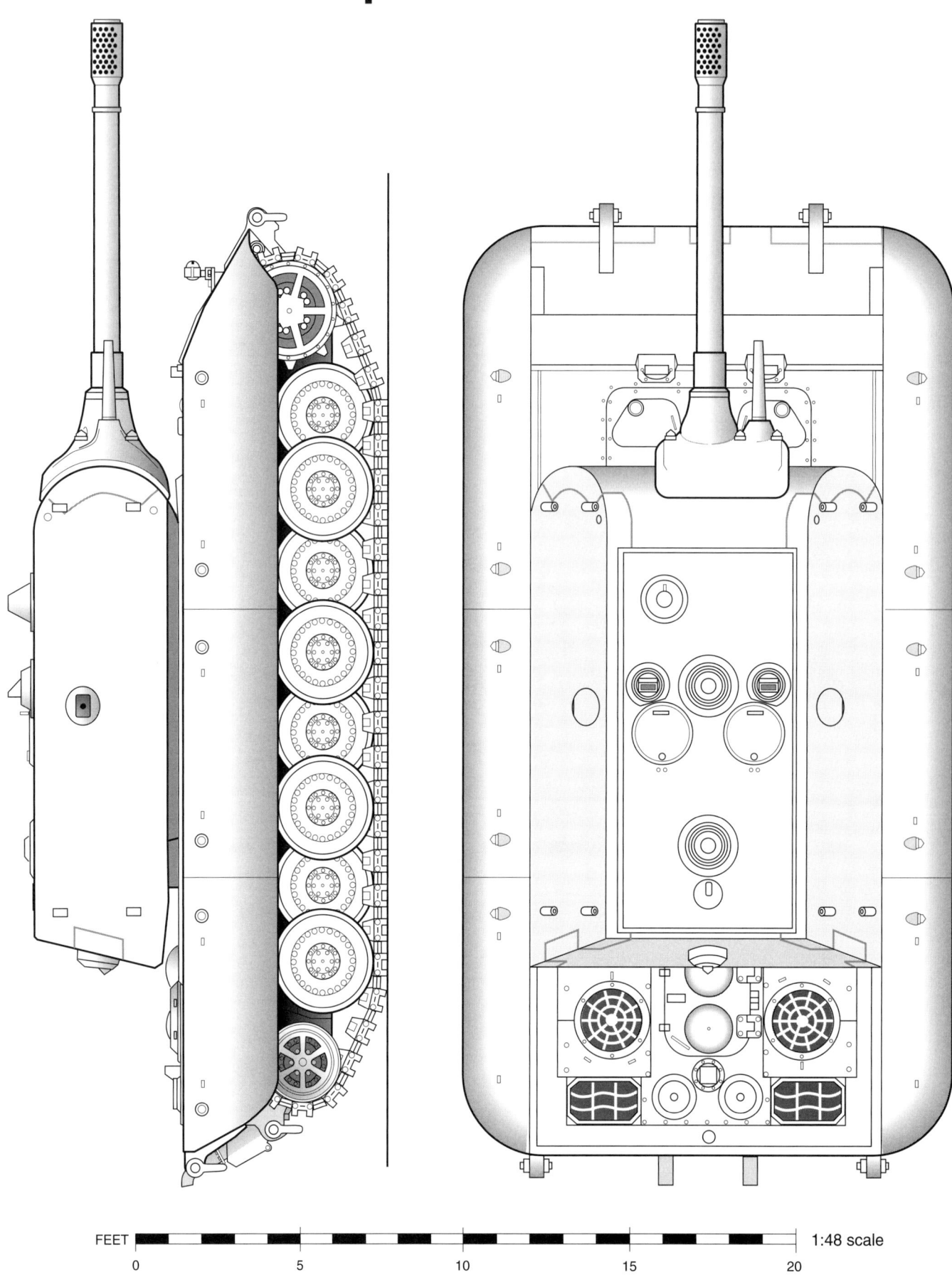

Pz.Kpfw. E-100

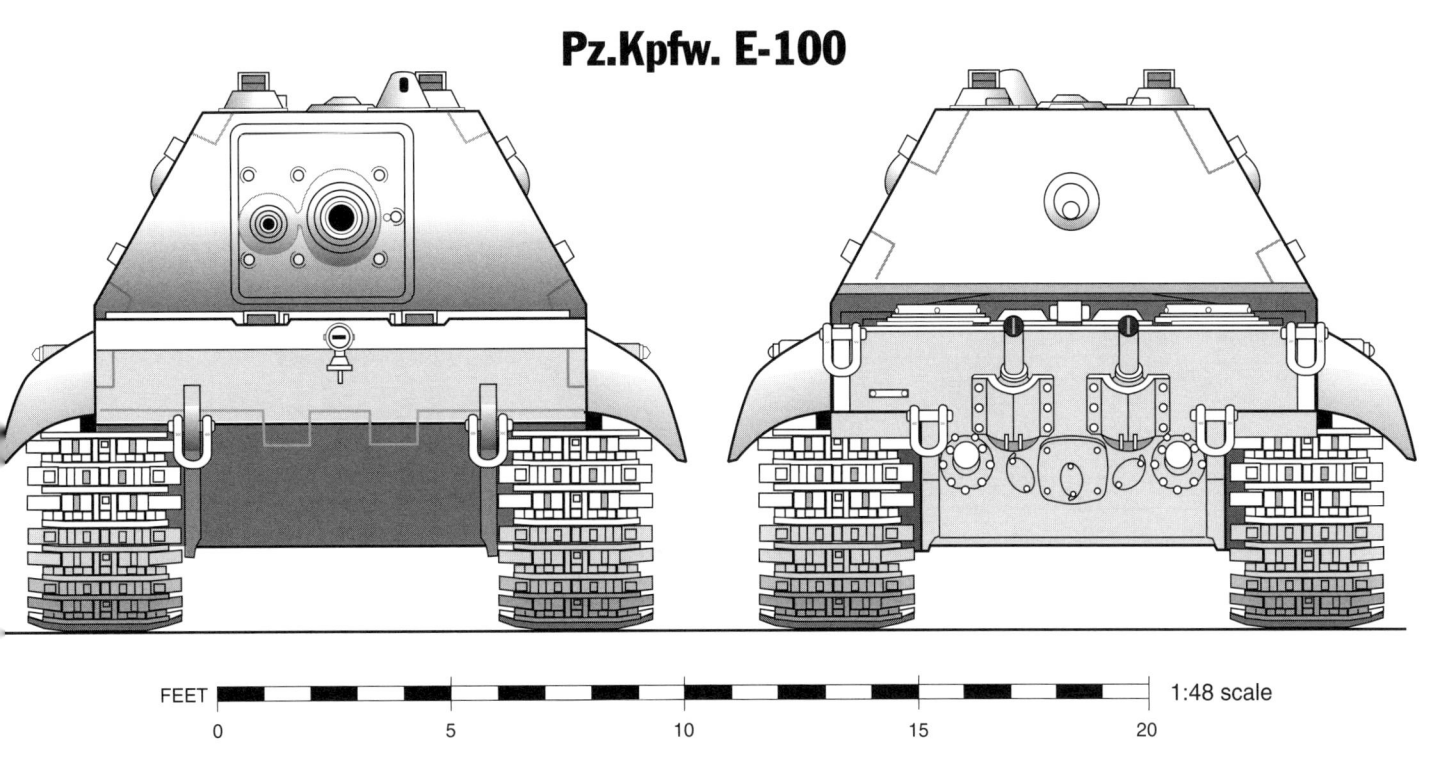

FEET 1:48 scale

Pz.Kpfw. E-100

FEET 1:72 scale

German Late War Armored Fighting Vehicles 89

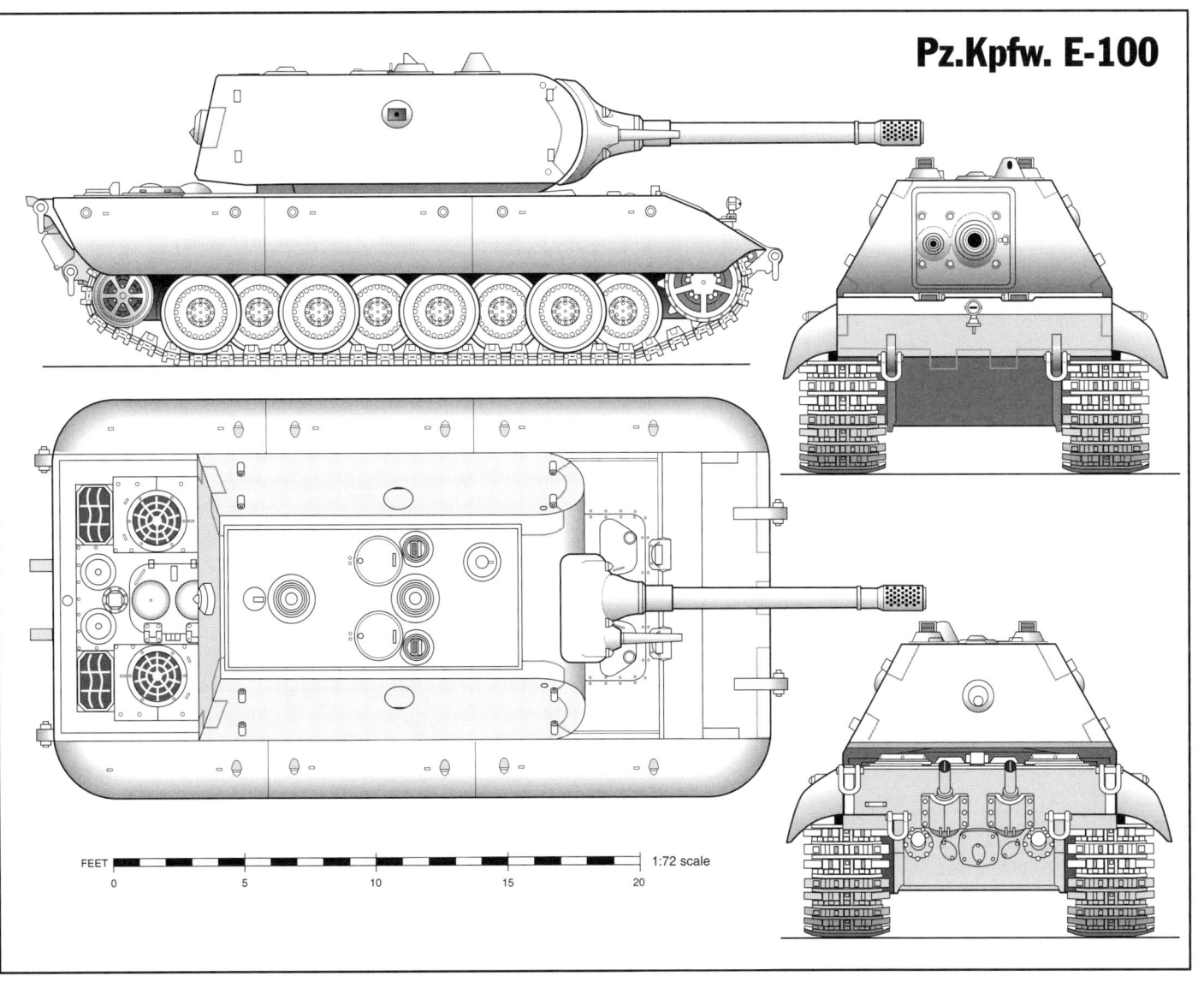

BMM/CKD "Kätzchen" Prototype
Recon and APC Vehicle

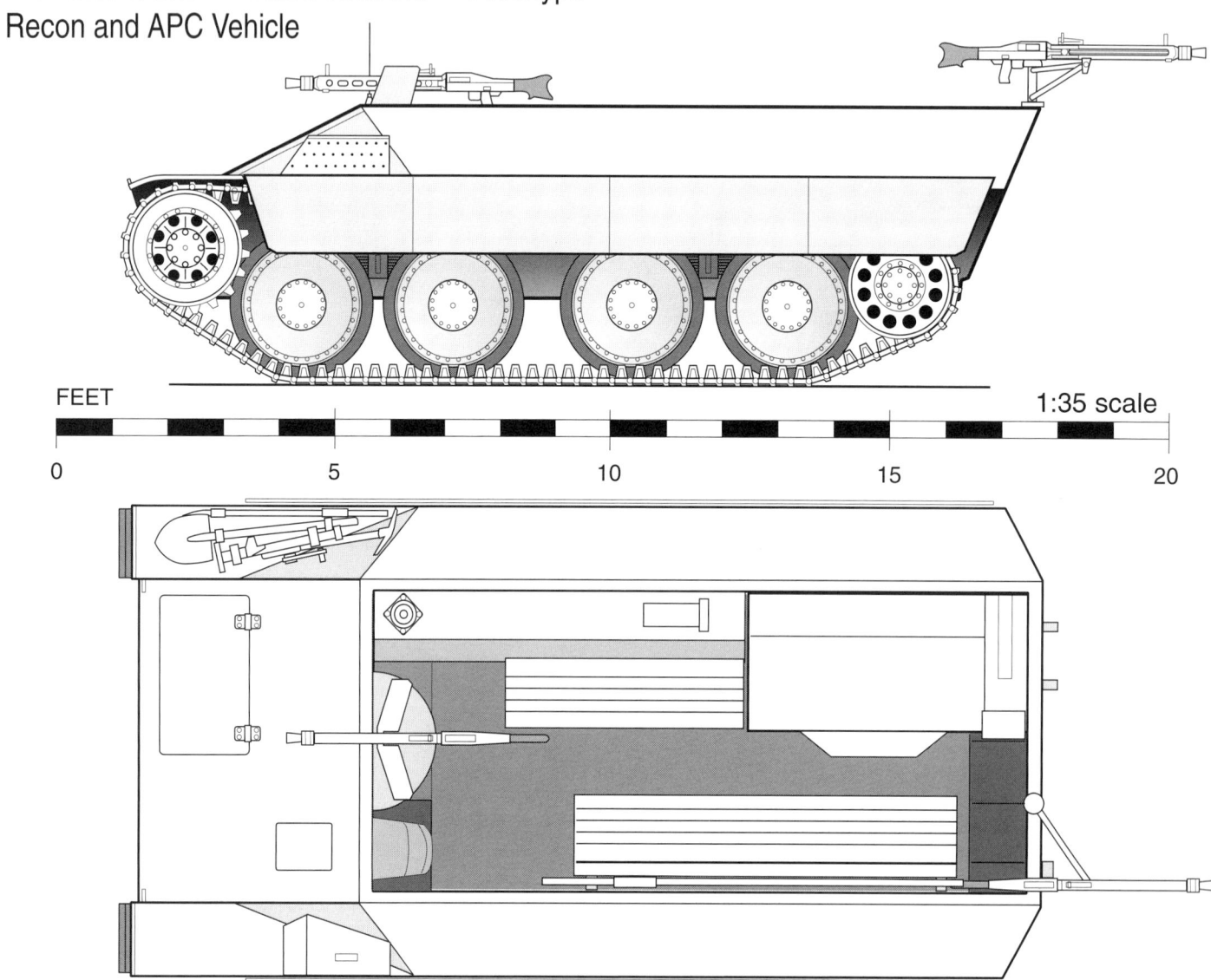

FEET   1:35 scale

0   5   10   15   20

This CKD design was one of two designs produced, in search of a new fully tracked reconnaissance vehicle capable of carrying 6–8 men. The other was the similar Auto Union version, of which two prototypes were built and tested in early 1944. The design proved ideal, but during the summer testing gear box problems arose which shifted favor to the CKD design. This was reinforced by the Sept./44 decision to limit chassis types to the Panther and 38(t).

This CKD of Prague prototype was built in 1944, but little is know of what became of it. The engine was a new Tatra 12 cylinder air-cooled Diesel with 280 hp at 2600 rpm, giving the vehicle a maximum speed of 64 km/hr on roads. Fuel capacity provided a radius of action of 600 km. The suspension was an improved version of the well tested Hetzer, with a Praga-Wilson gearbox. The unique aspect of this vehicle is that it appears to be the original forerunner of our modern day Armored Personnel Carriers.

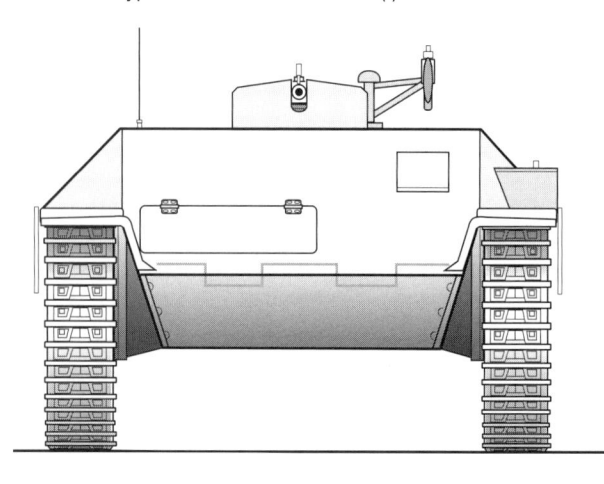

Weight:– 10.5 tons
Engine:– Tatra, 280 HP
Road Speed:– 60 km/hr
Front armor:– 50mm
Side armor:– 30mm
Rear armor:– 20mm
Crew:– 6 - 8 men
Armament:– 2 MGs

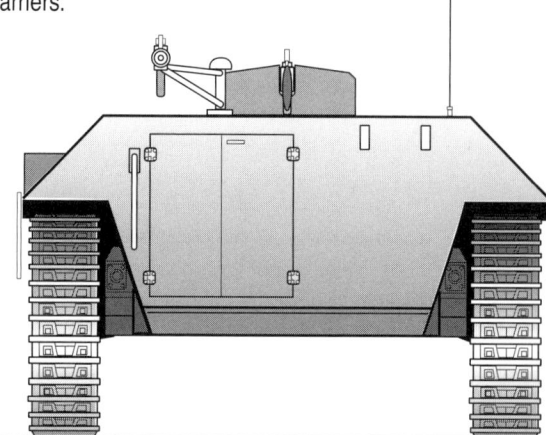

Bibliography

Chamberlain, P., and C. Ellis. *Pictorial History of Tanks of the World, 1915–45*. London: Arms and Armour Press, 1972.

Chamberlain, P., H. Doyle, and T. Jentz. *Encyclopedia of German Tanks of World War Two*. London: Arms and Armour Press, 1978.

Chant, C. *Artillery: Over 300 of the World's Finest Artillery Pieces from 1914 to the Present Day*. London: Amber Books Ltd., 2005.

Crowe, D., and R. J. Icks. *Encyclopedia of Armoured Cars*. Secaucus, NJ: Chartwell Books Inc., 1997.

———. *Encyclopedia of Tanks*. London: Barry & Jenkins Limited, 1975.

Doyle, H., and T. Jentz. *Panther Variants, 1942–1945*. London: Osprey, 1997.

Duske, Heiner F. *NUTS & BOLTS* series. Uelzen, Germany: Frank Schulz, 1996–2006.
  Vol. 1: *Jagdtiger (Sd Kfz 186)*. Duske, Greenland, Schulz.
  Vol. 2: *Wespe (Sd Kfz 124)*. Duske, Greenland, Schulz.
  Vol. 4: *Sd Kfz 222 & 223*. Duske, Greenland, Schulz.
  Vol. 5: *Saurer RK-7 (Sd Kfz 254)*. Duske, Greenland, Schulz.
  Vol. 6: *Kanonenwagen (Sd Kfz 251/9)*. Duske, Greenland, Schulz.
  Vol. 7: *Panzerjäger I (Sd Kfz 101)*. Duske, Greenland, Schulz.
  Vol. 9: *Raupenschlepper Ost (RSO)*. Duske, Greenland, Schulz.
  Vol. 10: *Hummel (Sd Kfz 165)*. Duske, Greenland, Schulz.
  Vol. 11: *PzKpfw. 35(t) (Sd Kfz 124)*. Rue, Duske, Greenland, Schulz.
  Vol. 12: *FAMO 18t (Sd Kfz 9)*. Hettler, Duske, Greenland, Schulz.
  Vol. 13: *Flakpanzer IV (Sd Kfz 161/4)*. Terlisten, Duske, Greenland, Schulz.
  Vol. 14: *Nashorn (Sd Kfz 164)*. Terlisten, Duske, Greenland, Schulz.
  Vol. 15: *Marder III (Sd Kfz 139)*. Andorfer, Block, Nelson, Schulz.
  Vol. 16: *sZugkraftwagen 12t (Sd Kfz 8)*. Hettler, Duske, Greenland, Schulz.
  Vol. 17: *Marder III/M (Sd Kfz 138)*. Andorfer, Block, Nelson, Schulz.
  Vol. 18: *Marder III/H (Sd Kfz 138)*. Andorfer, Block, Nelson, Schulz.
  Vol. 19: *15cm sIG (Sf) auf PKpfw I/B*. Wilhelm, Duske, Terlisten.

Feist, U., and B. Culver. *Tiger I*. Bellingham, Wash.: Ryton Publications, 1992.

Fletcher, D. *Tanks in Camera, 1940–1943*. Stroud, UK: Sutton Publishing Limited, 1998.

Forty, G. *Afrika Korps at War: The Long Road Back*. Shepperton, UK: Ian Allan Publishing, 1998.

———. *Afrika Korps at War: The Road to Alexandria*. Shepperton, UK: Ian Allan Publishing, 1998.

———. *A Photo History of Armoured Cars in Two World Wars*. Poole, UK: Blandford Press, 1984.

Ichimura, H. *Panzers at Saumur, No. 3*. Tokyo: Dai Nippon Kaiga Co. Ltd., 1992.

Icks, Robert J. *Tanks & Armored Vehicles, 1900–1945*. Old Greenwich, CT: WE Inc., 1967.

Jentz, T. L., and H. L. Doyle. *Germany's Panther Tank: The Quest for Combat Supremacy*. Atglen, PA: Schiffer Publishing Ltd., 1995.

———. *Germany's Panzer in World War II*. Atglen, PA: Schiffer Publishing Ltd., 2001.

———. *Germany's Tiger Tanks: D.W. to Tiger I*. Atglen, PA: Schiffer Publishing Ltd., 2000.

———. *Germany's Tiger Tanks: VK45.02 to Tiger II*. Atglen, PA: Schiffer Publishing Ltd., 1997.

———. *Panzer Tracts No. 1-1, Panzerkampfwagen I*. Boyds, MD: Panzer Tracts, 2002.

———. *Panzer Tracts No. 1-2: Panzerkampfwagen I*. Boyds, MD: Panzer Tracts, 2002.

———. *Panzer Tracts No. 10: Artillerie Selbstfahrlafetten*. Boyds, MD: Panzer Tracts, 2002.

———. *Panzer Tracts No. 13: Panzerspaehwagen*. Boyds, MD: Panzer Tracts, 2001.

———. *Tiger at the Front*. Atglen, PA: Schiffer Publishing Ltd., 2001.

Kliment, C. K., and V. Francev. *Czechoslovak Armored Fighting Vehicles, 1918–1948*. Atglen, PA: Schiffer Publishing Ltd., 1997.

———. *Hetzer Jagdpanzer 38*. Prague, Czech Republic: MBI, 2001.

———. *Marder III & Grille*. Prague, Czech Republic: MBI, 1999.

———. *PRAGA LT vz. 38*. Prague, Czech Republic: MBI, 1997.

———. *SKODA LT vz. 35*. Prague, Czech Republic: MBI, 1995.

Ledwoch, J. *SdKfz 251* Warsaw, Poland: Wydawnictwo Militaria, 1994.

Macksey, K. *Rommel: Battles and Campaigns*. Toronto: Thomas Nelson & Sons Ltd., 1979.

Münch, K. *Combat History of German Heavy Anti-Tank Unit 653*. Mechanicsburg, PA: Stackpole Books, 2005.

Milsom, J., and P. Chamberlain. *German Armoured Cars of World War Two*. London: Arms and Armour Press, 1974.

Pignato, N. *Atlante Mondiale dei Mezzi Corazzati*. Bologna, Italy: Ermanno Albertelli Editore, 1983.

Regenberg, W. *Armored Vehicles and Units of the German Order Police, 1936–1945*. Atglen, PA: Schiffer Publishing Ltd., 2002.

Schneider, W. *Tigers in Combat I*. Mechanicsburg, PA: Stackpole Books, 2004.

———. *Tigers in Combat II*. Mechanicsburg, PA: Stackpole Books, 2005.

Spielberger, W. *Der Panzer-Kampfwagen Panther und Seine Abarten*. Stuttgart, Germany: Motorbuch Verlag, 1978.

———. *Panzer IV & Its Variants* Atglen, PA: Schiffer Publishing Ltd., 1993.

———. *Sturmgeschütz & Its Variants*. Atglen, PA: Schiffer Publishing Ltd., 1993.

Trojca, W. *PzKpfw. V, Panther*. Vol. 1. Gdansk, Poland: AJ-Press, 1999.

Basic Tank Components

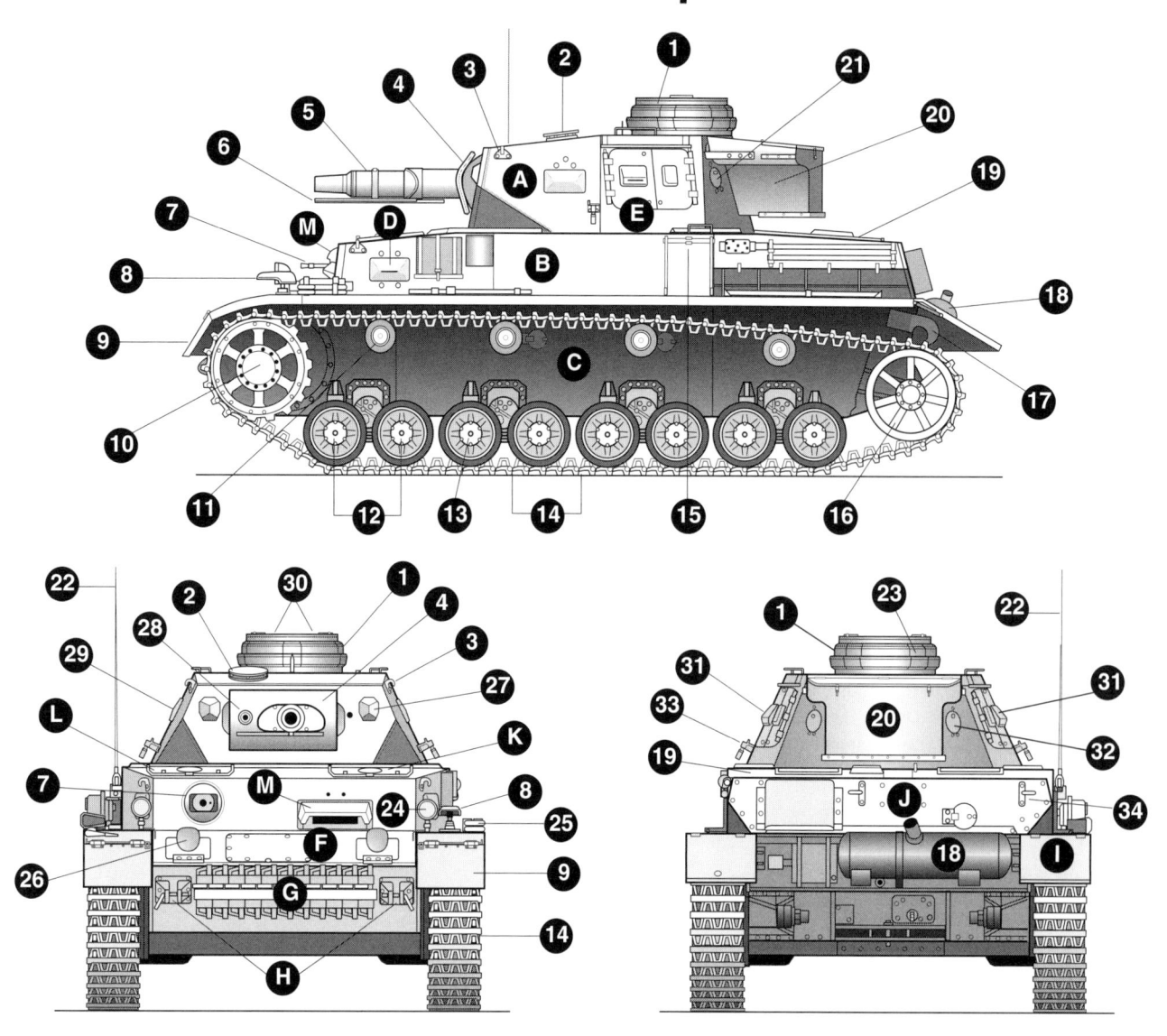

A. Turret
B. Upper Hull
C. Lower Hull
D. Hull View Port
E. Turret Side Hatches
F. Glacis Plate
G. Spare Tracks
H. Towing Pintles
I. Rear Fender Flap
J. Rear Plate
K. Driver's Hatch
L. Radio Op. Hatch
M. Driver's Visor

1. Commander's Cupola
2. Air Ventilator
3. Turret Lift Hook
4. Gun Mantlet
5. Main Gun
6. Aerial Deflector
7. Bow Machinegun
8. Notek Night Light
9. Front Fender Flap
10. Drive Sprocket
11. Return Roller
12. Bogie Suspension Unit
13. Road Wheel
14. Track Links
15. Fold-up Step
16. Rear Idler Wheel
17. Chassis Lift Hook

18. Muffler
19. Engine Deck
20. Turret Stowage Bin
21. Rear Pistol Port
22. Aerial & Mount
23. Commander's Cupola
24. Head Lamp
25. Tow Cable Hooks
26. Ventilator Cowls
27. Gunner's Vision Port
28. Coaxial Machine Gun
29. Turret Side View Port
30. Split Cupola Hatches
31. Turret View Port
32. Rear Pistol Port
33. Turret Hatch Stop
34. Cable Hanger Hooks

92 German Late War Armored Fighting Vehicles

VARIOUS MODELING SCALES

Scale	1 inch equals	1 scale foot =	1 scale meter =	Comments
1:4	4"	3"	250.0 mm	Flying Models, Live-steam Trains
1:8	8"	1 1/2"	125.0 mm	Cars, Motorcycles, Trains
1:12	1'	1"	83.3 mm	Cars, Motorcycles, Dollhouses
1:16	1' 4"	3/4"	62.5 mm	Cars, Motorcycles, Trains
1:20	1' 8"	19/32"	50.0 mm	Cars
1:22.5	1' 10 1/2"	17/32"	44.4 mm	G-Scale Trains
1:24	2'	1/2"	41.7 mm	Cars, Trucks, Dollhouses
1:25	2' 1"	15/32"	40.0 mm	Cars, Trucks
1:32	2' 8"	3/8"	31.25 mm	Aircraft, Cars, Tanks, Trains
1:35	2' 11"	11/32"	28.57 mm	Armor
1:43	3' 7"	9/32"	23.25 mm	Cars, Trucks
1:48	4'	1/4"	20.83 mm	Aircraft, Armor, O-Scale Trains
1:64	5' 4"	3/16"	15.62 mm	Aircraft, S-Scale Trains
1:72	6'	11/63"	13.88 mm	Aircraft, Armor, Boats
1:76	6' 4"	5/32"	13.16 mm	Armor
1:87	7' 3"	—	11.49 mm	Armor, HO-Scale Trains
1:96	8'	1/8"	10.42 mm	1/8" Scale Ships, Aircraft
1:100	8' 4"	—	10.00 mm	Aircraft
1:125	10' 5"	—	8.00 mm	Aircraft
1:144	12'	—	6.94 mm	Aircraft
1:160	13' 4"	—	6.25 mm	N-Scale Trains
1:192	16'	1/16"	5.21 mm	1/16" Scale Ships
1:200	16' 8"	—	5.00 mm	Aircraft, Ships

WORLD WAR II AFV PLANS

Technical artist and military historian George Bradford uses research of actual vehicles, official photographs, factory specifications, and, in some cases, the original design plans to produce precise scale drawings of the armored fighting vehicles of World War II. Each volume contains nearly 300 drawings of these steel chariots of war.

AMERICAN ARMORED FIGHTING VEHICLES
$14.95 • PB • 8 1/2 x 11 • 96 pages
0-8117-3340-8

GERMAN EARLY WAR ARMORED FIGHTING VEHICLES
$14.95 • PB • 8 1/2 x 11 • 96 pages
0-8117-3341-6

GERMAN LATE WAR ARMORED FIGHTING VEHICLES
$14.95 • PB • 8 1/2 x 11 • 96 pages
0-8117-3355-6

RUSSIAN ARMORED FIGHTING VEHICLES
$14.95 • PB • 8 1/2 x 11 • 88 pages
0-8117-3356-4

FORTHCOMING:
British Armored Fighting Vehicles
Other Axis and Allied Fighting Vehicles

WWW.STACKPOLEBOOKS.COM